GREAT MILITARY SIEGES

GREAT MILITARY SIEGES

Vezio Melegari

NEW YORK

To my sons

The love of peace
will not be saved
unless it be ordered
with the wish to act;
and life without danger
is not given
to a sovereign city
but to one already
conquered.

PERICLES

Modus hodiernus exstru:
endarum Munitionum.

Nulla fa|lus BELLO PACEM te|poſcimus omnes.

CONTENTS

INTRODUCTION

"Siege" is a harsh word, certainly less resounding than battle. *And it is correct that it be so, because battle is unchained violence and the uncertainty of fortune, just like a siege, but the latter possesses another element in the exasperation of time going by without one's being able to placate this violence, to solve this uncertainty. Furthermore, it implies the slow death of people in houses and streets made for peaceful everyday life. The siege is therefore connected with the suffering of civilians rather than the sacrifice of soldiers. For this reason this book is designed, above all, to give homage to the pain and sacrifice that history has demanded from these heroes without uniform. The reader will find in this work splendid examples of civilian bravery throughout the entire great scope of our narrative, which goes from the sunlit epochs of myth to the gray days of today's guerrilla wars. It would appear that legends tend to dwell upon the horrors of the siege and that, for protagonists, feminine figures are preferred. The chaste Digna of Aquileia who lets herself be carried away by the river rather than violated by a barbarian; the little shepherdess of Domrémy who frees Orléans; Jeanne Hachette, who captures a Burgundian standard on the bastion of Beauvais; Caterina Segurana, who, at Nice, equally humiliates a Turkish standard bearer; and Augustina of Aragon, who, at Saragossa, takes the place of her fallen betrothed at the gun are among the truest symbols of a "people's" siege, which often changes the outcome of great events and even the course of history itself, as opposed to the cold principles of the military engineering "schools" (according to which the siege becomes frequently little more than a dry geometrical problem).*

In a book such as this, tempted by the pleasure of dwelling on the rich material of human legends as well as unveiling some secret of old or new siege operations, what can one do other than try to establish an equilibrium between the warm interest of an anecdote and exact historic and technical information? Illustrations are very helpful in this sense and certainly the collection of illustrations among the following pages, without, however, overemphasizing rigorously scientific aspects of the material, will amply explain whatever points may need some clarification for the reader from the text. In discussing particulars referring to fortifications an elementary terminology has generally been used, easily identifiable in a simple dictionary. And when mention is made of ravelins and cavalry crescents, covered routes and counterscarps, pincers and parallels, circumvallations and countervallations, care has been taken to explain at each point exactly what is meant, in such a way as not to distract the reader from the course of the narrative.

Therefore this book is not a manual but a se-

lection of episodes whose historical importance is supremely evident: this is the purpose of this book.

It certainly does not make the presumption of being, in this sense, a complete work. One does not have to be a specialist to notice the lack of a chapter on Ostend or on Famagusta, on Querétaro or Almería, on Calais or Rouen, on Lucknow or Strasbourg: but a selection was necessary.

Besides acceding to the tyranny of space, the author had to strike a balance between the greater or lesser importance of each siege to be included. In this case as well one does not need an expert knowledge of the material in question to be able to calculate the differences in the difficulties of the siege of Jerusalem by Titus, Napoleon's difficulties at Toulon, and the difficulties of the legations in Peking. And certainly some readers may be surprised not to find mention of the end of Amalfi or the resistance of Jarabub, the epic of the Alamo or the beautiful page of Makallé. In fact a true siege should not be confused with encirclement, surprise, or massacre; and small garrisons crushed by overwhelming forces make a part of history by themselves, which eventually should be told, but which has nothing to do with the history of sieges.

All this does not diminish the epic quality of the "great" sieges, although perhaps of a "greatness" which is both bewitching and monstrous. In each case, man is there, to say what he has to say. And often a single word offers a view of history itself. There is, for example, the "I envy you" of the conquering Russian Gurko to Osman Pasha, the luckless defender of Plevna; the gesture of Eugene of Savoy, wishing to divide his siege rations with the vanquished Bouflers; and the cry of Pietro Micca impelling his comrade to safety.

Today there are many who consider military honor lacking in good sense or even an indication of insanity. But the examples quoted, and especially such instances as the desperation of Jenot when he lost his place in Napoleon's esteem after the defeat of Vimeiro and Nogi's hara-kiri in a depression caused by the memory of the blood shed by his infantry at Port Arthur, are quite apart from any polemics and are not affected by such rhetoric. Perhaps the best reply to all such reactions is the ancient saying that an act of courage is always the best gesture; or rather, to adhere more closely to our theme, the words which Thucydides attributes to Nycias on the eve of the Athenian disaster near Syracuse, "It is men that make cities, not walls without defenders."

Acknowledgments

The author has made wide and valuable contacts with students, collectors, and directors of art and cultural institutes who have greatly aided him in the collection of editorial and illustrative material. Particular thanks are due to General Robert Nicolas of the French Engineering Corps; to General Giuseppe Vasile, former Director of the Central Military Library of Rome; to Colonel Frederick P. Todd, former Director of the West Point Museum; to Lt. Colonel Guido Amoretti, of the School of Arms of Turin; to Lt. Colonel Alessandro Gasparinetti, Secretary-General of the International Center of Military Prints and Uniforms of Rome; to Mlle. Madeleine Barbin, Curator, Bureau of Prints, National Library, Paris; to Philip Warner, M.A., Senior Lecturer, Royal Military Academy, Sandhurst; to Dr. Georg Schreiber, of Vienna; to Professors Elio Bolognesi of Genoa and Elio Nicolardi of Piacenza; to Dr. Laura Sechi, Organizer of the Civic Naval Museum of Genoa-Pegli; to Monsieur R. Lemaire, of the Municipal Library of Beauvais; to Don Trinidad Cruzate Espiell of Barcelona; to Dr. Hegebert Ewe of the City Archives of Stralsunde; to William Y. Carman, Delegate Director of the National Army Museum of London; to Olaf Hällström, Director of the Soumenlinna Museum, Helsinki; to the Directors of the Museum of Dijon; to Professor Nino Lamboglia, Director of the International Institute of Ligurian Studies, Bordighera; to Professor Carlo Costamagna, Director of the State Archives of Genoa; to the Cattaneo-Adorno family of Genoa; to Professor Vitaliano Rocchiero of Genoa; to Commander Ugo Speranza of Aquila; to Dr. Roberto Simari of the Provincial Library "S. Tommasi" of Aquila; to the Directors and personnel of the Civic Print Collection "Achille Bertarelli" of Milan, proven once more a source of study and research without equal.

TROY (1194-1184 B.C.)

A horse destroys the "city of beautiful horses"

Homer's *Iliad* is the necessary point of departure for the consideration of Troy and the siege. On the other hand, the poet lived almost certainly in the IX century before Christ, that is, two or three hundred years after the siege. His most ancient biographers state that he was born in Asia Minor, either in Smyrna, in Chios, or in Colophon. It is therefore almost certain that he was able to consult some authentic record or some valid proof from an historical point of view. In other words, his interpretation of the coming of war between the Greeks and Trojans could possibly be based not only on fantasy, but also on history, on vestiges of memory still alive at his time and in the places where he must have lived.

It has been noted that excavations carried out by Heinrich Schliemann in the second half of the 1800's at Hissarlik, which other scholars had already identified as the site where Troy once reared its towers, uncovered quite new strata corresponding to the other Troys. Which was the Homeric city, the one destroyed by the Greeks of Agamemnon?

This was later identified as the seventh stratum (from the bottom), bearing traces of a fire which, according to Homer's story, ended the siege. Archaelogists and ancient historians agree on the date of this conflagration: 1184 B.C. It was therefore during the late Bronze Age, when the Greeks had only sharpened un-tempered weapons and observed the custom of burying, not burning, their dead. It was therefore not during the Iron Age, although we find certain references of Homer to forging weapons of iron and to the incineration of the dead. This is a proof that Homer could not have lived during the times of his heroes.

According to him, and also according to history, those who attacked Troy ten years before the fatal date of 1184 B.C., were Mycenaeans, that is, descendants of those "mainland Greeks" who, around 1500 B.C., fell upon the "Cretan Greeks" or Minoans. It was these who gave their own warlike and virile character to Greek history and established in the Hellenic world their belief in *areté,* individual excellence, the goal of human existence. In 1194 they attacked Troy, resolved to destroy her. What had this city done to deserve death?

It had grown great in an ideal position to dominate the commercial routes between the Orient and the Occident, like a sentry at the entrance of the Hellespont, with its commerce of gold, silver, iron, timber for the construction of ships, flax, hemp, dried fish, oil, and above all, grain, all at a low price. Moreover, Troy was not alone. She had allies among the neighboring cities and with them had formed a confederation which represented a menace to the Mycenaeans. These latter were not accustomed to allow menaces to continue to threaten them.

Trojan helmet with swastika. The most ancient use of this symbol, considered a protection against the evil eye, has been traced to the Elamites, who inhabited the left bank of the lower course of the Tigris, and near the Trojans. To the right: An ancient geographical representation of the Trojan domain, showing its great extent and its strategic importance to the ancient world.

According to Homer, the pretext for attacking Troy was the rape of Helen, wife of Menelaus, King of Sparta, by Paris, the son of Priam, King of Troy. This may be true, but then historical reasons are not so clear. "Helen" was also the name of the Spartan moon goddess, in whom we easily recognize the Great Goddess who, in the most ancient religions, represented the very summit of divinity. Mythology has complicated matters, saying that Helen was also kidnapped by Theseus. A Sicilian poet of the VI century B.C., named Stesichorus, claims that Helen never even reached Troy and that the long war was fought for a "phantom" made in her own image by Hera (Juno) with a cloud. Many chroniclers of the myths believe that while fleeing with Paris (while Menelaus was in Crete for the funeral ceremony of his grandfather Catreus), Helen took with her her son Plistenes, the greater part of the court treasures, and three talents of gold from the temple of Apollo.

Perhaps the one authentic vestige of truth in all this story is that of the stolen treasure, with or without Helen. The Trojans, under the leadership of Paris, transformed an official visit to the King of Sparta into a piratical raid, doubtlessly to avenge themselves for something similar that the Greeks had done to them, to

One of the most dramatic moments in the siege of Troy, according to a reconstruction of the XIX century (Milan, Bertarelli Collection). In the background we see Hector leaving for his fatal encounter with Achilles while, in the foreground, Priam consoles Hector's wife Andromache, who carries her son Astyanax in her arms. At Priam's right is his daughter Cassandra who, after the disaster, will become Agamemnon's prize of war and victim of Clytemnestra's jealousy.

their loss. In brief, the Trojan War could perhaps be classified as a "squaring of accounts" between pirates.

In any case, the war took place and the siege ended it. Again according to Homer, the rape of Helen provoked the indignation of all Greece. Each city replied to the call of Menelaus, sending men and ships and placing them under the orders of Agamemnon, King of Mycenae, brother of the same Menelaus. One thousand two hundred ships set sail against Troy, transporting men and demigods, whose names were destined to immortal fame, in the greatest undertaking of heroic times. Among many, certain heroes were especially notable, such as Achilles, King of the Myrmidons of Thessaly, and Ulysses, King of Ithaca. The heroes of the Trojans were no less great; among them Hector, son of Priam, and Aeneas, son of Venus and Anchises.

Still following the Homeric account, we will remember that the Greeks tried to take the city by assault. They were not successful however, and suffered many losses.

Thereupon Agamemnon decided to lay siege. The ships were pulled up on land, according to ancient custom, and protected by entrenchments. Afterwards they commenced to pillage the neighboring cities and to make raids into Trojan territory. A quarrel which broke out between Achilles and Agamemnon divided the forces of the Greeks. This allowed the Trojans to attack the entrenched camp where the ships were

beached and, under the command of Hector, successfully to set fire to many ships.

Patroclus, the friend of Achilles, having put on the hero's armor, as the latter had openly declared that he would not fight following the above quarrel, met Hector but did not survive the encounter alive. Hector killed him and took Achilles' arms and armor from him, with the result that Achilles, aroused at last and attired in new armor, threw himself into the struggle and saved the day for the Greeks. Hector fell beneath his blows and Achilles, in his chariot, dragged the corpse three times around the walls of Troy. Old Priam asked for a

parley with Achilles and, in order to get back the mangled body of his own son, fell on his knees before the enemy.

A short time later, an arrow shot by Paris, guided by Apollo, wounded Achilles mortally in the heel, the one vulnerable spot in the hero's body. Achilles thus left the scene of the war, soon followed by another Greek hero, Ajax, taken by madness. The situation needed to be resolved as soon as possible. It was at this point that Ulysses had the idea of the horse. Under his guidance Epeos, a famous sculptor, constructed an enormous equine statue of wood, in whose belly Ulysses

Laocoön, priest of Apollo, brother of Anchises (and therefore uncle of Aeneas), thrusts his lance against the wooden horse abandoned by the besiegers to show his opposition to the unanimous decision of the Trojans to bring the horse within the city walls. The episode is illustrated here in a miniature taken from the famous Virgilian Codex, preserved in Florence, at the Riccardiana Library. It is noted in the Virgilian version (Aeneid, II), that shortly thereafter, while the priest with his young son was performing a sacrifice to Poseidon, the goddess Athene caused two monstrous reptiles to come out of the sea, crushing in their coils Laocoön and his sons, and convincing the Trojans that bringing the horse into the city was the will of the gods and that the priest, in opposing it, had deserved divine punishment.

The funeral of Hector and below, *Cassandra according to an ancient engraving (Milan, Bertarelli Collection).*
On the following page: *The burning of Troy, in a picture of the XVIII century, preserved at the Castello Visconteo of Pavia. In the upper center one can see Aeneas carrying his father Anchises on his shoulders and accompanied by his son Ascanius.*

and a certain number of warriors hid themselves. The other Greeks put to sea in their ships and set sail toward their own land. The Trojans thought that the Greeks had given up the struggle, believed in their retreat and brought the horse into the city, considering it to have religious significance. During the night, Ulysses and his companions crawled out of the wooden model and signalled the fleet to return. Troy was thus taken by surprise, her people killed almost while they slept, and the buildings pillaged and then burned. Some were able to flee, like Aeneas who, after a long voyage, found a refuge in Italy where he started a new lineage which, in turn, founded Rome.

The subject matter of the twenty-four chapters of the *Iliad* refers only to the last of the ten years of siege. Other sources give earlier particulars which, although casual and disconnected, are of very great interest.

Meanwhile, the landing of the Greeks was certainly preceded by Greek incursions along the coast of Thrace and Asia Minor. Besides, a Greek military base located at the mouth of the Scamander River would inhibit the arrival of Trojan reinforcements from the Mediterranean Sea.

However, it is possible to read in the *Iliad* itself that the siege did not cut off the city completely. The routes to the interior were not cut off except occasionally, by the raids of Achilles and sometimes, a particularly amusing detail, by Greek washerwomen who risked their lives in order to do their laundry at a fountain within bow-shot of the walls. In addition, Trojan units occupied Sestos and Abydos, assuring the possibility of obtaining reinforcements from Thrace. The decisive tactics of Agamemnon, after the failure of the initial assault, was therefore that of a war of attrition. A certain exhaustion of the Trojan reserve took place as even Hector admits, again according to the *Iliad.* The Greeks as well had difficulty in obtaining reinforcements and it was really a question of provisions which caused the dissension between Ulysses and Palamedes, who died somewhat unjustly as a traitor, without being able to see the end of the long war.

Various conjectures have been made about the final military operation of this war; according to some, the fall of Troy was caused by a moveable tower of wood, covered with wet horsehide, against which the burning arrows, shot by the city's defenders, would extinguish themselves. The place where this may have happened could have been on the western part of the wall where, according to Andromache, the wife of Hector, the weakest part of the wall was to be found; near the fig tree where, according to the *Iliad*, the Greeks under Ajax tried three times to force their way into the city.

The legend of the horse arose somewhat later. The most ancient commentators of Homer seemed to be of the impression that it referred to a machine for battering down the walls. Others think that it refers directly to a horse, painted on the secondary gate of the city, opened to the Greeks by the Trojan traitor Antenor; still others consider that it refers to a cavalry attack which caused the fall of Troy, or else that the Greeks, in order to distinguish each other from the enemy, in the darkness and confusion of the battle, had worn an emblem in the form of a horse.

In Greek mythology the horse is a symbol of the passage to the hereafter. It can also be that of the Greek victory over the city which demanded sacrifices and trials and superhuman suffering from the heroes who came from Mycenae.

BABYLON (539-538 B.C.)

"I am against thee, o thou most proud: thy day is come."
(Jeremiah 50:31)

The surrender of Babylon to the forces of Cyrus the Great in 538 B.C. brought the Persian Empire and the Archaemenid power to its apogee. For the Hebrews, thanks to the magnanimity of the conqueror, it represented the end of the Babylonian Captivity, begun fifty years before under Nebuchadnezzar. There exist, for this reason, numerous biblical references to the undertakings of Cyrus, which began toward 550 B.C. with the conquest of Ecbatana and the annexation of Medea. After a victory over an African-Aegean-Mesopotamian coalition (Egypt, Lydia, Babylonia and Sparta) in a campaign culminating in 546 B.C. in the battle of Sardis—in which the Lydian King, Croesus, called "The Rich," was decisively defeated—Cyrus turned toward Chaldea and Babel, or Babylon, its capital.

As soon as the army was assembled under the walls, cutting off the city on all sides (this was in the summer of 539 B.C.), Cyrus personally circled the entire city on horseback, accompanied by his most faithful collaborators. This inspection convinced Cyrus that the city could not be taken by direct assault but by hunger. He gave orders to the army to leave the walls and to go back to camp.

After he had made camp, Cyrus called his officers to a conference and ordered the construction of a line of circular trenches and a system of ditches to be filled with water at an opportune moment. The water was to be that of the Euphrates, the river which crossed the city, and the ditches were constructed in such a way that only a dam divided them from the great river. During the autumn and part of the winter the Persian engineers were occupied in completing the work of excavation, as well as adding towers made of palm trees (some of which grew in the vicinity to more than ninety feet high). Cyrus was attempting to get the Babylonians to believe that he was conducting a siege by blockade, with the intention of causing the fall of the city through hunger. This simply gave rise to new outbursts of hilarity within Babylon, where there were ample food supplies for twenty years. But Cyrus' plan was something else.

This plan came to fruition on a certain winter's day of 538 B.C., on the occasion of a festival scrupulously celebrated by the Babylonians, while the inhabitants of the city were beginning their ritual evening libations. This was the feast referred to by the author of the Book of Daniel in the Bible (5:1 et seq.) when he describes the famous dinner of King Belshazzar, disturbed by the prophetic apparition of a man's hand writing on the wall the three terrible words: *Mene, Tekel, Upharsin.*

Daniel was called upon to explain to the terrified King the meaning of the message "*Mene*: God hath numbered thy kingdom, and finished it; *Tekel*: Thou art weighed in the balances and found wanting; *Upharsin*: Thy kingdom is divided, and given to the Medes and Persians." That same night, as recounted in the biblical story, Belshazzar, King of Chaldea, was killed when "Darius the Median took the kingdom, being about three score and two years old." It is now certain however (as proved by non-religious documents) that Belshazzar was not the King, but the son of the King (Nabonadius) and that Darius the Mede was an invention or a mistake of the biblical chronicler. For his name should be substituted the name of Cyrus, who, when the evening of the fateful day arrived, gave the order to break the dam of the Euphrates at the pre-established point. The river,

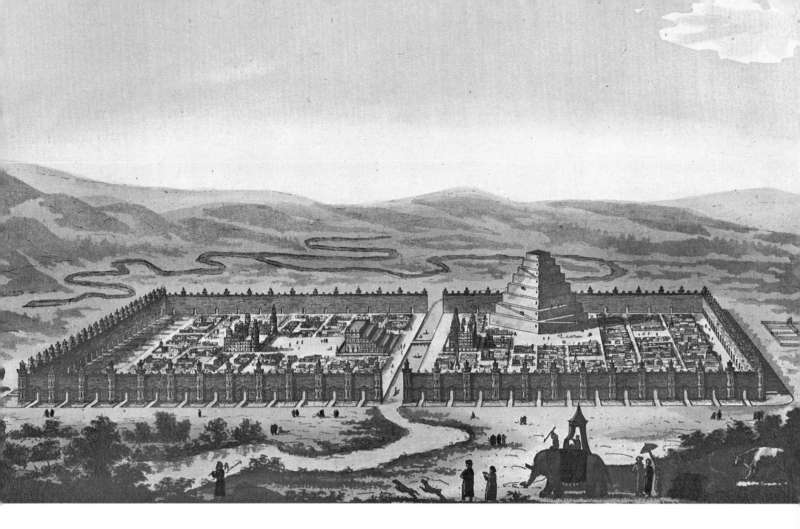

On facing page: *A Persian archer in a reconstruction of Ludovico Menin (Milan, Bertarelli Collection).* Above: *An ancient view of Babylon. The city, whose name means "The Gate of God", was fated to suffer other sieges before and after that of Cyrus. In November of 691 B.C. it was taken and destroyed by Sennacherib of Assyria. In September of 519 B.C. a certain Naditabira, who pretended to be Nebuchadnezzar, after having liberated Babylon from Persian control, was besieged there by Darius for a year and seven months. When the city was taken, he was killed.* Below: *In a beautiful engraving of Ludovico Cheron (Milan, Bertarelli Collection) Cyrus superintends the work of changing the course of the Euphrates.*

as has been mentioned, trasversed the city, cutting through the walls of Babylon in two places. Its waters were so deep that the break in the walls did not represent a danger from outside enemies. But with the unexpected diversion of the waters into the Persian canals the level of the river became so low that it was possible not only for cavalry but also for infantry to advance along the edges of the river .

What happened thereafter, besides the death of Belshazzar (also noted by Xenophon), is vigorously narrated in the furious prophecy of Jeremiah (51:30 et seq.): "And Babylon shall become heaps, a dwelling place for dragons, an astonishment, and hissing, without an inhabitant." In a word, much blood flowed, notwithstanding a Babylonian clay cylinder which states textually: "I, Cyrus, King of all the World, entered peacefully into Babylon in the midst of joy and ovations...."

The task of taking possession of the royal palace was entrusted to two sons of Cyrus, Gobrias and Gadata. They were easily able to overcome the guards, taken by surprise while they were drinking around the fire, and to find Belshazzar and to kill him with all his followers. Thereupon, according to Xenophon, they ran to kiss the feet of Cyrus "shedding tears of tenderness."

ROME (508 B.C.)

The eternal city's first siege

It is now universally accepted as certain among scholars that, in its most ancient period, Rome was governed by a monarchy and that it had seven kings. The monarchical order lasted from 753 to 509 B.C. and under it Rome advanced to a firm position of ascendency over Latium. The advance of Rome, however, was interrupted by the Etruscans who, for some time, held the city under their sway. The last kings, the Tarquins, are generally accepted to be Etruscans by the most authoritative historians. Since the Tarquins acted to weaken the patricians (the second ruler of the Tarquins was called the Proud because he never consulted the senate), the nobility of Rome reacted strongly and, in 509 B.C., were successful in expelling them and in founding the republic.

The Tarquins found refuge in Clusium near the lucumon, or king, Porsenna, and did their utmost to convince him to attack Rome and to restore them to the throne. It was an example, they said, that had to be given to the world. To expel the kings and to install a republican regime—this was a grave offense to the gods, from whom the institution of monarchy was (according to them) an obvious emanation. Porsenna hesitated for a time. Finally, considering a war to give an Etruscan king to Rome to be undoubtedly more convenient than letting such a dangerous power wax ever stronger through peace, he ordered his army to prepare to march.

When the news reached Rome, the senate trembled: according to Livy, as never before, the patricians, who were in power, were afraid that the plebeians would exchange, through fear, their liberty for peace and open the door again to the monarchy. It therefore became generous in largesse and promises, reducing duties and tributes and fighting against speculation in such commodities as salt, which was put under state monopoly. All this reinforced the unity of the citizens and the prestige of the republic. It was not difficult to organize the city for defense, the main part of which, in those times, had not yet extended its borders beyond the Tiber. The river, therefore, constituted the principal barrier against the enemy, and the Janiculum Hill, arising across the Tiber, was an advanced defense point. A little more than a century before, King Ancus Martius had strengthened it with a garrison and had joined it to the city by means of the Sublicium Bridge. But the Janiculum Hill did not stop Porsenna, who conquered it by assault. Encouraged by their success, the Etruscans swarmed down the hill and made for the bridge. On their arrival they found there three men with their weapons in hand. History has handed down their names to us: they were Spurius Lartius, Titus Herminius, and Horatius Cocles. History has justly reserved the greater fame for

the latter. It was apparently his decision to sacrifice himself at the bridgehead, to give time to other members of the bridge guard to destroy the only possible means of reaching his native city. The others stood by him, a point of honor when the rest of the Roman forces had wished to flee at the sight of the Etruscans rushing down from Janiculum Hill. Horatius Cocles had inspired this fellow soldiers with his words and example, urging them to destroy the bridge while he slowed the enemy.

The Etruscans, when they saw what was happening, stopped for a moment in surprise and wonder. Then, angered by the mocking words of Horatius, they let forth a swarm of arrows, which he stopped with his shield. Thereafter they advanced and engaged the defenders with their swords. He fought valiantly until he felt the trembling of the bridge which was about to fall. He then made an invocation to "Father Tiber" and threw himself into the river, which he swam across despite the weight of his armor and the arrows of the enemy, until he happily reached the Roman shore. He received, as a reward, as much land as he could himself plow within the space of a day. And every Roman felt himself obliged to give him part of his own ration of food. Lartius and Herminius were saved as well.

On the facing page, above the title: *In a fresco on the ceiling of the Palazzo Braschi, Rome, present location of the Museum of Rome, Horatius Cocles confronts the Etruscans of Porsenna while his comrades cut the bridge over the Tiber.* Above: *A Pinelli engraving, Clelia with her companions, crosses the river to bring back the prisoners. These two episodes are scarcely credible from a historical point of view.* Below: *Etruscan weapons and armor according to a reconstruction of the early XIX century.*

According to legend the incident on the Sublicium Bridge convinced Porsenna to abandon the idea of taking Rome by force. Instead, he invested it by siege and expected it to fall through hunger. With this in mind he blockaded part of the Tiber with warships, cutting off the city from the mountains and valleys of the other side and besides transporting raiding parties across the river into the fertile countryside which extended up to the walls of Rome. The activity of these raiders forced the Romans to keep their herds shut within the city and prevented the people from going outside the gates.

It was the first siege in the history of Rome and this fact troubled the thoughts of a noble youth, Caius Mucius. To him the siege seemed to be a dishonor for Rome, an intolerable burden, a shame to be erased through a noble gesture. He took the decision to accomplish this by himself alone, in the very middle of the enemy camp. In order that his fellow citizens would not think that he was deserting, Caius Mucius explained his plan to the senate. Having obtained the consent of the republic he selected a well-sharpened dagger and hid it within the folds of his robe and departed.

When he reached the Etruscan camp he mixed in with the soldiers gathered around King Porsenna and his record keeper, who were distributing pay to the soldiers. King and record keeper were dressed in almost the same way and Caius Mucius could not distinguish one from the other. He could not find out which was which without betraying himself so he took a chance. He approached the one who seemed more frequently to speak to the soldiers and, hoping it was Porsenna, thrust the dagger into his breast. It was, however, the paymaster. Captured and brought before the lucumon, the young man was far from intimidated and shouted that all Rome was ready to repeat his action and that Porsenna was not destined to enjoy a long life. Then, almost as if he wished to punish the hand that had erred, he plunged his right hand in a brazier which was kept burning ready for sacrifice, and left it there until the fire had consumed it. Porsenna arose from his seat, horrified but

Caius Cordus Mucius, popularly known as Mucius Scevola, puts his hand in the brazier to punish it for having killed the record keeper instead of Porsenna. Porsenna observes with wonder the sacrifice of Mucius which, from that time on, will endow Mucius and all his descendants with the name of Scevola, that is, the left-handed (actually scaevola *was the name of an amulet against the evil eye). This is another fresco from the Museum of Rome. As in the case of Horatius Cocles and Clelia, illustrated in the preceding pages, this one, Mucius Scevola, represents an attempt by Livy to give a heroic and positive imprint to events which, in reality, must have been contrary to the rising fortune of Rome. In the Gigli Hall of the Palazzo Vecchio in Florence a fresco of Scevola by Domenico Ghirlandaio (1449-1494) has been preserved while on the façade of the Bentivoglio-Savelli and Ricci Palazzi in Rome two more by Polidoro da Caravaggio (1500-1546) can be admired. Left: Etruscan warriors with Greek helmets, in vigorous attitudes.*

struck with admiration. This gesture, he said to his followers, gave Mucius the right to be treated as a soldier, not as an assassin. And he allowed him to return to Rome free, where the hero received the name of Scevola, meaning left-handed, from *scaeva* (the left hand), as well as the gift of a field from his grateful country.

A short time afterward, Porsenna made an offer of peace to the Romans. He attempted to impose the return of the Tarquins, more to honor his word to them than from conviction, and, after the first Roman refusal, he did not insist on this point. Instead he asked for a certain number of hostages in exchange for the abandonment of the Janiculum Hill by the Etruscan garrison. Among the hostages was a certain Clelia, famous for having organized the flight of a group of girl hos-

tages from the Etruscan camp. Porsenna, in admiration, wanted to have her back simply for the pleasure of liberating her personally. The Romans gave her back to him; and the lucumon, praising her courage, offered her the opportunity of taking back with her to Rome other hostages that she might choose. Clelia chose the children and went back to her city with them. In Rome there awaited her an unbelievable honor for a woman: that of being portrayed in an equestrian statue. On the highest point of the Sacred Way, according to Livy, was placed the statue of the young girl mounted on a horse. The same story relates a deed rare in the history of sieges: Porsenna, moved by the misery to which Rome had been reduced, gave to the Romans his own camp, well provided with Etruscan grain.

PLATAEA (428-427 B.C.) *The useless bushes of Mount Cyteron*

The long Peloponnesian War (431-404 B.C.) was characterized by cruelty and betrayals committed in the name of loyalty to either bloc engaged in the struggle: Athens. The beautiful Beotian city decided to remain exuberance, and on the other side, Sparta, harsh, tenacious, and conservative to the point of narrow-mindedness. In 433 B.C. in a quarrel between Dyrachion, Corinth, and Corcyra, Athens came to the aid of Corcyra, while Sparta upheld Corinth. The Spartans offered an agreement but Athens, following the advice of Pericles, refused to negotiate. It was war.

At the beginning of the third year of conflict, that is, in 428 B.C., Archidamos, King and Commander of the Spartans, turned his attention to Plataea, an ally of Athens. The beautiful Beotian city decided to remain true to the alliance and not to open its gates to the Spartans. Archidamos thereupon took measures to besiege it. He caused a palisade to be built completely around the city and ordered the construction of an embankment which would equal the height of the walls. Using timber from Mount Cyteron and filling in with bundles of twigs, branches, earth, and stones, within the space of seventy days and seventy nights the embankment was ready to bear the weight of assault machines. However, the Plataeans in the meantime had heightened the circling wall in proportion to the embankment, raising a wall of wood, reinforced with brick and earth, which they gathered not only from their own dwellings but even daringly from territory held by the enemy, under which they had built a tunnel. In addition, behind the wooden superstructure, protected by dampened hides against incendiary missiles, they erected another semicircle. If the enemy forced a passage through the first circular defense, he would have to start again from the beginning. From the embankment, the battering rams of the Peloponnesians (as Thucydides called the Spartans and their allies) tried in vain to destroy the huge superstructure. More than one machine was wrecked in the struggle, with its bronze head broken off by the chained beams which the Plataeans let fall from the top of the wall.

Archidamos then tried his luck with fire. He had the short space between the embankment and the wall filled with faggots and had others thrown within the city. Then, with incendiary arrows he set fire to the bundles. The Plataeans thought they were lost, but providential showers of rain put out the flames, while the Peloponnesians had one more reason to inveigh against their bad fortune.

September of 428 B.C. had almost arrived and the good season for warfare was about to end. Archidamos substituted the primitive palisade with a double wall around the city. Within Plataea there were now besieged four hundred combatant Plataeans, eighty Athenians, and one hundred and ten women, adept in the making of bread. The rest of the citizens (women, old people, and children) had been sent to safety in Athens some time previously. Archidamos left a Spartan garrison to guard half the wall (the other half was guarded by Thebans) and then gave leave to his allies to spend the winter at home.

During the winter some Plataeans attempted to leave the city and reach Athens. The night was dark and stormy, with showers of rain and gales of wind. The fugitives placed ladders on the wall erected by Archidamos without being seen. When the Peloponnesian sentries realized that they were being attacked, it was too late: two hundred Plataeans were on the march to safety, toward Athens.

When the good weather returned it was not necessary to renew the attacks. Plataea fell from hunger and opened the gates. There ensued a curious procedure. After the establishment of a court composed of five judges who had arrived from Sparta, the Plataeans were called upon to answer, one after the other, the same question: If, in the war that had just ended for them, they had done anything to the advantage of Sparta and her allies. Whoever replied "no" found the executioner waiting for him as he left the court.

In this way the remaining Plataeans perished. The hundred and ten women were sold as slaves. The city was left to the Thebans who razed it to the ground. This was in the year 427 B.C. Plataea and Athens had been allies for ninety-three years.

A

VEII (404-396 B.C.)
A Latin Iliad

Veii was one of the most important cities of ancient Italy. She was raised in a well protected position, high on a cliff of southern Etruria, at two and a half hours' march from Rome. Her walls were powerful and the city rich in temples and marble buildings. She was populous and civilized, rich and strong. She was, in fact, too rich and too strong for Rome, which considered her the most serious menace to her growing power and the most annoying neighbor on the right bank of the Tiber.

War fatally arrived and marked a turn in Roman history: it was the first war conducted beyond the borders of the original Latin people, the first in which operations were not suspended during winter, the first in which the State paid its soldiers a daily stipend.

The war against Veii made such a deep impression on the Roman spirit that it became legendary. Historians have noted cases of divine intervention, superhuman deeds of heroes, and celestial vendettas after the victory, obtained at last after ten years, in a curious analogy with the account of Homer: almost a Latin *Iliad*, still awaiting its own poet.

Although encounters between the Romans and the inhabitants of Veii are mentioned toward the end of the Age of Romulus, the decisive impact did not happen until the end of the V century B.C., after a forty-year truce, given by the Romans at the request of the Veientines. An uncertain truce at best, broken, for example, in 444 B.C. (310 from the founding of Rome), when the Roman colony of Fidenae came under the control of Veii. The representatives of Roman government at Fidenae received the order to kill themselves and could only obey. The Roman reprisals, conducted by Aulus

Cornelius Cosso, were severe and long lasting. Fidenae was taken three years later, through a stratagem which today seems to have been the dress rehearsal for the siege of Veii: an underground passage cut through the rock. Messengers from Veii were sent over all Etruria in search of support against the wrath of Rome. But the reply was negative. Veii had broken the truce on her own initiative and would have to bear the consequences.

Veii's isolation did not cease even when the Romans, angry at some slight provocation, lay siege to the city.

It was 404 B.C. (350 from the founding of Rome). The last decade of independence was beginning for Veii, troubled by internal strife which convinced the rest of Etruria not to interfere. Resolved to come to a final decision, the Romans established a winter camp in the field, overriding considerable opposition in their own ranks. Appius Claudius, the military tribune with power of consul, defended this decision firmly as well as that of war to the end.

Appius Claudius was helped by an unexpected night sortie of the Veientines who, within a very short time, destroyed siege works which had cost months of effort to the Roman engineers. This news put an end to discord and encouraged patricians and plebeians to form a new army composed of volunteers, who, in a short time, reconstructed what the Veientines had destroyed.

But disappointments had not finished their course: two Etrurian cities of Capena and Falerii, considering

Crested Etruscan helmets equipped with fixed and mobile visors, according to an ancient representation reproduced in watercolor in the first half of the XIX century.
Below: *An engraving of Bartolomeo Pinelli: Roman women sacrifice their jewels to the common treasury to enable it to bear the cost of war. The print is a part of the* Gran Quadro della Storia di Roma Antica, *published in Venice in the first half of the XIX century (Milan, Bertarelli Collection). Such incidents were frequent in the course of Roman history, especially during the Republic.*

le Dame Romane si privano delle loro gioie

that Veii was about to fall and that the Roman menace would fall on themselves, suddenly attacked the Sabine camp nearest to Veii, under the military tribune Marcus Sergius. The Veientines, believing that all Etruria was coming to their aid, in turn launched their own sortie. In spite of the surprise attack the Romans held, in the hope of reinforcements from the main camp. This, however, was under the command of Lucius Virginius, unfriendly toward Sergius due to petty rivalry. The former, learning of the situation, withheld sending help under the pretense that Sergius should ask for it; Marcus Sergius, under the influence of his pride, did no such thing and, considering the day already lost, ordered a retreat all the way back to Rome. This was in the year 401 B.C. (352 from the founding of Rome). One year later, the Romans recaptured the former positions at Veii and held them without difficulty until 398 B.C., when Capena and Falerii repeated their attack. But the hesitation of Sergius and Virginius had at least served some purpose. At the first alarm reinforcements rushed to the walls of Veii from the main camp and the contingents from Capena and Falerii were met separately and annihilated. The Veientines, after having made once again a sortie, were obliged to flee back within their walls and close the gates even before all of their troops had returned.

This success raised somewhat the spirits of the Romans, so beset by calamities that they seemed to be the target of the anger of the gods: a severe winter which froze the water over the Tiber, an unusually hot summer, accompanied by pestilence. The Sibylline Books were consulted and the feast of the *Lettisternium* was celebrated for the first time in the history of Rome. This very ancient ceremony, of unknown origin, consisted of a solemn banquet in honor of the gods. The patricians, who during the annual elections for military tribune held during the previous year, following the shameful behavior of Sergius and Virginius, had been able to obtain the election of only one tribune, succeeded in getting the public to believe – according to Livy – that the wrath of the gods was also caused by the unexpected electoral success of the plebeians, who had cast opprobrium on so many noble families. The electorate did not hesitate: the new military tribunes of 398 B.C. were all patricians. One of them, elected to the tribunate for the second time, was named Marcus Furius Camillus. Since he was fated to be the conqueror of Veii, we must accept the possibility that the gods were indeed placated. The Romans, however, who did not know that they had finally found the man of destiny, were still somewhat apprehensive. Rumors were current of other prodigies, an indication of persistent divine anger. Principal among these was the unusual rising of the water level in the Alban lake. Emissaries were sent to Delphi to consult the Oracle: but the reply was sent directly back to Veii. One day, while the opposing sentries were engaged in exchanging taunts and insults, in their usual manner, there suddenly appeared on the wall of the besieged city an old man who had the air of one inspired. The

exchanges between the sentries ceased while he, in a tone of prophecy, shouted in the ensuing silence that the fall of Veii would not come until the waters of the Alban lake found an outlet for the overflow. A Roman soldier who was particularly religious and affected by the prophecy, noting that the speaker was a haruspex, requested from the Veientines permission to consult with the soothsayer. The meeting took place on the "no man's land" between the walls of the besieged city and the most advanced trenches of the besiegers. The old man, however, did not have the chance to speak. The young Roman seized hold of him and, using him as a shield against the horrified and indignant Etruscans, dragged him back within his own lines. A few hours later, the haruspex found himself in the presence of the Senate of Rome where he was called upon to repeat his prophecy and to explain that the gods that day were angered against Veii and for that reason had inspired him with the fatal words. He was not believed until the emissaries from Delphi had returned and given the same reply: for the capture of Veii it would be necessary to cause the waters to flow from the Alban lake by artificial means. The work was therefore begun which resulted in the flooding of the nearby territory. The Romans, however, still found reason for a certain amount of nervousness inasmuch as serious news was arriving from Etruria: from the north contingents were coming to the fray from a people with whom the Romans were

In 444 B.C. Fidenae, then a Roman colony, fell under the sway of Veii. The Roman reprisals, conducted by Aulus Cornelius Cosso, were long and severe and ended with the reconquest of the rebellious city in 441 B.C. A stratagem was used in the capture of this city which was probably a rehearsal for that later used in the conquest of Veii: the excavation of a tunnel into the rock. Above is a view of the supposed entrance, cut by the Romans during the Veii campaign right to the temple of Juno. The noise of the final blows of the invaders' pickaxes was smothered by the chants of the inhabitants of Veii, gathered within the temple invoking the protection of Juno for the city soon to be taken.

Various types of scaling ladders in use since remote antiquity. The ladder remained for centuries the assault apparatus which was the most simple and often the most efficient. We will find it again in use at Dien Bien Phu in 1954 (see page 242). At right: A tower. From what has remained of the walls of Veii it is not clear that they were reinforced by towers. It is possible that the parts of the city which jutted out from the rest, which followed the curve of the cliff on which the city was built, took the place of towers, which alliwed the Veientines to strike the enemy on the flank while he attempted to scale the walls. Below: The Battle of Camillus by Gaspare Celio (1571-1640), an oil painting preserved in the Galleria Borghese in Rome. Camillus, had a long and fortunate life. He is said to have died of the plague in 365 B.C., when he was more than eighty years old. His fame has come down to us notably in the episode of Brennus during which the famous phrase "Woe to the conquered!" was pronounced.

not yet familiar — the Gauls — while the Etrurians, who were now making a united front against the new terror, had decided to help Veii and to settle accounts, once and for all, with their oldest and most pressing enemies, the Romans.

The Romans were also thinking, now that the gods were placated, of hastening the end of this great conflict. Marcus Furius Camillus, having been made Dictator, selected, according to his right, Publius Cornelius Scipio, a man in whom he had great confidence, as *magister equitum* or commander of the cavalry. Levies were raised and for once there was no resistance.

The new army won its first victory over the troops of Falerii and Capena: their camps were completely destroyed. The booty was immense, but Camillus gave only a small part to the soldiers and sent the rest to Rome where, once the war was finished, it would be employed according to public will for the restoration of a temple already dedicated by Servius Tullius to the Mother Matuta, goddess of the morning light.

When Camillus arrived at Veii, he put an end to patrol encounters in "no man's land" and employed all his soldiers in reinforcing the siege works and in building another one which would later prove decisive: a passage from the Roman lines cut into the rock under the enemy.

Camillus was now so certain of victory that he wrote a letter to the senate to request advice on the disposition of the booty. Inasmuch as this would be the greatest among the many acquisitions won by the Roman armies, it was suggested to permit the rank and file to pillage

PARTE ANTERIORE DEL VASO VEIENTE

PARTE POSTERIORE DEL VASO VEIENTE

Figures from Etruscan jars showing warriors engaged in combat (left) and, on the right, in the process of mounting a chariot. The ornaments and style greatly resemble the style of classical Greece. In effect, Greek myths appear frequently in Etruscan tombs, especially notable in their sensitive and aesthetic treatment by this people so dedicated to the pleasures of life.

as they wished. And this was the opinion that prevailed, implying also some astute political calculation. If the booty were divided into equal parts and individuals were assigned their share by the state — as some suggested — it would perhaps give rise to suspicion by the plebeians that something had remained in the coffers of the quaestors, and that there would thereupon be a pretext for a new distribution. It was therefore more useful for all, and more favorable to the senate's popularity, for everyone to take what he could.

The result was that Camillus saw half of Rome ar-

rive on the field. He gave the order to his soldiers to hold themselves ready and then the Dictator raised a solemn prayer to the gods.

He then gave the order for the attack and the entire multitude rushed toward the wall with a fury which unnerved the Veientines, already somewhat disconcerted by the end of the skirmishes in "no man's land." The invocations to Juno in the temple dedicated to her on the rock cliff of Veii were interrupted by the intrusion of Roman soldiers bursting forth suddenly from the tunnel and shielded by the outside clamor. They were chosen shock troops and they carried on their work without pity and with controlled vigor: in short moments everyone was at his post, either on the wall in back of the defenders, or engaged in opening the gates, or in setting fire to houses in order to stop the showers of stones from the roofs, a refuge for the terrorized women and slaves.

When the city was well within Roman hands, Camillus, in not too great haste, gave the order to spare the defenseless and to commence the pillage. Since the booty turned out to be much greater than had been calculated, he took the occasion to raise a prayer to the gods which was often done when mortals, having been granted almost an excess of good fortune, feared somehow to offend the feelings of the gods and to thereby induce them to send new disasters down to earth. He begged that the gods send some small misfortune to him and the Roman people, to take the place of or avert the chance of a major calamity. He had hardly finished when suddenly he slipped and fell. He got up again, it is said, satisfied that part of his prayer had been answered. As for the Roman people, the requested disaster arrived some years later, but it was scarcely a slight one: it came with the tortures of the Gauls as they set fire to Rome, destroying it to such a point that, when its rebuilding was discussed, there were those who proposed to transfer the sacred Penates to another city that, although ruined, was still standing: this city was Veii.

TYRE AND GAZA (332 B.C.)
The impossible sieges of Alexander the Great

The lightning-like career of Alexander the Great is not lacking in examples of brilliant siege operations. However, those of Tyre and Gaza in 332 B.C. are the most impressive.

He was then twenty-four years old and had been on the Macedonian throne for four years. In 335 B.C. we find him along the Danube putting down a rebellion of the Thracian tribes, then in Illyria and finally in Thebes, also in revolt. After the capital of Boetia had been razed to the ground and his control reestablished over Greece, Alexander, in the summer of 334 B.C., resumed the war against Persia, which had already been begun by his father. Crossing the Hellespont with a force of thirty thousand infantry and five thousand cavalry, he had beaten the Persian army on the Granicus River and had thereupon begun the conquest of Asia Minor. After having overcome Darius III at Issus in 333 B.C., he informed the army of his plan to conquer Egypt. The idea appeared to be unusual, inasmuch as it interrupted a victorious march to the

east with a dangerous digression to the south. But Alexander knew what he was doing. He needed to occupy the Mediterranean ports in order to have a place for his own fleet of one hundred and sixty ships and, at the same time, to inhibit the Persian army from having bases at its disposal from which to launch an attack on Greece. The Syrian campaign was therefore an operation to reinforce the Macedonian flank, for the thrust toward the east and toward Babylonia.

Tyre was then a double city; part of it lay on the coast (near the present Lebanese village of Es-Sur), the other part rose from an island, separated from the mainland by an arm of the sea about twenty-two hundred feet wide; in effect a citadel constructed on inaccessible rock one hundred and forty feet above sea level and protected by massive walls.

Two centuries before Alexander, the great Nebuchadnezzar of Babylon had besieged it for thirty years in vain, receiving the one serious setback of his life.

After the part of the city built on the mainland had

been easily captured, in the beginning of 332 B.C. Alexander summoned Dyadis the Thessalian, who was in command of the Macedonian Corps of Engineers, and entrusted him with the construction of a causeway destined to cross the twenty-two hundred feet which divided the fortress city from the mainland. It was a memorable undertaking: as we shall see, in a later siege, Cardinal Richelieu would remember it at the siege of La Rochelle thirteen hundred years later, and would get inspiration and know-how from Alexander.

The famous forests of Lebanon provided the beams for the foundation on which the construction was based. The buildings of mainland Tyre, demolished to their foundations, furnished the material to fill it in. The entire army collaborated in the undertaking and, according to tradition, Alexander personally carried stones on his shoulders.

Ships equipped with archers came out from the fortress from time to time to harass the Macedonians while they were working. Alexander thereupon ordered the construction of two immense towers, one hundred and fifty feet high, equipped with catapults and other hurling machines. These advanced toward the fortress as the causeway progressed until it was over two hundred feet long and meanwhile attacked the ships which were interfering with the work of the engineers. One night the Tyrians sent two fireships out against the towers and the causeway. The wind was favorable and the towers burned like torches.

On opposite page and above: *Two moments during the siege of Tyre by Alexander the Great. These are miniatures from a manuscript of the XV century preserved at the Petit Palais in Paris and entitled* Histoire du Grand Alexandre. Below: *A reconstruction of a siege tower used in antiquity for attacks from the sea. From the* Poliorceticon *of Justus Lipsius, the Latinized name of the Flemish humanist Joost Lips (1546-1606), author of numerous works about the ancient Roman world.*

Alexander the Great shown in a XVI century representation exulting in his military triumphs. At Tyre and Gaza the great Macedonian conducted two sieges which became famous through the cyclopean works carried out by his engineers. The causeway erected to join Tyre to the mainland became the inspiration to Cardinal Richelieu during the siege of La Rochelle in 1627.

Alexander immediately had two more towers constructed. Then, leaving the command of the siege to his lieutenants, Perdiccas and Craterus, he went to Sidon for the purpose of preparing a fleet which would permit him to protect the causeway from the attacks of the Tyrians by day and night. Soon he was able to count on two hundred and twenty-four ships, collected from the Sidians, from Gerostratus, the King of Arados, from Emilios, the King of Byblos, from Rhodes, from Solois of Cilicia, and from various cities of Lycia and Cyprus. Four thousand hoplites sent from Greece under the command of Cleander were distributed among the ships; and thereupon the fleet set itself in motion. Arriving in front of Tyre the fleet was arranged in battle order with Pnitagoras in command of the left wing and Alexander himself in command of the right wing. The besieged, having heard about the formation of the fleet, had decided to sally forth and give battle. But when it appeared on the horizon in all its power, they changed their minds and restricted themselves to defensive oper-

ations. The two harbor entrances of the island city, the northern one called the Sidonian Harbor and the southern one called the Egyptian, were both very narrow. The entrance to the first was two hundred feet wide and the second, three hundred and thirty. Several ships, fastened together sidewise, in flanking position, were sufficient to block both entrances. Alexander concentrated his major forces against the Sidonian harbor, but without any result other than the foundering of three triremes of the blockade. The besieged thereupon removed the blockade of triremes and substituted it with great iron chains. Although it was no longer possible to use ships to damage the causeway, the besieged were far from being discouraged. The forward section of the causeway was now in fact within the range of their catapults. They proceeded to bombard it with a new type of projectile: burning sand. Then they put into action machines which were later called "crows" which had a tremendous effect: through the use of sharpened hooks they fell suddenly on the Macedonians while they were at work, hooking them like fish and carrying them up to the wall. Here they were tortured in full view of their horrified but impotent comrades.

Alexander's men worked in an atmosphere of terror, under incessant attacks by the Tyrians who sometimes, in a single night, succeeded in destroying the labor of many days. Finally the causeway was completed and the battering rams were ready to begin their work against the walls. But the walls, however, were so solid that attacks with the battering rams obtained practically no results whatever.

At first the operations of battering rams mounted on ships and attacks from the open sea gave no better results. Then, suddenly, the first breach was opened. The infantry poured in, but were repulsed. The battering rams were returned to the task incessantly, continuing without interruption and, at last, a good section of the wall fell into the sea. Thereupon ships equipped with boarding gangways made fast below the city and that was the end of Tyre. The Macedonians entered the city and there began a furious massacre. The pent-up wrath of seven months of suffering and torment exploded and no quarter was given to the Tyrians. Eight thousand were killed during the attack and two thousand were hanged immediately afterwards. Thirty thousand survivors, including women and children, were sold into slavery. The entire city was destroyed, except those parts which were considered of specific use for the naval base which Alexander wished to construct on the site.

After having settled accounts with Tyre, the Macedonian army continued its march toward Egypt. After proceeding one hundred and fifty miles, it found itself confronted with another obstacle which had to be eliminated: the strong fortress city of Gaza.

Situated across the sole route between Syria and Egypt, erected on a rocky hill, Gaza enjoyed great strategic importance. The foresight of its inhabitants had fortified it with strong walls, thanks to which the Persian garrison, under the command of the courageous Batis, was able to refuse the Macedonian command to open the city gates, and to engage in warfare with Alexander with some hope of success. The refusal of Batis, and even more, the apparent indomitability of the stronghold, piqued the self-esteem of the young Emperor and sharpened his political calculations. If he were able to take the city his prestige would ascend to the realms of divinity: the world would have to acknowledge his power of accomplishing miracles. On the other hand, to leave in the hands of the Persians such a strong position to his own rear would be an unforgivable military error. Therefore it was necessary only to call for Dyadis and to give him new orders. This is what Alexander did. The plan he laid out was supremely simple; to raise a ramp entirely around the city in order to facilitate the placement of siege machines which would be able to batter the walls from the proper elevation; in other words, to buld a huge hill.

Mindful of their arduous experiences suffered on the causeway of Tyre, the Macedonian soldiers set themselves

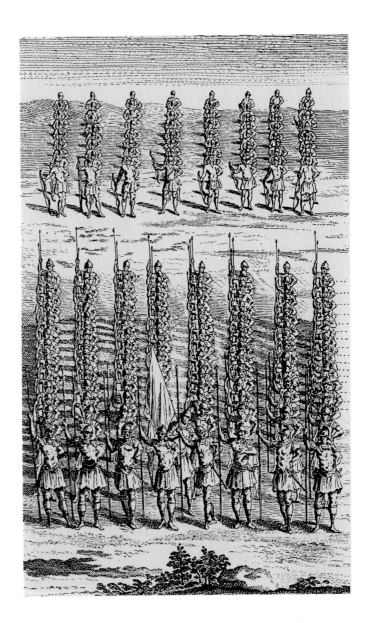

A XVII century print from the library of the Musée de l'Armée of Paris showing the deep array of the soldiers in the phalanx, the typical fighting unit of the Macedonian army.

to their labor with decided vigor and in less than two months Gaza was surrounded with a Cyclopean rampart topped by a huge platform. The machines were set up upon this and shortly thereafter, within the houses of Gaza, the people of the city began to hear the sinister booming of rams against the walls. But the walls were very strong, and the desired breaches were not opened. Alexander thereupon ordered his soldiers to begin what is called, in terms of siege warfare, mining operations. Mine passages were dug under the walls to weaken the base and facilitate their fall.

The Macedonians then put their scaling ladders into place and it was impossible to stop the impetus of their attack. The walls and streets were covered with dead and wounded. Batis was among the latter who continued to fight until he fell from loss of blood.

With one of his typical and unexplainable gestures of cruelty, Alexander had him tied to a cart and dragged around the walls. When the horses began their course, Batis was still alive.

SYRACUSE (213-212 B.C.)

Archimedes' "iron hand" against Marcellus' "sambuca"

Following the dark days after Cannae, Rome appeared definitely to have lost the contest against Carthage. But unfortunately for the great African power, Hannibal, its leader, did not seize the favorable moment that was offered to him and fortune thereafter turned away from him. Marcus Claudius Marcellus, having received the consulate for the third time, won a victory over him at Nola while Hannibal was tarrying in Campania awaiting help from his homeland. Marcellus then moved to Sicily, where Appius Claudius Pulcher, praetor of the army, was attempting to keep the city of Syracuse from falling under the Carthaginian sphere of influence.

In 215 B.C., with the death of the Syracusan tyrant, Hiero, a faithful ally of Rome, the city had fallen into the hands of his young and dissolute nephew, Hieronymus, who, because of his cruelties, was eliminated by a conspiracy in the same year. Syracuse changed its government to a democratic republic, establishing a regime in which, thanks to the maneuvers of Hannibal, the pro-Carthaginian faction prevailed over the pro-Roman one. The leaders of the pro-Carthaginian faction were Hippocrates and Epicydes, two brothers who were natives of Carthage but of Syracusan extraction. These two, with the support of the Carthaginians, were planning to establish their power throughout the entire island.

The city of Leontini, where Hippocrates had caused the death of many Roman citizens, was another reason for discord between Syracuse and Rome. Marcellus, when he arrived in Sicily, took possession of Leontini, protecting it from Carthaginian control, as an example, punishing Roman citizens who had supported Carthage by having them beaten with rods and then executed. He spared, however, natives who were not Romans. Hippocrates, however, spread the report that Marcellus, once he had occupied Leontini, had massacred all the inhabitants, even children. Making use of the natural resentment of the Syracusans, he forced them to appoint him and his brother as praetors of the city.

When the Roman consul arrived under the walls of Syracuse, he pitched camp and sent emissaries to inform the citizenry about what had really happened at Leontini. His version was not believed, however, and thereupon hostilities broke out.

Having received timely help from the Carthaginian fleet in the form of men, horses, and elephants, the Syracusans prepared to resist the Romans. Appius Claudius Pulcher, commander of the infantry, approached the walls from the land while the consul Marcellus from his position with the fleet, made up of sixty-eight quinqueremes, blockaded and attacked the city from the sea. Both sides began to put into operation devices and strat-

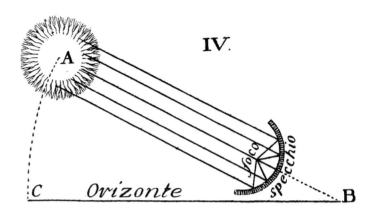

A diagram of the mirror supposed to have been used by Archimedes during the siege of Syracuse for focusing the rays of the sun on the ships of Marcellus, causing them to burst into flames. The first support of this thesis comes from Claudius Galenus (129-201), the famous doctor of Marcus Aurelius, followed shortly afterwards by the medieval Byzantine historians, Giovanni Zonara and Giovanni Tzetze. But the major historians, Polybius, Livy, and Plutarch do not even mention it. Below: A map of ancient Syracuse from the Tabulae Geograficae by various authors, published in Padua in 1699. On facing page: The death of Archimedes, in a painting by an unknown artist, according to the traditional version, as reported by Cicero. Tzetze, however, reports that the Roman soldier killed the scientist because the latter was attempting to attack him with some machine he had invented.

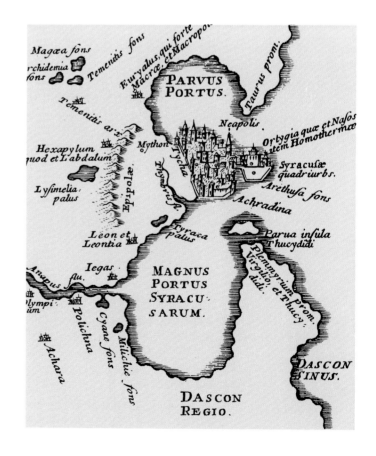

agems destined to become famous and even legendary. The Romans, for example, attached eight ships together making a new assault machine from which a kind of bridge could be projected so that the infantry could enter into direct contact with the defenders.

The defenders, under the wise guidance of Archimedes, who was now seventy-four years old, were no less active: in order to reach ships that were somewhat distant catapults and ballistas were arranged in batteries of long and medium range, while assault ships were attacked by use of various devices which have contributed to the well-merited fame of the Syracusan mathematician and physicist. The most efficient of his inventions was a kind of crane which came out over the walls and by means of a grapple (popular called "the hand of iron") hooked onto the ships and then, through the use of counterbalances, hoisted them up in the air. Finally it let them fall again with effects that can be easily imagined. By means of still other devices the Roman ships were vigorously pulled onto the reefs, where they broke up; and still another stratagem involved the dropping of great weights on the enemy ships which broke through their

decks. One of these huge boulders also fell upon Marcellus' machine, already described, which was formed by the use of eight ships. It was called a "sambuca" (since it resembled somewhat a harp-like musical instrument of the same name). The massive rock, according to Plutarch, weighed ten talents (about 670 pounds) and that was not the only one which fell on the sambuca putting it, in fact, *hors de combat*. Thereupon the consul ordered operations to be suspended and summoned officers from the land and sea operations to a council of war. It was decided to try a night attack from the sea which would permit soldiers to advance very close to the walls, in a safe corner as far as shots from the Syracusan war machines were concerned, inasmuch as these machines, in effect, seemed to have their best effect on attackers who were at some distance. The night attack took place, although without success.

The Roman losses and damages were considerable, while the Syracusans had suffered none at all. Archimedes had opened many spaces within the walls and behind them soldiers, from in effect a protected area, launched boulders and stones by means of "scorpions" – small

artillery pieces of forceful impact but short range.

When we speak of Archimedes' inventions, we should not skip the famous and much-discussed "burning mirrors," by which he is supposed to have set fire to the ships of Marcellus. Despite the fact that the more important historians do not mention them, the mirrors have always been part of the story of the siege. Descartes and Buffon demonstrated the impossibility of constructing a weapon of this kind but an experiment performed in the following century by the French physicist Jules-Antoine Lissajous (1822-1880) seems to have been definitely successful.

Having failed in the attempt to take the city by storm, Marcellus immediately established a strict and unrelenting blockade. His hope was now that the Syracusans would shortly suffer from lack of food supplies. In the meantime, the consul carried on other operations in the neighborhood. He conquered Megara and surprised Hippocrates' army while it was about to make camp near Acila. Plutarch claims that on this occasion Hippocrates lost more than eight thousand men.

One day a Roman ship captured at sea a certain Damippos, a Spartan captain, who, according to Titus Livius, the Syracusans were sending to Philip of Macedon in order to ask for help. As the besieged were very anxious to ransom the prisoner they approached Marcellus for a parley, who thereupon began a long negotia-

Two types of tolleni, *assault devices composed of a beam in counterweight mounted on a mast. A large wicker or wooden basket attached at the end of the traverse beam was hoisted up to the top of the wall, enabling troops to make an assault or even a simple reconnaissance.*

Roman ships equipped with scaling ladders. More ships fastened together were used to form the so-called "sambuca," which can be seen in the colored picture above near the top under the point of the sword of the soldier engaged in killing Archimedes.

tion. In order to discuss the question, he had frequent meetings with the Syracusans near the tower of Galeagra, which he observed to be not very strongly guarded and whose height he calculated with an expert eye.

A short time afterward there occurred the period for the feast of Diana, which in Syracuse was celebrated with three days of festivals. The populace and the defending soldiers took part in them with great enthusiasm. The sentries relaxed their vigilance to the profit of Marcellus, who chose a thousand warriors who were not only brave but skilled in the use of scaling ladders. He ordered them to climb up the tower which he had so attentively observed during the parleys. It was a complete and successful surprise: the sentries fell transfixed by the swords of the Romans who spread out along all the walls. Before it was day, they had broken in the Exapilian Gate and from the outer port had penetrated into the larger port of the city, between the island of Ortigia and the new city. However, the part of Syracuse called Achradina, surrounded by walls like a citadel and divided

into two parts, Nea and Tiche, was still free. But the alarm experienced by the Syracusans allowed the Romans to occupy this land as well. Thereafter, at dawn, Marcellus entered the city through the Gate of Exapilus. He was able to admire, surrounded by his captains, the greatness and beauty of the city.

In other zones of Syracuse, some pockets of resistance stubbornly held out. It was not until the summer of 212 B.C. that the city was completely occupied and put to the sack. In spite of the firm promises of the Roman consul not to make a slave of any Syracusan citizen and not to burn the city, the population suffered outrages by the victors and Syracuse was given over to the flames.

Archimedes died along with the city, Syracuse. As everyone knows, a warrior, ignorant of his identity, taking as a sign of arrogance the old mathematician's brusque demand to be allowed to finish some calculations he was working on, killed him with a blow of his sword. Marcellus was deeply affected by his death and refused thereafter to look on the face of his slayer.

CARTHAGE (149-146 B.C.) *A "final solution"*

The Third Punic War (149-146 B.C.) was shorter than the preceding two and took place almost entirely around the fortifications of Carthage. The destruction of the city was ordered by the votes of the Roman Senate, due also to the implacable insistence of Cato and of his celebrated phrase: *"Delenda est Carthago."* But there were some who, like Scipio Nasica, thought that letting Carthage live would be a stimulus for competition on the part of Rome.

The new conflict was brought about through a quarrel between the King of Numidia, Masinissa, ally of Rome, and Carthage itself. Masinissa was engaged in extending by force the territory which he had inherited from his father. Carthage, after having requested Rome without success to mediate, declared war against Masinissa in 150 B.C. and dispatched against him an army under the command of a general named Hasdrubal (not to be confused with other Carthaginian personages of the same name). This was in violation of one of the points of the treaty of peace, according to which Carthage could not declare war without the authorization of Rome. The latter did not lose any time. A strong Roman force commanded by the two consuls, Manlius

Manilius, responsible for the army, and Lucius Marcius Censorinus, responsible for the fleet, set sail for Utica and prepared to invade Carthage.

Carthage, frightened by the appearance of the Roman war machine, put her fate in the hands of the consuls. The Carthaginian envoys, when they presented themselves in the Roman camp, were informed that they were obliged to give over their fleet, their war machines, and their arms. Since the city would henceforth be under the protection of Rome, it would no longer need arms with which to defend itself. The harsh conditions were accepted: the fleet was burned before the city itself, portable arms (two hundred pieces were reported) and two thousand catapults ended up in the Roman camp.

At this point the consuls dropped their masks and informed the envoys what the final decree of the Roman Senate was: the city was to be destroyed and rebuilt at any place in its territory "as long as it was at a point eighty stadia from the sea."

The envoys listened to this last disposition with dismay and desperation: some were even unable to find enough courage to bear the sad news back to their

CARTHAGINIS OBSIDIO.

On facing page: *The siege of Carthage according to a XVI century engraving.* Above: *A shield called "The Taking of Carthage" which belonged to Charles V.* Right: *Armed Carthaginians according to a reconstruction of the XIX century by Ludovicus Menin and based on ancient pictorial sources. (Milan, Bertarelli Collection). Note the club held by the first warrior on the right. The conflict between Carthage and Rome began in 264 B.C. Although beaten several times, the city of Dido always recovered. It became clear that only a "final solution" would be able to settle the conflict, which was by this time a question of spheres of influence which could not be limited. This explains the stubborn repetition by the censor Cato of the words "Delenda est Carthago."*

own citizens and asked to be allowed to remain in the Roman camp. The others returned to the city with their spirits completely crushed. The people of Carthage were anxiously awaiting them along the top of the city walls. When they saw them arrive, they crowded around them to hear the results of their mission but the envoys would say nothing until they came before the senate. They were willing to declare only before the supreme council, with indignation and sorrow, the irrevocable decrees of the Roman consuls.

The people of Carthage were seized by despair and many of them turned against the senators who had advised submission and also against the envoys themselves who, they considered, should have attempted to dissuade the Romans or not come back. But then there came about a controlled calm on the part of the strong and a common decision on the part of those who were previously divided: the great gates were shut and the entire city was transformed into one tremendous factory for the making of arms. The Carthaginians freed the slaves and dismantled houses to obtain the wood for getting ready a new fleet. To make new weapons, in addition to working in iron and bronze, they even used precious metals. Women offered their hair to make cords for the catapults. Appianus reports that men and women, eating together in large groups and working in day and night shifts for the manufacture of weapons, were successful in turning out a daily production of one hundred shields, three hundred swords, five hundred spears, and a thousand arrows.

The Roman consuls, secure in their belief that they had already disarmed the Carthaginians, awaited the return of the envoys who, in accord with a request of the Carthaginians, had been sent to Rome in the hope of obtaining less harsh conditions. They were unaware of what was going on in Carthage and its citadel of Byrsa.

The city was surrounded by a triple line of bastions, along the width of which were located positions for infantry and cavalry, stalls for horses and elephants and storehouses for provisions and forage. There were two harbors, merchant and military, the latter being permanently barred by means of a heavy chain. An inner lake, which was connected by a narrow passage with the sea, constituted another natural protection. When the consuls finally realized what the situation was, they decided to take the city by assault. Manilius, advancing from the land, and Censorinus, attacking from the sea, caused scaling ladders to be placed on the walls at the spot which they considered to be the weakest, where the walls made a corner toward the port zone. The first and second asaults were repelled by the Carthaginians with great spirit. The consuls decided thereupon to fortify the camps and to make new war machines to increase the supply at hand. Censorinus sent out an expedition in search of lumber but was surprised by Himilcon, called Famea, the prefect of the Carthaginian cavalry, who inflicted on the Romans the loss of five hundred men and many weapons. Nevertheless Censo-

rinus got the wood he was looking for and was able to construct war machines and ladders.

Two of these machines, equipped with rams, were of huge proportions. One of these was operated by special groups of rowers from the fleet. A breach was

Roma apud
Carolum Losi
anno 1773.

GEORGIVS PENCZ
PICTOR NVRNBERG
FACIEBAT ANNO·M·D·
M·XXXIX·

The Fall of Carthage *by Giulio Pippi, known as Giulio Romano (1492-1546), one of Raphael's most assiduous disciples. The print, which dates from 1733 and is part of the Bertarelli Collection of Milan, reproduces one of the frescos of the famous painter. It contains themes from the sixteenth century, especially in architecture, as well as a realism which the painter must have personally experienced. He was, in fact, present at the sack of Rome in 1527. In popular tradition the story of Carthage closes with these scenes and with Scipio weeping over its ruins. But already twenty wears after the "final solution," in the time of Caius Gracchus, the foundation of a new colony there was already under discussion. Caesar would carry it out.*

opened in the walls as a result of their operation but the Carthaginians repaired it in a single night and then, in the course of a very successful sortie, set both machines on fire and put them out of operation. On the following day the Romans, although they saw the Carthaginians waiting for them in the breach with their weapons ready, tried again to penetrate within the city. On this occasion the military tribune Publius Cornelius Scipio Aemilianus, distinguished himself for the first time. He rushed in with a small group and managed to rescue legionnaires who had gone within the walls in former attacks.

On a dark night the Carthaginians attacked the tower on the sea and, once more, Scipio avoided the danger through a stratagem. He came out with ten cavalry squadrons, with each man carrying a lighted torch. The maneuvering of the squadrons struck fear in the Carthaginians who, fearing a general attack, departed.

Without giving up the siege of the city, Manilius thought it more wise to begin by eliminating the danger represented by Hasdrubal and turned his attention to him, with decision and also with swiftness. At a crucial moment during the crossing of a ford, Hasdrubal attacked, causing many losses in the Roman ranks. These would have been even more serious if Scipio had not launched two cavalry charges against the enemy which had the effect of diminishing the Carthaginian pressure against the legionnaires, who were able to recross the river and retreat.

A new attempt of Manilius against Hasdrubal had a much more positive effect inasmuch as in the course of the action Famea's Carthaginian cavalry went over

Carthage had a triple line of walls around it which were almost fifty feet high and so thick that, as partly shown in this ancient illustration, they contained stalls for three hundred elephants and four thousand horses, as well as quarters for twenty-four thousand soldiers and space for arms, equipment, harness, and machines of war. Under the Roman pressure even the temples of the city were transformed to military use and into factories for the production of weapons.

to the Romans. This was a contingent composed of two thousand two hundred cavalrymen, including Gallusa, the son of Masinissa. Scipio and Famea were sent to Rome where they were received with great honors.

In the spring of 148 B.C. the new consul of the army, Calpurnius Piso, and that of the navy, Lucius Mancinus, arrived under the walls of Carthage. They employed the majority of their forces against the different minor cities located on Carthaginian territory. They sacked many of these, although they suffered setbacks at others. When the summer was almost over, Piso retired to Utica to spend the winter.

Meanwhile, back in Rome, Scipio had been elected consul of the people, at the age of thirty-seven years, although the law required that the holder of the office be at least forty-three. He set sail for Africa in 147 B.C. together with reinforcements gathered from the new levies and landed at Utica.

While Piso had been inactive on the continent, Mancinus had attempted another blow against Carthage. He had reached a fortified position and now, with few men and with short rations, he was at the mercy of the enemy.

Scipio freed some Carthaginian prisoners so that they might inform the Carthaginians of his arrival and thereupon set sail from Utica to Carthage. Mancinus and his followers were rescued from the uncomfortable position in which they found themselves and taken aboard ship.

Mancinus returned to Rome, since Serranus, who was to relieve him of the command of the fleet, had already arrived and Scipio immediately moved the camp next to Carthage.

Publius Cornelius Aemilianus, the son of Lucius Aemilius Paulus, and member through adoption of the Scipio family on the part of the conqueror of Hannibal, forced Hasdrubal to take refuge within Carthage and thereupon blockaded the city with many fortifications.

The hour for the "final solution" of the Carthaginian problem struck at the beginning of spring 146 B.C. Using deserters as guides, Scipio overcame the triple line of fortifications and penetrated within the city itself where, fighting from house to house for six days and six nights, through a labyrinth of narrow and tortuous streets, he opened the way to the bottom of the Byrsa, the hill on which the citadel was erected.

It was a terrible week. The struggle was conducted from house to house and since almost all the houses were six stories high, each floor meant a separate battle. There were three streets leading to the Byrsa and in each one the struggle was carried on with the same bitterness, both on the roofs and on the pavements. Fire was not applied to the houses in order not to endanger the legionaries who were fighting on the roofs, but once the Byrsa was reached, Scipio ordered all the houses to be set on fire. The flames spread rapidly throughout the city. Houses collapsed, taking with them in their fall the living, dead, and dying, children, old people, and fighters who had established themselves in the innermost

recesses of the buildings and who could not get out in time because of their wounds.

The engineers charged with leveling the streets for the reinforcements who were arriving for the assault on the Byrsa filled the holes with debris and also with the bodies of the fallen, whether alive or dead.

After the seventh day of this inferno, some of the citizens came to Scipio and asked him if he would spare the lives of those who wished to leave the Byrsa. Scipio agreed to spare the lives of all except the Roman deserters. Thereupon fifty thousand people left the Byrsa while nine hundred Roman deserters remained therein. These rushed to the temple of Aesculapius, which was located at a high and steep point, together with Hasdrubal, followed by his wife and sons. Seeing that the end was near, the survivors came out on the roof of the temple and decided to sell their lives dearly. Hasdrubal, however, who had treated the Roman prisoners during the siege so ferociously, killing them, mutilating them, and throwing them from the walls while still alive, now that Scipio bade him open the gates, showed himself capable of unbelievable cowardice. He threw himself at Scipio's feet, begging for his own safety. While the survivors, who now found themselves without hope,

According to Vitruvius, when the Carthaginians in the capture of Cadiz wished to demolish rock constructions, they took a beam and manufactured what later would become the battering ram. A certain Pephas Menos, a Tyrian, a smith by profession, is said to have invented the counterbalance device which gave the beam its effective movement. Cetras of Chalcedon is reputed to have perfected it, adding a floor and the wheels, if not the covered roof. Because of the slow rate of progress of the machine as well as the general aspect, the Carthaginians called it "the tortoise." The name of "battering ram" (aries) was given to it by the Romans, who also employed such arms without counterbalances.

set fire to the temple, the wife of Hasdrubal, dressed in her richest garments, came out on the roof with her sons, made a salute to the conqueror, and after having killed her two sons with a sword, followed them onto the funeral pyre while still declaiming against the dishonorable conduct of her husband. She died, as Appianus reports, "No longer as the wife of Hasdrubal, but as the consort of the last leader of Carthage and the last matron of the free Phoenician race." Besides the famous tears shed by Polybius, who was present at the massacre, a tear was said to have been observed on the face of Scipio as well, at the sight of the utter ruin to which he had so greatly contributed.

NUMANTIA
(134-133 B.C.)

A patriotism without equal

While Hannibal, resting in Capua, dissipated the fruits of his victory, Rome pushed its advances into Iberia, extending its sway first along the coasts, already under the dominion of the Carthaginians, and then into the interior. As they arrived on the central plateau and in the mountains of the north, the Romans came upon a type of people both wild and uncultivated, of archaic dress and civilzation, but strongly determined to maintain their independence. These were the Celtiberians and the Cantabricans, peoples used to every hardship and ready for any sacrifice, fearing neither cold nor hunger and preferring to fight day and night rather than to fall into slavery, and determined not to give the legionnaires of Rome a moment's truce. This was when the legions

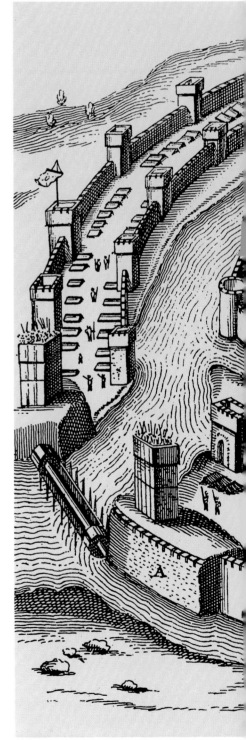

Cantabrian and Celtiberian cavalry and infantry according to two illustrations from the Album of Spanish Infantry *and* Album of Spanish Cavalry, *by Lt. General Conde de Clonard published in Madrid in the last century under the patronage of the army and the navy. These were the men that the Romans had to deal with at the time of the siege of Numantia 134-133 B.C. Right: The besieged city showing the two lines of circumvallations (A) and counter-embankment (B) erected by Scipio Aemilianus. Between the two lines, drawn according to the principles of classic siege operations, can be observed the camp of the besieging army (C). In the two bends of the Duero, the river which flows by the city, can be seen the barrages of beams with iron points as planned by Scipio.*

encountered nerve shattering guerrilla warfare, a new element to those not accustomed to this type of combat. Their enemies appeared sometimes directly before them, sometimes within the camp itself, sometimes within the city, whether the troops were on the march or resting in the open field, and always characterized by fierce, quick, and pitiless attacks. The chief of these guerrilla bands was Viriathus, the first Spanish national hero.

This was the setting for the tragic events of Numantia. This city troubled the sleep of the Romans from 143 B.C., the date of the first siege laid against it by Quintus Cecilius Metellus, until 134 B.C. when Publius Cornelius Scipio Aemilianus, with a final definitive siege, at last was able to cause its fall.

The position of the city, situated on a bluff over the River Duero in the middle of precipitous cliffs, combined with the bravery of its inhabitants, made it particularly difficult for the Romans to establish their dominion over Numantia. Perhaps, as far as the Romans were concerned, a point of some importance was that of the choice of leaders, who were not always suitable for this very difficult and harsh conflict.

After the unsuccessful siege conducted by Metellus in 143 B.C., a new siege was instituted by Quintus Pompeius, who obtained as a result, however, only a treaty by virtue of which the city was able to maintain its independence. In 139 Pompeius violated the treaty and tried once more to decide the matter by force. The city

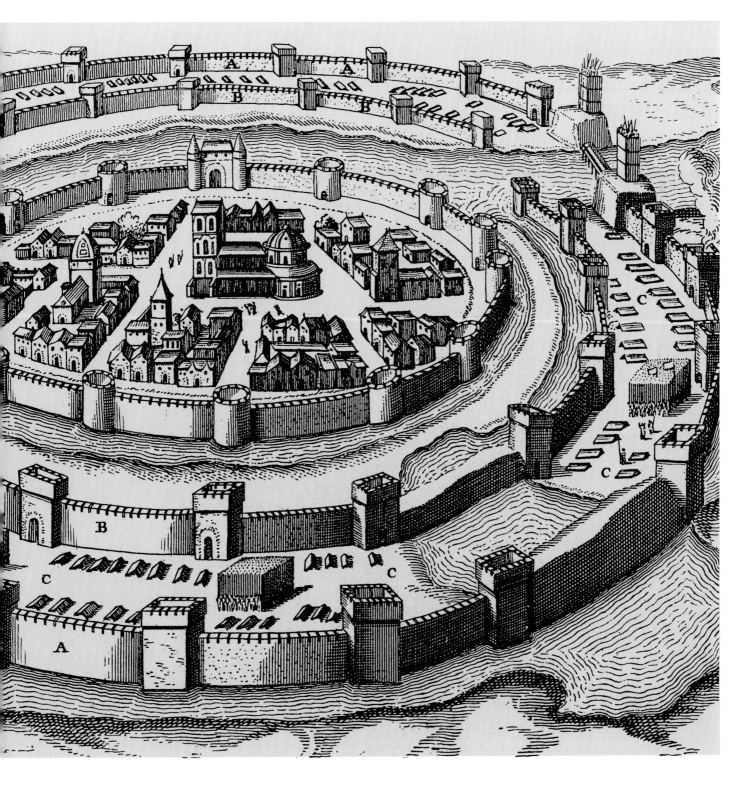

appealed to the Roman Senate but the Senate ordered Pompeius' successor, Marcus Popilius Lenatis, to continue the war and to put the city once more to siege. Numantia continued to resist and command passed to the consul Caius Hostilius Mancinus, who in turn was repulsed various times by the city. Finally he fell into an ambush and was forced to make peace.

The Roman Senate, nevertheless, did not recognize the new treaties and hostilities continued. In 136 Lucius Furius Filus, and again in 135, Quintus Calpurnius Piso were repulsed by this indomitable city, although its inhabitants no longer could count on the leadership of Viriathus, who had been killed traitorously by two of his officers who had been bought through the offices of the consul Cepio.

Finally, in 143 B.C., Rome sent to Numantia Publius Cornelius Scipio Aemilianus. The arrival of the man who had already triumphed over Carthage sealed the fate of Numantia, but two years of suffering and desperation were still fated to take place.

When Scipio arrived in Spain he found the morale of the army to be extremely low and discipline incredibly relaxed.

With his profound knowledge of men, he made his first aim the reestablishment of discipline. The legionnaires were again assigned to the proper carrying out of military details and forced to undergo a severe physical and technical preparation. Scipio imposed long marches on his soldiers and caused them to continually dig trenches and make embankments and then to remove them. The entire summer of 134 B.C. passed in this preparatory training with some isolated encounters all of which gave back to the legionnaires a secure belief in their final victory and, at the same time, took from the enemy their now excessive confidence.

When his army had thereupon been sufficiently brought back into fighting trim, now composed of sixty thousand men (including the auxiliaries of Jugertha, the nephew of Masinessa, who had some war elephants with his troops), Scipio renewed the attack on Numantia. Inasmuch as the fighters of Numantia hated inaction and never hesitated to risk their lives if it involved combat, Scipio thought that it would be more advisable to condemn them to inaction, through the conduct of a siege by a blockade. Famine would then complete the operation. He constructed near Numantia two principal entrenched camps, and increased them later by another five; all of them possessing walls ten feet high.

Scipio then reinforced the encircling walls with seven towers from which, as well as from the walls, the slingers and archers held the enemy constantly within their range. As there existed a swamp close to the city as a natural obstacle and as it was not possible to build a wall there, he dammed it up with an embankment which grew to the height of the walls themselves and completely encircled them. This had a length of approximately seven and a half miles, more or less double the perimeter of Numantia's walls.

For the protection of this line of embankments, Scipio had a very long and deep trench excavated.

The only means of communication open to the city was the Duero River, which flowed past the city at its most rocky sections: the inhabitants of the city were in the habit of crossing it by swimming, despite the rapid current and the width of the river. In order to shut off this last means of communication as well, Scipio had two towers constructed across the two banks of the river and connected with cables and beams equipped with sharp blades. This resulted in an insuperable obstacle not only for a boat but also for anyone who might attempt to swim the river. Hunger soon began to affect the inhabitants as well, another disadvantage for the people of Numantia for whom a battle in the open field was the only way that they could hope to escape annihilation. One day, they got themselves drunk with strong draughts of *coelia*, their favorite beverage, which was made of barley, and they attempted a desperate sortie which was repulsed. Through envoys that they then sent out they declared that they were ready to surrender if they could keep their liberty. Scipio, however, insisted on an unconditional surrender. The Numantines, now reduced to a state of desperation, began to nourish themselves with dead bodies, which led to even more atrocious events: the stronger killed the weaker and ate him. Finally pestilence broke out and claimed many other victims.

To a certain point the citizens discussed the possibility of surrender: but before offering it to the Romans they were inclined to wait for death to remove from them the shame of their defeat. Husbands killed their wives and children and set fire to their homes. Since they no longer had the force to defend their city in case it were attacked, they adopted the extreme decision of burning it. Their chieftain, Rhetogenes, wished also to die in the flames.

Three days later the survivors threw down their arms and surrendered themselves to Scipio. There was no longer anything human about them: their looks showed the fatigue they had suffered, the anger, sorrow, hunger, labors, and perhaps also the remorse at having survived their kindred.

All this, as well as the heroic decade which preceded the end, made Numantia a symbol of Iberian independence. So it is considered, for example, by the Spanish historian Pablo Orosio, who, in his *Historiarum adversus paganos libri septem*, has left us a fiery eulogy to the spirit and sacrifice and heroic resistance of his compatriots. Numantia still stands forth as a deed of heroism without equal and an eternal lesson of patriotism.

An illustration by Ludovico Pogliaghi for the History of Italy *by Bertollini, showing the entry of the Romans into Numantia. Famine had already overcome the heroic resistance of its inhabitants, destined to remain a symbol of the stubborn desire for independence of the Iberian people from foreign dominion. When surrender had been decided upon, many of the Numantines killed their own families and then themselves, having first set fire to their houses. Their chieftain Rhetogenes threw himself alive into the flames of his own house.*

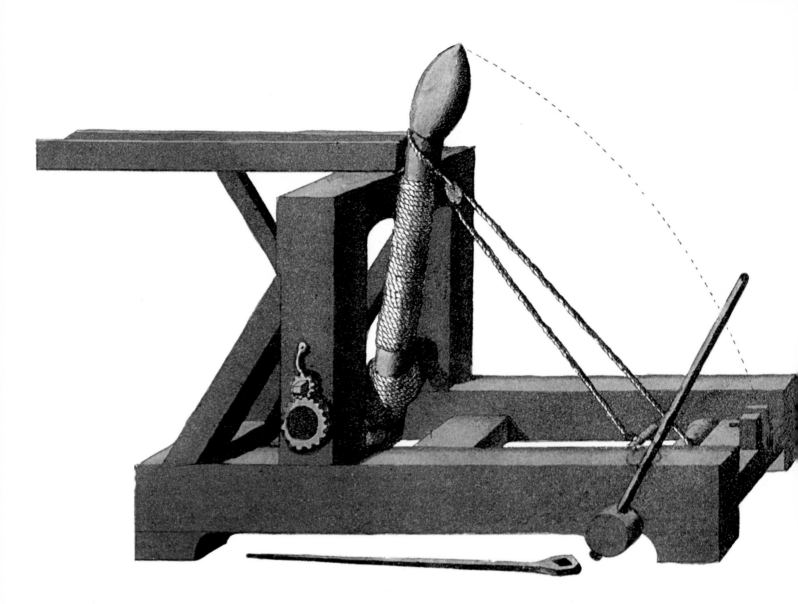

ALESIA (52 B.C.) *"Vir fortissime, vicisti!"*

In the winter of 52 B.C., while he was at Ravenna, the notice reached Caesar that his "great friend" Vercingetorix had revolted, placing himself at the head of a revolution of the tribes of Gaul against Roman rule. Caesar made one of his habitual lightning decisions and, accompanied by four cohorts, crossed the Alps in the dead of winter and arrived unexpectedly once more to assume command of the legions in Gaul.

Notwithstanding the difficulties caused by the winter weather, in little more than a month he had taken possession of the cities which had instigated and encouraged the revolt. The city that resisted most strongly was Avaricum (today Bourges), which was besieged by the legionaries for a month, shivering with cold, tormented by hunger and hardship: when it was captured, it was destroyed and its inhabitants massacred.

It was of prime importance to Caesar to destroy the army of Vercingetorix which was, however, still intact. The chieftain of the Gauls, avoiding encounters in the open field, scoured the countryside with his cavalry, destroying supplies of grain and hay in order to weaken the enemy.

When he had squared accounts with Avaricum, Caesar returned to Alvernia with six legions for the purpose of occupying its capital Gergovia (today Clermont-Ferrand), and sent Labienus with the rest of the army to fight in the north against the Senoni and the Parisii.

Gergovia, the native city of Vercingetorix, was located on a hill which was not only difficult to climb but also protected by strong fortifications. The chief of the revolt rushed immediately to the defense of his own city but limited his activity to guerrilla warfare. Caesar, in order to put an end to the wasting away of his forces, ordered an assault on a favorable position, from which he intended to proceed to the decisive attack on the city. The position was taken and the legionaries, encouraged by their success, kept on going. Heedless of the orders they had received, they climbed the walls. The Gauls rushed to meet them and the result was a massacre.

Seven hundred Romans remained on the field. This setback resulted in serious consequences. The Edui, the only tribe among the Gauls who were still faithful to Rome, joined the forces of rebellion. Caesar was now practically surrounded, without reinforcements, and without any foreseeable possibility of being joined by Labienus.

Vercingetorix then decided to invade Provencia still faithful to Rome, but Caesar, with another of his impromptu decisions, prevented him. He crossed the territory of the Edui, forded the Loire and was able to join Labienus: all Vercingetorix's plans collapsed.

At this point the chieftains of the different barbarian contingents consistently demanded an opportunity of confronting the Romans in the open field. They obtained what they desired but they had cause to regret it. The legions, with the aid of German cavalry, completely routed the Gauls.

Vercingetorix, surprised by the unexpected outcome of the battle and attempting to re-form his battered squadrons, ordered the survivors, in the number of eighty thousand, to retreat to Alesia.

On facing page above the title: *A Roman catapult. The use of ballistic artillery, according to Livy, was introduced in the Roman army in the latter part of the regime of Servius Tullius.* Below: *A view of Alesia during its siege by the Romans. Beside the two lines of embankments and counterembankments there can be seen different obstacles constructed to slow down, if not to impede, the advance of a rescue army from without as well as to impede a sortie of the enemy from within.*

In the past there have been lengthy discussions regarding the location of Vercingetorix's last refuge. The excavations made by Napoleon III at Alise-Saint-Reine, at a distance of sixty kilometers from Dijon, on the route to Paris, finally settled all doubts. Alesia was located in that general locality. This has been ascertained by archaeological finds in great numbers as well as hundreds of Gallic and Roman coins and other objects. All this notwithstanding, we find that in the spring of 1949, on the occasion of the two thousand year anniversary of Vercingetorix, the "problem" of the location of Alesia was still being discussed in France in no less important a place than the National Assembly.

To return to our account, we can say that Alesia, placed on a hill in the environs of what is now Alise-Sainte-Reine, was located in a good position but, considering all the people for whom food had to be provided, not more than a month of resistance could be contemplated. Caesar, from the first moment that he put the city under siege, had, in fact, thought to take it through famine.

He immediately undertook construction of the great field fortification works of eternal fame and which he described in several of the chapters of Book VII of the *Gallic Wars*. The legionaries set to work with great spirit and continued with tireless zeal to work day and night, under the eye of their commander, to whom Caesar had given precise orders. There were nine thousand men at work under the orders of Labienus, Mamurra Antonius, Decimus Brutus, Caius Trebonius, and others, whose names Caesar was pleased to record.

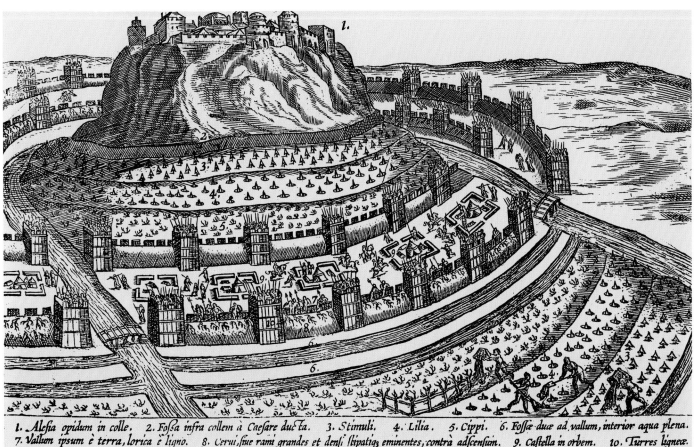

1. *Alesia opidum in colle.* 2. *Fossa infra collem a Caesare ducta.* 3. *Stimuli.* 4. *Lilia.* 5. *Cippi.* 6. *Fossae duae ad vallum, interior aqua plena.* 7. *Vallum ipsum e terra, lorica e ligno.* 8. *Cervi, sive rami grandes et densi stipatiq; eminentes, contra adscensum.* 9. *Castella in orbem.* 10. *Turres ligneae.*

A bronze coin bearing the effigy of Vercingetorix. It was discovered at the foot of Mount Rhea in the time of Napoleon III. Another gold coin has since been found, of the same design.

Within six weeks the great siege works had taken definite form while Vercingetorix looked on without making any definite move. However, before the circle could be closed completely and inexorably, he called together all his cavalry and sent it out through the opening that remained to him. Before releasing the cavalry, his favorite arm, he gave them precise orders with a warning of severe punishment for those who did not carry them out: part of the warriors were to be employed to guard the supplies needed for a city in which eighty thousand men were concentrated, without counting women and children; part were to hasten to all the settlements and tribes of Gaul with orders for a mass levy of all available warriors. All men capable of bearing arms should therefore come together in a great army and bring help to the besieged.

Caesar learned all this from the interrogation of some prisoners and he prepared himself in time. The siege works against the city were soon finished: a wide and deep ditch was established all along the internal perimeter of the walls connecting with two water courses which ran along the foot of the hill on which the city was built. Right in front of this first enclosure, a line of counterembankments was constructed with two ditches in front, one of which was filled with water. With the same rapidity Caesar constructed an outer line of encircling embankments to be ready for Vercingetorix's expected army of liberation.

Secondary works had been set up by the legionaries and proved to be of great utility. Still other works, of a passive defensive nature, were aimed away from the city in order to impede the eventual advance of the relief army. In front of the circumvallations there were also placed *chevaux de frise*, and iron spikes. The legions were stationed between the two lines of circular embankments and counterembankments.

The Roman cavalry as well as the German auxiliary cavalry were kept constantly busy on scouting expeditions for the purpose of keeping Caesar informed about the Gallic troop movements, while from the walls of the besieged city soldiers and women watched the horizon in the hope of seeing the great army expected by Vercingetorix which would come to vanquish the Romans.

What happened was that the Gallic princes, convoked to a conference, had determined to contribute to the army of liberation not, as they had been asked, all men able to bear arms, but selected quotas proportionate to the numbers of each tribe. Together they formed a colossal army of two hundred and twenty thousand infantry and eight thousand cavalry (according to Caesar; less, according to others). Four generals were in command: Commius, Viridomarus, Heporedorix, and Vercassivellaunus. There was a certain amount of discord between them and, moreover, there was the constant problem of supplies for so huge an army.

Supplies were far from abundant even for the besiegers. One of Caesar's first measures was, in fact, the ordering of reduced rations for the legions. But the food situation for the besieged was graver still, since they had almost a hundred thousand mouths to feed. In Alesia some elements were already thinking about surrender but others entertained the most warlike plans. Among the latter was Critognatus, cited by Caesar as having made a memorable speech during which, after having railed at those who proposed surrender and rebuking the ardent spirits who proposed an immediate sortie, tried to convince everyone to resist desperately while awaiting the allied army. When the food reserves gave out, Critognatus suggested, the besieged should eat the flesh of those among them who could no longer fight: old people, women, and children. This terrible proposal, reminiscent

Facing page and above: *Two XIX century prints from the drawings of Andrea Paladio among the illustrations of a XVI century work dealing with the campaigns of Caesar. The first shows a military bridge in the process of construction and the other a typical formation of the barbarian forces for a frontal attack on the Roman camp. The Romans placed a special effort in the building of their camps even though they would be constructed for a single night. The work of fortifying the camps (as opposed to permanent fortifications) was concerned with protecting it from surprise attack.*

of the horrors of Numantia, was offered by the barbarian chieftain with absolute convinction. In order to incite his fellow citizens to greater resistance, he pointed out that the Romans were working day and night to strengthen their forces from the outside; and this was a sure sign that the long awaited army was approaching. In order to offer an alternative to the proposal of Critognatus, the council decided that all persons incapable of bearing arms should leave the city. Thus there took place the expulsion of the "civilians" who wandered about the "no man's land" rejected by both contestants.

At this time the rescue army arrived, and made camp on a hill not very far from the Roman fortifications.

On the following day the barbarians commenced their attacks on the fortifications of Caesar, while within the besieged city there grew a general rejoicing, and the conviction that their liberation was at hand. The assaults and counterassaults lasted for seven days but were constantly rebuffed with bloody fighting: the Germanic cavalry, by means of constant charges, overcame the Gallic horsemen. Commius' infantry, after having experienced the fatal traps prepared by the legionaries, fled from the field leaving weapons and prisoners, with-

out even having seriously menaced the Roman fortifications.

On the last day of these scattered attacks, while Caesar fought in the front line, Vercassivellaunus himself was captured by the legionaries. The Gallic army, thrown into confusion, left seventy-four standards in Caesar's hands.

In the most critical moment of this great battle, Vercingetorix, from within Alesia, had launched a sortie against the right wing of the Roman army. Labienus, however, saved the situation and again the besieged were thrown back.

Caesar could now use all of his forces against the besieged city, since he had cut their army to pieces. But the situation was now impossible for the Gauls. Vercingetorix, displaying his nobility of soul and his heroic nature, offered to leave the fortress and to confront Caesar, taking upon himself all consequences of surrender.

The King of the Averni, wearing his best armor, and mounted on his finest war horse, presented himself before Caesar. Throwing down his arms at Caesar's feet, he is supposed to have said, according to Florus: "Habe: fortem virum, vir fortissime, vicisti." (Here I am: you, O most strong, have conquered the strong.)

The Siege of Alesia *by Henri Motte. This French painter, who lived from 1846 to 1922, has portrayed in this oil painting, now at the Musée de la Tour de l'Orle d'Or at Sémur-en-Auxois, France, the Roman line of counterembankments during a sortie by the besieged. These can be seen on the left, in the background, engaged in attacking a Roman tower which they have set on fire. In the center foreground a sling catapult is about to launch its projectile against the enemy from another Roman tower. A basket full of other projectiles is being mounted up to a machine placed on the upper level.*

JERUSALEM (A.D. 70)

"They shall fall by the edge of the sword and Jerusalem shall be trodden down of the Gentiles" (Luke 21:24)

The siege of Jerusalem in A.D. 70 has been narrated by the historian Josephus Flavius with a wealth of detail, owing to his personal presence at the events. Josephus, who had fought against the Romans in the revolt of A.D. 66 and, in the following war against Flavius Vespasianus, was made prisoner in Galilee, where he was governor, and then was freed by the same Vespasianus when the latter became emperor, at which point he was able to adopt for himself the name of Flavius. The historian thereupon followed the son of Vespasian, Titus, at the siege of Jerusalem and left us a testimony of the city's agony and destruction.

Vespasian, in two campaigns, had subdued Palestine and its principal cities, except for Jerusalem. It fell to the lot of his son Titus, with eighty thousand men and powerful equipment of war machines constructed on the spot, to capture this metropolis, the heart and symbol of religion and the state.

The city was protected by a wall 35 feet high constructed in such a way that the walls jutted forward and then receded, a measure purposely taken so that any attackers would expose their flank to the fire of the besieged. The two principal hills, Zion and Acra, were also fortified by means of thick surrounding walls strengthened by high towers. The citadel of Zion, with its seventy towers, was practically unassailable, thanks to the precipices which surrounded it. From the hill of Zion the wall continued up to the Hippicus tower and to the Temple. The Acra wall, which was the middle wall, with fourteen towers, continued up to the fortress

of Antonia. A third wall from the Hippicus tower went on to the Psefinus tower, and from there to the bastion of Bezetha and then joined the wall of Zion. The Psefinus tower was octagonal in shape, over ninety feet high, while the Bezetha bastion was surrounded by ninety towers. The Hippicus, Phasaelus and Mariamne towers caused the amazement of the Romans themselves because of the magnificence with which they had been constructed. Instead of using stones in their building, blocks of marble had been employed. The Temple complex as well, surrounded by a triple wall, porticos, and crowned by the tower of Antonia, constituted in itself a practically impregnable citadel.

Within the city a Jewish sect called the Zealots held sway. The Zealots, animated by a fanaticism that was both religious and nationalistic, were the principal opposition to the Romans and were unwilling to make any compromise whatever. Under the leadership of John the Levite, a native of Gischala in Galilee, they called for help from the Edomites, a warlike tribe, in order to oppose the coming siege by Titus with the utmost force. The Edomites, however, had no sooner entered Jerusalem than they gave themselves over to a ferocious slaughter of all those who had opposed their entry, until the Zealots, tired of the overbearing tyranny of John, put themselves under the command of Eleazar, an already celebrated chieftain from the Israelite revolt against the rule of Rome. John was left the command of the Acra citadel. The confusion of the moment was increased by the sudden appearance beneath the walls of the Holy

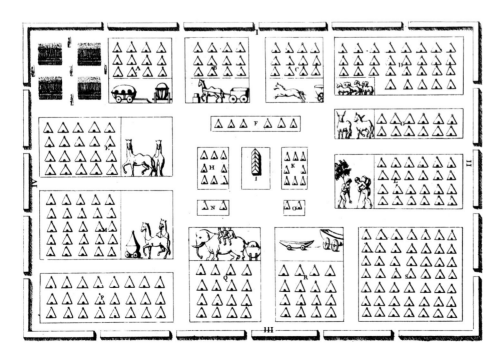

A camp of the Hebrews according to a reconstruction of the XIX century by Ludovico Menin (Milan, Bertarelli Collection). Elephants can also be seen here. These were much employed in the battle of Betzur or Betzacara (165 B.C.) by Antiochus V Eupator of the Seleucidae, against whom the Hebrews, under the command of Judas Maccabeus, waged a revolt which gave ample proof of their outstanding military qualities. A Victory of Judas Maccabeus is illustrated in the picture reproduced on the following page, the work of François-Joseph Heim (1787-1865), now at the Magnin Museum of Dijon. The anti-Roman rebellion of A.D. 66, which led to the siege of Jerusalem in the year 70, would confirm the Hebrews' stubborn desire to resist.

City of another fierce leader, Simon of Jona, with twenty or thirty thousand fighters from Galilee. These entered into the city and occupied the Zion citadel and some points of the lower city. It is said that Simon's Galileans, a perverse and corrupt group, would dress up as women and, imitating the gestures of prostitutes, would walk around the streets of Jerusalem attracting and then attacking the citizens who approached them, and then robbing them or occasionally killing them.

Part of ancient Palestine according to a XVII century map. The rebellion of 66 started with the capture of the Roman garrison of Jerusalem by the Zealots, who represented an extremist faction. The revolt spread throughout the entire country and ended with the siege of Masada, where the last of the Zealots were to kill their own families and then themselves so as not to fall into the hands of the Romans.

Finally, three factions were engaged in internecine warfare within Jerusalem even while Titus was advancing against the city with his legions. The danger from without did not mitigate the fierce and pitiless combat they waged against each other. As an additional blow, numbers of pilgrims came to the Temple with the approach of Passover, causing thereby a serious food shortage, made even more serious by the outbreak of a sudden fire which destroyed some of the warehouses.

In April of 70 the Roman advance guard closed all communications between the cities and the countryside. A short time later, the main army arrived before the city and established a state of siege. The northern and western sides of the city were the only ones against which an attack was possible: the deep ravines which surrounded Jerusalem on the other side did not permit either the use of war machines or the establishment of camps for the soldiers. Titus thereupon established one legion (the Tenth) on the Mount of Olives in front of the tower of Psefinus, while the other legions (the Twelfth, the Fifteenth, and the auxiliary troops) made camp on Mount Scopus.

From April to September Jerusalem was subjected to the incessant attacks of the Roman legions, while within the city the struggle between the three factions as well as hunger continued to aggravate the situation. The Hebrews undertook a series of determined sorties which caused the legionaries no little difficulty. Even the famous Tenth Legion (the Fretensis) had to be saved under such circumstances by the timely intervention of Titus himself.

The struggle between the different factions, for a moment, seemed to take a turn toward solution. A surprise attack against the Temple on the part of John eliminated many of the followers of Eleazar. The factions were now reduced to two which were, however, still unable to agree. John, with eight thousand five hundred men, and Simon with fifteen thousand, conducted a personal war against the Romans. The latter methodically razed to the ground the suburbs of the city and cut down all the surrounding trees. They continued to build towers and to construct machines for the hurling of projectiles, with which they bombarded the center of the city while the great bronze-headed battering rams shook the walls incessantly. The first and then the second walls were stormed within twenty-four days. The ditch before the walls was filled in after fifteen days of hard labor. Continuous hand-to-hand struggle permitted the Romans to win possession of a good part of the city, but the proportion between the number of men sacrificed and the results obtained, the bitterness of the house to house struggle, and the fear of not being able to overcome the last inner bastions into which the city was divided, convinced Titus to start over again from the beginning and to seek a solution through a blockade.

He thereupon ordered Jerusalem to be surrounded with a battlefield embankment or wall about four and a half miles long, reinforced with thirteen forts; and he waited for hunger to do the rest. And to make the

blockade even more severe, Titus ordered that anyone who should venture outside the walls, even to pick up as much as a blade of grass, should be immediately crucified on the spot.

Within the city, famine was soon joined by disease. It was then necessary to throw the dead bodies down from the walls both to get rid of the pestilential smell as well as to inflict them on the enemy. Simon and John were among the last to lack for rations, and it is reported that the besieged, in order to allay their hunger, ate harnesses and the leather from belts and the fastenings of shields. The struggle went on unceasingly: the defenders burned the enemy's war machines, they built new walls to oppose the battering rams, and they repulsed the legionaries in a series of fierce hand to hand encounters.

The end came in the first part of July, when the Romans, in a sudden attack, surprised the sentries while they were asleep and took possession of the tower of Antonia, which Herod had built at great expense. It was there that Jesus Christ had heard pronounced his death sentence.

Day by day the destruction was getting nearer to the Sanctuary. It was the wish of Titus to spare this magnificent monument but a legionary hurled some burning brands through a window and in a short time the flames devoured everything. Amidst the noise of crashing masonry could be heard the piercing cries of those who had sought refuge within the Sanctuary and who were now being massacred by their own defenders who, in close combat with the Romans, dazed by the smoke of the burning building and crazed by their despair, consigned the enemy, old people, women and children to a common fate.

Detail of a painting of the Flemish school now at the Museum of Fine Arts of Ghent. It represents the siege of Jerusalem by Titus. In the right foreground are represented two of the most shocking episodes of the siege, that of the mother eating her own child and that of the tortures inflicted on the inhabitants by the followers of John and Simon, to rob them of their food and money. According to the report of Josephus Flavius, an eyewitness of the events, the rebels "dragged food out of the mouths of those who were eating it" (Wars of the Jews V, 10). Again according to Flavius (ibid., VI, 4), the unnatural mother was a refugee coming from a village beyond the Jordan. Below: A type of hoist, the war machine already described on page 42.

AQUILEIA (452) *From the ashes of her heart, Venice arose*

On the twenty-fourth of August, 410, Alaric, King of the Visigoths, conquered Rome, which from the times of Brennus and Camillus had never known the shame of foreign occupation. Ten years afterward, following the fixed settlement of other barbarian tribes in certain parts of the Empire of the West, it was reduced to half of its former territory. When Honorius died in 423, the imperial title passed to his nephew, Valentinianus III, to whose ineptitude have been attributed two other mortal blows suffered by the Empire: the invasion of the Vandals in Africa and that of the Huns in Gaul and Italy. One of the best known episodes of the first invasion was the siege of Hippo in 430, marked by the death of Augustine, one of the most famous scholars of the Church. The most vivid memories of the second invasion include the battle of Campi Catalaunici, near Troyes, in Champagne, in 451, and the siege of Aquileia in 452.

Attila, the fierce and warlike king of the tribes of Mongolian Huns (he would later be called "The Scourge of God"), was now at the head of a vast empire centered in Pannonia, the Roman province corresponding more or less to Slovenia and western Hungary. A prime concern of Attila was the expansion of his borders toward the Empire of the East. However, after having confronted the valiant Emperor Marcianus, the King of the Huns altered his plans of action and turned to the Empire of the West, first attacking Gaul, where he was stopped although not completely beaten, by Aetius, who had always maintained ties of friendship with the Huns and who thought it would be possible, in leaving them possibilities of retreating from Gaul, to be able to maintain friendly relations and therefore use their warriors as mercenaries against other barbarian tribes, then in a dangerous ferment. This proved to be a tragic delusion, as it induced Aetius to leave the passes of the Julian Alps unguarded, permitting Attila suddenly to appear in 452, with a great army, on the Paduan plain.

The army of Huns continued to advance, marking its path with ferocious destruction; and while Aetius and the Emperor were abandoning Italy, the Huns laid siege to Aquileia.

This city, now a municipality of the province of Udine, was then a very important commercial center,

having grown from an early Roman frontier post established in 181 B.C. In its six centuries of history it had undergone more than one siege, but it had never been captured. In 248 it was besieged by the orders of the Emperor Maximinus, who wished to capture two usurpers who had taken refuge within the city. But Maximinus was killed by his own soldiers under the walls of the city and once more Aquileia was spared.

Attila himself found that he was in difficulty in his plan to capture the city, probably because of a lack of an adequate supply of war machines among his forces, in which all emphasis, as was suitable for an army of nomads, was on the cavalry. It appears that Attila thereupon decided to wait.

This delay on the part of Attila under the walls of Aquileia gave rise to two legends, recorded by the Lombard historian Paulus Diaconus in his *Historia Romana* as well as in other sources. One of these concerns the storks which Attila is said to have seen rising in flight from the roofs of Aquileia, carrying their young in their beaks. Instinct was said to have been the reason that these birds, sensing the imminent ruin that was approaching the city, considered it necessary to search for new nests elsewhere. The second legend concerns a young woman, named Digna, "forma eximia sed candore puditiae amplius decorata," that is, of great beauty and of unassailable virtue. Her house was located near the walls and under her windows flowed the River Natissa. It was therefore easy for her to observe the enemy and to understand that these were people who could only be classified as "the most sordid" and to further realize that once they had succeeded in forcing their way into the city they would take her by force as well. When the first Huns, after repeated attacks, appeared on the walls, Digna threw herself into the river.

Aquileia was a total ruin. It is said that even after a hundred years it was difficult to find the place where Aquileia once stood. The survivors looked for a refuge among the islands within the lagoon and founded a colony which later developed into the city of Venice.

In reporting the episode of the storks, Paulus Diaconus claims that when this happened Attila had been besieging Aquileia without interruption "continuo triennio," that is, for three years. In reality Aquileia's resistance lasted only a few months. After this a great terror spread over all Venetia. Padua, Vicenza, Verona, Brescia, Bergamo, Pavia, and Milan also fell to the enemy. At Milan Attila saw a painting showing the Roman Emperors of the East and West, sitting on golden thrones, at whose feet lay the bodies of some dying Scythians. He summoned a local painter and had himself painted also on a throne, with the two Emperors at his feet, not dying, but in the act of offering him a sack of gold.

He returned to Pannonia and died soon afterward. When his warriors heard of his death they cut their hair and slashed their faces with their swords so that, as the story goes, "the greatest of all warriors should not be mourned with wailing and tears, as women do, but with the blood of men."

On facing page, above the title: *Refugees from Aquileia, destroyed by the Huns, search for a refuge on the Venetian Lagoon, where they will construct the first nucleus of the future Venice. This is one of the one hundred and fifty pictures of the* History of Venice *by Giuseppe Gatteri (Venice, 1867).* Above: *Attila in a nineteenth century print from the* Mausoleum Regni Apostolici Regum et Ducum. *Apart from the legend which has presented him as the "Scourge of God," Attila appears to have been a man of genius, able to affirm authority throughout the Hunnish Empire and form his people into a force capable of conquering half of Europe.*

NICEA, ANTIOCH, JERUSALEM

(1097-1099)

The Crusaders up to their knees in blood

Bottom of preceding page: *Combats by the walls of Antioch in the Flemish miniature of the XV century (Geneva, Public and University Library).* On facing page next to title: *According to ancient paintings, scenes from the battle between Christians and Moslems. The first siege undertaken by the Christian forces was that of Nicea, followed by the battle of Dorylaeum (July 1, 1067) and then the siege of Antioch. This rich and beautiful city aroused the cupidity of the leaders of the Crusade, particularly Bohemond of Taranto who, to further his personal ambition for riches, engaged in intrigues with the enemy.*

The first Crusade, which occurred between 1096 and 1099, can be divided into two campaigns from a military point of view. The first campaign, conducted in Asia Minor, includes the sieges of Nicea and Antioch. And, between these two encounters, the battle of Dorylaeum. The second campaign, waged in the Holy Land, includes different minor operations and a decisive one, the siege of Jerusalem.

In order to reach the Holy City, it was necessary to follow routes through Asia Minor directly to the south. Nicea was located on one of these and was an important strongpoint. It was indispensable to capture it.

Toward the end of April of 1097, while the Turks were employed in certain operations on the eastern border of their empire, a Crusader army advanced on Nicea under the command of Godfrey of Bouillon, proceeding from Constantinople, which was the base of the Christian forces. He was accompanied by a detachment of Byzantine engineers with assault machines, under the command of a certain Taticius. Godfrey was joined at Nicomedia by an Italian-Norman army under the command of Tancred of Altavilla. The two united armies continued their march toward the south, through the passage of Dracon, where they passed the whitening bones of the followers of Peter the Hermit, annihilated on the spot by the Turks on October 21, 1096; a tragic conclusion of the so-called "Beggars" Crusade. On May 6, 1097 Godfrey and Tancred were under the walls of Nicea. On May 6 Raymond IV of Saint Gilles, Count of Toulouse and Marquis of Provence joined the camp for the purpose of completing the envelopment on the southern side. Bohemond of Taranto, destined to become the most celebrated military figure of the enterprise, had already taken his post beside Tancred, his nephew, on the eastern side of the wall, while Godfrey was camped along the northern side. To the west were the waters of Lake Askanius, which reflected the city of Nicea. On June 3 there arrived Robert II, Duke of Normandy, and Stephen, Count of Blois and of Chartres. By now the army of the Crusaders was entirely assembled. But there was not a supreme command over the army and decisions were taken in council by the princes.

A Turkish relief advance guard, arriving at camp on the western boundary a little after Raymond, attacked him without success. On May 21 Raymond found himself before the main body, under the command of Sultan Kilij Arslan, the same one who had destroyed the Beggars' Crusade. The Sultan was repulsed, to his great surprise, and compelled to leave Nicea to its destiny. The Crusaders cut the testicles off the enemy bodies and hung them on pikes before each gate. Others they threw over the walls. The walls were extraordinarily strong. Raymond and Ademar de Monteil, Bishop of Le Puy (a man bearing the full confidence of Urban II and moral preceptor of the enterprise), organized a mining operation, and had a gallery dug under one of the towers of the southern enclosure. But they obtained only negligible results. Meantime it had been discovered that the besieged were receiving reinforcements from across the lake. A small flotilla would be enough to cut off such communication and the Crusaders could have it from the Emperor Alexius who had one ready, but wanted the Crusaders to ask him for it in a manner befitting his dignity. He wished the Crusaders to understand, on every possible occasion, how indispensable was the help of Byzantium. Meanwhile, he was in secret contact with the city through the commander of the fleet itself and of the detachment of imperial engineers, Manuel Butumites. In fact it was to Alexius first that the request of the Niceans for surrender was addressed, and this happened as soon as the Byzantine ships were glimpsed from the walls.

At dawn on July 19, while a general Crusader attack was developing against the city, suddenly the colors of the Roman Empire of the East appeared on the battlements. During the night the city had opened the gates facing the lake to the mercenary troops who, paid by Alexius, made up the armed force carried on board the ships of Butumites.

There was considerable resentment in the camp of the Crusaders, especially among the troops, who were counting on the rewards of pillage. But Alexius softened the blow, generously distributing food to the soldiers, and gold to their leaders.

One week after the fall of Nicea, the Crusader army moved south. It was divided into two parts, one under

A miniature from the Roman de Godefroi de Bouillon *(Paris, National Library). Godfrey of Bouillon is generally considered to have been the head of the First Crusade and the Conqueror of Jerusalem. In reality he was simply one of the chieftains who directed the undertaking together.*

the command of Bohemond and the other Raymond of Toulouse. A day's march divided the two contingents. On June 30 Bohemond pitched camp on the plains of Dorylaeum. The following morning, at dawn, came the sound of Turkish trumpets as the Turks rushed down the hill with Bohemond leading the charge. From the Crusaders camp a messenger departed with breakneck speed to Raymond's camp to urge him to hurry. The others remained for six long hours under a rain of arrows and resisted as well they could. Raymond arrived at midday and without great difficulty broke the encirclement and joined forces with Bohemond. Now the Crusaders launched their counter attack and hesitation and dismay was first noted in the Turkish ranks. Suddenly they fled in disorder, frightened by the appearance in their rear of the Provençal contingent under the leadership of the Bishop of Le Puy in one of history's most effective encirclements. Their camp fell intact into the hands of the Crusaders with the treasure of Sultan Kilij Arslan. He retired to the hills, devasting the surrounding country so that the Crusaders would not be able to find supplies along their route. In effect, the Crusaders marched through a land of absolute desolation during the entire month of July and half of August. They finally reached Iconium (now Conya) where they found fresh streams and luxuriant orchards. After having recovered its forces and treated its wounds, the army turned again to its task of marches and conquests. Tancred demonstrated his rebellious nature by breaking off from the main body and taking a route with his Italian and Norman troops which the Byzantine guides counselled against. He was followed by Baldwin the brother of Godfrey, together with some Flemish and Lorrainian levies. It was inferred from the aforesaid that their plan was to seek a piece of territory over which they could reign. This base plan to win a crown caused a quarrel which cost the lives of hundreds of men from both groups. The deed was too serious and the reaction, even on the part of the Christians in the area, was such as to induce Tancred and Baldwin to make a reconciliation. Tancred thereupon proceeded south and, having taken Alexandretta, returned to the main part of the Christian army which was then encamped below the walls of Antioch. Baldwin, however, continued off to the fabulous adventure which would end with his ascension to the throne of Edessa.

The city of Antioch, governed by Yaghi Siyan, a Turkoman, was rich and well fortified, and had aroused the cupidity of the chiefs of the Crusaders. Bohemond, in particular, felt the need to make it his and engaged in dealings with the enemy, as Alexius had done at Nicea. In Antioch, however, the situation was different. The Christian community itself was not certain that it was really advisable to transfer the city from Turkish dominion to that of the Crusaders or of Byzantium.

Yaghi Siyan, who up to that moment had abstained

from any action because he had fewer men than were necessary to sufficiently guard the walls, regained his courage and began to attempt some sorties, especially since he knew that reinforcements were coming.

The Crusaders, however, reported some notable successes, such as capturing the nearest port, Saint Simeon, owing to the arrival of thirteen Genoese ships, bearing men and materials. Lack of provisions had caused a serious situation. Autumn had begun (it was November of 1097) and the campaigns had not advanced to any extent. Anyone going out from camp in search of food risked falling into a Turkish ambuscade. By Christmas the camp of the Crusaders was a prey to hunger. The Council of Princes was forced to make new decisions: Bohemond and Robert of Flanders were sent, with twenty thousand men, to make a grand raid to the south. Yaghi Siyan, soon informed about this project, made a determined sortie and almost upset the situation. Raymond of Toulouse who, with the Bishop of Le Puy, remained on hand to direct the siege (Godfrey was seriously ill), made an energetic counterattack and only chance kept him from taking the city by assault, just as, in spite of Bohemond, he had always dreamed of doing.

Two hurling machines used by the Crusaders: on the left the more simple form of a torsion catapult. The arm with the sack loaded with stones is attached to the base by a skein of twisted rope, the torsion of which gives the arm, when let loose, the necessary force to launch the projectiles. In the more complicated types the arm is lowered through a winch which does not appear here. On the right, a counterweighted device somewhat schematically represented.

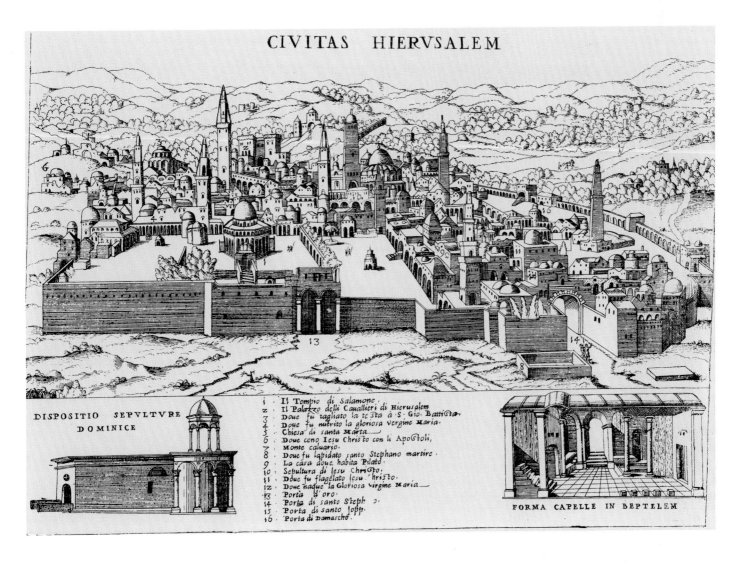

CIVITAS HIERVSALEM

DISPOSITIO SEPVLTVRE DOMINICE

1 · Il Tempio di Salamone.
2 · Il Palazzo delli Cauallieri di Hierusalem
3 · Doue fu tagliato la testa à S. Gio. Battista·
4 · Doue fu nutrito la gloriosa Vergine Maria·
5 · Chiesa di santa Marta·
6 · Doue cenò Iesu Christo con li Apostoli,
  Monte caluario·
7 · Doue fu lapidato santo Stephano martire·
8 · La casa doue habita Pilato·
9 · Sepultura di Iesu Christo·
10 · Doue fu flagelato Iesu Christo·
11 · Doue naque la Gloriosa Vergine Maria·
12 · Porta d'oro·
13 · Porta di santo Steph 。·
14 · Porta di santo Jopp·
15 · Porta di Damascho·

FORMA CAPELLE IN BEPTELEM

A picture of Jerusalem after the Crusades sufficiently indicative of the strength of the walls which, through the centuries, have caused so much trouble to those who have tried to capture it, from Sennacherib to Saladin.

Bohemond, in the meanwhile, found himself automatically cut off by the army which Yaghi Siyan's son was leading from Damascus. In the encounter which followed, the Crusaders were victorious. The forces from Damascus retreated and Antioch was still without help. But the Christian army was so battered that it had to give up the raid and return to Antioch with empty hands.

There then began a slow loss of men and especially horses, and desertions began. Among these desertions was an especially notable one, that of Peter the Hermit, who fled one night in January in 1098, with a certain William, called the Carpenter. They were followed and brought back by Tancred and sternly reprimanded by Bohemond. Thereafter a veil dropped over the whole affair, considering that the reputation and prestige of Peter could not be lowered without loss to the whole undertaking and to the morale of the troops, which was already low enough.

In the first part of February Taticius, the Byzantine, also abandoned camp, destroying the last appearance of feudal subjection on the part of the Crusaders to the Emperor.

Finally even Bohemond showed some signs of leaving, justifying his plan by political reasons of necessity connected with his presence in Italy. But it was a maneuver: in fact, he let it be understood that he would give up his plans to leave if he were assured rule over Antioch. This move pleased the troops who were afraid of being left without a chief such as he but it was rejected by the Princes. Bohemond, however, remained and his presence permitted the Crusaders to repel a second relief army. The merit of this victory belongs above all to those of the Crusaders who, on the 8th of February, were still able to mount their horses: seven hundred in all. Their charge was sufficient to save the day.

On March 4, an English fleet from Constantinople dropped anchor at Saint Simeon. It brought Italian pil-

This fresco, located in Genoa, in a room of the Palazzo Cattaneo-Adorno, and now the premises of the Passadore Bank, is the work of Lazzaro Tavarone (1556-1641). It illustrates the decisive contribution of Guglielmo Embriaco to the capture of Jerusalem. Left: One of the mobile towers constructed by the Genoese who arrived with two ships at Jaffa, June 17, 1099. Center: In the foreground Guglielmo Embriaco encourages the crossbowmen (a specialty of Genoese armament) while the infantry break through one of the gates of the city. This marks the end of the Crusade and the beginning of a terrible massacre. Below: A mobile assault tower. The greatest problem for the constructors of the towers was that of the weight of the machine. As they came near the walls, the towers often had to advance across the difficult terrain formed by ditches or moats filled with water. Their weight was capable of causing them to sink. The smallest towers were sixty feet high and with a base of about twenty-two feet per side.

grims as well as Byzantine assault machines, the latter generously furnished by Alexius.

April went by and then, in May, the news was received that Kerboga, a Turkish leader of great fame, Lord of Mosul, was marching on Antioch with an enormous army for the purpose of freeing the city. The Crusaders sent messengers to Alexius to implore his help. This was against the advice of Bohemond, who was afraid that the presence of Imperial troops would keep him from taking the city himself, and it is probable that he again threatened to leave. Nevertheless he made the following compromise with his colleagues: if his troops were the first to enter the city and if the Emperor did not personally come to the camp, Antioch would be his.

Events worked in his favor. Kerboga, inexplicably worried at the prospect of having Edessa on his right flank, stopped for three weeks to besiege Baldwin and his men. These were three very precious weeks for

Bohemond, who had the chance to plot with an Armenian named Firuz who, after having given up his faith and become a Moslem, had reached a position of certain eminence in the entourage of Yaghi Siyan. Now he betrayed him through envy, selling the city to Bohemond. The latter said nothing about this, and when the news came that Kerboga had lifted the siege of Edessa and was marching on Antioch the incidence of desertions reached a frightening point.

On June 2, Firuz sent word to Bohemond that everything was ready. If the Prince would pretend to leave with his army, as if he were going off to meet Kerboga, and then return secretly during the night, he would be able to mount the walls with a ladder on the tower of the Two Sisters and enter Antioch by that means. Bohemond finally informed all his colleagues about his plans. The first sixty men went up under the leadership of Folco of Chartres. Firuz assigned to them the other two towers under his command and nervously waited Bohemond and the main force. The latter entered by the nearest gates, forced by Folco's men. But Bohemond wanted to enter by the scaling ladder and took rather a risk since it broke suddenly afterward.

With the dawn of June 3 his vermilion banner was flying aver Antioch, whose streets were already covered by bodies.

Kerboga was successful in infiltrating warriors into the citadel and in making it a base for the attack. The Crusaders, however, were able to isolate it from the other fortifications of the city and all the Turkish assaults from the citadel were repulsed. Kerboga therefore decided to tighten the ring around the city and to take it with the aid of famine.

The situation seemed lost for the Crusaders. The sad spectacle of desertion again became evident, while

A supposed picture of Caffaro di Rustico (1080-1166), a famous Genoese historian and soldier who lived with the Crusaders from 1100 on and could therefore describe the events of the First Crusade with a wealth of detail.

the more faithful to the cause of the Holy Spirit placed all their trust in one hope: the arrival of Alexius, who, it was reported, had already left Constantinople.

A certain Peter Bartholomew, a servant of a pilgrim from Provence, declared that Saint Andrew had revealed to him that within the church of Saint Peter, in Antioch, was buried a precious relic: the Holy Spear, the iron point of which had pierced the side of Christ. An excavation was made at the place indicated, and a rusted fragment of iron was, in fact, found. The cry arose that a miracle had transpired and the Holy Spear was trustfully accepted as a symbol of imminent victory.

Victory came on June 28, when the entire army of the Crusaders came out of the city and challenged the Turks to a combat in the open field. Kerboga accepted and began the battle with a calculated withdrawal, in order to lure the Crusaders to a point more favorable to the Turks. But the advance of the Crusaders could not be stopped. Moreover, many emirs, tired of the dominion of the Lord of Mosul, chose that very moment to leave him by deserting with all their followers. Kerboga set fire to the underbrush in front of the Crusaders in order to gain time, but from that point on the day was lost for the Moslems.

Meanwhile, Alexius' forces had been joined by deserters and, perturbed by their reports, Alexius ordered his army to make an about turn. Antioch was already in the hands of the Crusaders when they learned of this. The Christian leaders delivered themselves of bitter comments concerning the Emperor's behavior and decided that by now they were authorized to solve territorial problems themselves.

The army finally took the part of Raymond, when he decided to continue the march to Jerusalem. But this did not take place until six months after the surrender of Antioch, January 13, 1099. When Raymond and his followers, dressed in pilgrims' garments, turned at last toward Palestine, behind them burned the flames coming from the city of Maarat-an-Numan, the last center of resistance in Asia Minor. Raymond had ordered it to be sacked and burned as a symbol of the impossibility of a retreat. By February 14, the Crusaders were before the walls of Arga which they immediately besieged. Tancred was again among them, having joined Raymond and accepted his authority for a sum of money.

At Arga, when the siege tended to languish, the legend of the Holy Spear began to lose much of its previous enthusiastic acceptance. Peter Bartholomew, thereupon, in order to defend himself and the relic against the increasing incredulity of the Crusaders, offered to undergo an ordeal by fire. This barbarous ordeal took place on Good Friday, April 18, 1099. Peter left the flames so injured that he died twelve days later. After this, only the fervent Provençal troops of Raymond continued to venerate the relic found in Antioch.

On May 13, Raymond lifted the siege and crossed the River of the Dog, which then served as a boundary between the Kingdom of the Seljuk Turks and the Caliphate of Cairo, ruled by the Fatimides. Following

D· BAPTISTÆ CINERES, MIRR ÆA
TRANSVEHVNTVR CIƆ· IIC

In the lunettes placed around the fresco described on pages 70-71 Lazzaro Tavarone has depicted other moments in the life of Embriaco. We reproduce here one showing the famous captain presenting to the Archbishop of Genoa the ashes of Saint John the Baptist, found in 1099 in the monastery of Myra in Asia Minor. The accompanying text notes the contribution made by Embriaco's war machines to the success of Godfrey of Bouillon in the assault on the walls of Jerusalem.

the coast, May 20 found the Crusaders at Sidon; on the 24th they were at Acre; on the 26th at Caesarea; the 3rd of June at Ramleh, after having turned their backs to the sea near Arsuf. And on the 7th they were before the goal for which they had suffered so long — Jerusalem.

The wells and cisterns around the walls were poisoned and the heat was suffocating. It was neccessary to make haste. On the day of the 12th the first attack was launched, with disastrous results. It was clear to all that they needed to construct new scaling ladders and war machines. But the necessary material was not available until the 17th, when six ships entered the port of Jaffa, now abandoned by the Egyptians.

Guglielmo Embriaco and the Genoese put their abilities to the service of the Crusade and in three weeks the army could count on a large number of mangonels, siege towers, and scaling ladders, sufficient to attempt another assault. The first attack occurred at night between the 13th and 14th of July. At that moment the Crusaders could muster somewhat more than thirteen thousand men able to bear arms. One thousand three hundred of these composed a cavalry force, the others fought on foot.

On the morning of the 15th Godfrey of Bouillon was successful in placing one of the towers against the wall and in establishing a bridgehead into the city. The Crusaders were finally able to set foot within the Holy City. The Moslems then retreated toward the mosque of El Aqsa but they did not have time to prepare their defenses. Tancred, impetuous as ever, was upon them with a rush and forced their surrender, at the same time promising to spare their lives.

The other Moslems of Jerusalem, however, were slaughtered in their houses, in the mosques, and on the streets. No exception was made even for those within the mosque of El Aqsa, under the protection of the standard and the given word of Tancred. After the slaughter, the pool of blood within the mosque reached knee high. The Jews of Jerusalem fared no better. Shut within their principal synagogue, they were all burned together with their temple.

When the massacre was finished, the Christians sheathed their swords and went to the Holy Sepulcher to take part in the singing of the Te Deum.

LISBON (1147)

Portugal lays siege to its own capital

A knight standard bearer participant of the Second Crusade of which the siege of Lisbon, then held by the Moslems, was a curtain raiser. Below: A Moorish mounted archer of the XII century. The two prints are taken from the Library of the Musée de l'Armée in Paris.

In 1147, in an attempt to establish a worthy capital for his growing kingdom of Portugal, Alfonso I (Henriques) solicited the aid of the army which, in the late spring of that year, was descending from the north of Europe to establish itself in the Holy Land to wage the Second Crusade. The forces which made up this army, English, Flemings, Normans, Frisians, and Germans, assembled by sea in front of the destined capital, the beautiful and flourishing Lisbon, on the 16th of June of that year, and determined to take it from the Moors.

The Flemings and Germans camped on the east side of the city, Alfonso I and his troops established themselves on the north, that is, on a mount overlooking the city, while the English and Normans made their camp to the west. From the beginning there arose a discussion concerning the division of the eventual booty. Herven de Glainville, Constable of the Suffolk and Norfolk forces, attempted to throw oil on the waters, troubled especially by two pirates named Wilhelm and Radulph, who were part of the expedition. He made an agreement with Alfonso to the effect that all the booty would become the property of the Crusaders, including the price of the eventual ransom of the prisoners.

Before the beginning of assault operations however, a deputation was invited within Lisbon to consider conditions for peaceful capitulation. The Archbishop of Braga, an important Portuguese city, joined the Crusaders in this mission.

The Moors were certainly not in a position to come out of the city and to meet the enemy in the open field; in spite of the density of the population and the prosperity of the city they had not under arms more than five thousand men, while the besiegers had about thirty thousand; nevertheless the offer to surrender was refused. The English, under the command of Savery d'Arcelles, were able to occupy a suburb of the city within a short time, from which the Moors were not able to expel them in spite of their furious defense during the various desperate sorties. A fire, breaking out in back of the defenders, worked to the advantage of the besiegers, obliging the besieged to abandon that part of the city, where the grain warehouses were located.

In order to keep the besieged from receiving reinforcements by sea, Alfonso had eight ships constructed. Some of the Moorish sorties from the seaport caused considerable damage to the English sector, without obtaining any decisive success. The Arabs could only wait for the worst. Meanwhile, from the height of the wall

they hurled fiery insults on the Crusaders and the Portuguese. At the end of July Alfonso I again offered capitulation but once again was refused.

The Crusaders then began construction of more powerful siege machines: the Anglo-Normans and Germans constructed two mobile towers and five catapults. The Saracens defended themselves with shots from missile hurling mangonels and incendiary arrows which soon succeeded in setting fire to the mobile towers.

Meanwhile within the city the scarcity of food made itself dramatically felt.

In Lisbon it was no longer possible to bury the dead. The stench of corpses increased along with hunger and the danger of an epidemic became menacing.

The Flemings became specialists in a barbarous sport; they were wont to capture the besieged by putting out food as bait near the walls. The besieged were unable to resist the temptation to get at the food, and the Flemings then captured them by snaring them in nooses.

On the 29th of September a confrontation took place when the mine gallery being dug by the Germans opened into a countermine of the Saracens, with disastrous results for the latter. The digging continued and on the 17th of October the timberwork which supported the vault of the excavation dug under the wall was set afire: a large section of the wall fell with a crash which was heard far out at sea. The Crusaders quickly advanced through the breach but were met by the Saracens with the courage of desperation and the struggle, lit by the flames of the fire, lasted for ten hours. The Crusaders were repulsed, and they had no better luck later.

On the other side of the city the new tower had been set up and all the attempts of the Moors to set

The assault on Lisbon in an old print (Milan, Bertarelli Collection). The Second Crusade was proclaimed by Bernard of Clairvaux when news of the fall of Edessa reached Europe. It was led by two of the most powerful rulers of the time, Louis VII of France and Conrad III of Germany.

it afire had met with failure. In the fighting around this tower the Pisan who had invented it was wounded by a missile from a mangonel, which carried away his leg. At last the machine was brought up next to the wall and the Crusaders set up their bastions. The Moors decided to surrender, but they were still in command of the city and therefore able to make certain conditions.

Fernando Captivo and Herven de Glainville were invited to listen to the proposals of the defenders of Lisbon. In the meantime riots broke out in the Crusaders' camp, which was not helpful to the negotiations. In effect, the Christians were attempting not only to assure themselves that they would obtain the booty but also to prevent its disappearance before they got it. At length the Moslems agreed that three hundred men-at-arms only (a hundred and sixty German-Flemish and a hundred and forty Anglo-Normans) would enter the citadel and that all would have in their hands their money and possessions, having sworn to have withheld nothing.

On the 23rd of October, while the Crusaders approached the appointed place, King Alfonso, preceded by the Archbishop of Braga, entered Lisbon. The solemnity of the moment and the seriousness of the agreement were however disturbed by the Flemings and the Germans, who, in violation of the pacts, entered the city through the breaches, abandoning themselves to pillage and to a massacre of indescribable violence.

CREMA (1159)

"Blessed are those who have the opportunity to die nobly."

Otto of Freising, a famous German medieval historian, has left us a vivid description of the time of the Italian communes or city states, which he himself was familiar with since he followed Frederick Barbarossa on this first descent into Italy. According to his account: "The city dwellers are so totally devoted to their liberty that, in order to avoid the growth of a dictatorial power, they are governed by means of consul ... Since the population is divided into three classes, that is, great feudal lords, small noblemen, and the people, they choose their consuls from all three classes, so that one will not predominate over the others. The consuls remain in office only one year, so as to avoid the formation of personal power ... This is why cities of this kind surpass the others in richness and power."

In effect, the autonomous Italian city states were, during the first half of the XII century, continually growing. Besides the maritime republics of Genoa, Pisa, Venice, and Amalfi, other cities such as Milan, Trani, Bari, Naples, and Gaeta had freed themselves from subjection to kings, emperors, and feudal lords. They were undoubtedly helped by the economic advantages which followed contacts between the west and the east, established from the time of the First Crusade. But the city states had also enjoyed to their own advantage the weakening of imperial power in Italy, caused by the dynastic disputes which had arisen in Germany when, at the death of Henry V, the Franconian dynasty became extinct. With this there arose the supporters of the dynasty of Bavaria, founded by Welf (and for this reason referred to as Guelph), and, in opposition, those who favored the dynasty of Swabia, based at Weiblingen (therefore called Ghibellines).

Lothar II and Conrad III, the Emperors who were trying to rule in that political quicksand, had very little time to devote to Italy. And for this reason, as we have seen, the communes were able advantageously to strengthen their own autonomous institutions. In truth, this development found more serious obstacles in other directions. The great feudal lords, for example, were naturally hostile to any increasing power from the city. And even among the city states themselves, the less fortunate or badly governed among them harbored hostile feelings against others whose greater power they were obliged to recognize and endure. Como and Lodi, as we shall see, were doggedly opposed to Milan. In Rome the free city movement took on the character of a revolt against the Pope and found its tribune in Arnaldo da Brescia.

Such was the situation in the Italian peninsula when, in 1152, the Empire passed into the hands of Frederick I of Swabia, later called Barbarossa. Strongly influenced by the Imperial Roman concept ("quod principi placuit legis habet vigorem") he wished to apply it in a sudden and decisive manner. On the occasion of his first arrival in Italy in 1154, he held a diet at Roncaglia, near Piacenza, and demanded homage and aid from the cities. Milan, which decisively refused such demands, suddenly became the adversary that must be overcome.

Before turning to Milan, however, the Emperor attacked the cities allied to this chief city of Lombardy. In 1154 he burned Rosate, Galliate and Trecate. In 1155 he laid siege to and destroyed Tortona (with the aid of the Pavians). In 1158 he finally tightened a siege around Milan, which surrendered on September 7th, after resisting for a month. The Emperor then convoked a new diet at Roncaglia. There, beneath a magnificent tent, a gift of Henry II Plantagenet, King of England, the jurists from the legal academy of Bologna manifested to Frederick their legal approval, declaring that the imperial demands were perfectly in accord with Roman law, and not that the city should have power on a par with the Empress. Milan again refused to obey and was thereupon put under the ban of the Empire. And once more, the first to pay the price were its allies. In 1159 it was the turn of Crema to undergo a siege that will always be memorable.

The siege began on July 7th of that year with the participation of Imperial German forces and contingents sent from Cremona and Pavia, always accessible as co-belligerents in the struggle against Milan. From the height of the wall, the defenders of Crema aimed their hurling machines against the war machines of Barbarossa and especially against a tower, still in the process of construction, destined for the decisive assault. The losses suffered by his troops irritated the Emperor to the point of suggesting an inhuman vengeance. He ordered that the hostages from Crema that he had in his power be tied to the tower so that, if the defenders of Crema struck at the tower they would be also striking at their fellow citizens who were tied to it. And, in fact, this is exactly what happened. When the tower was moved to the walls, loaded with warriors who were using the defenseless bodies as a shield, none of the defenders hesitated. The eight hostages perished under the blows of their own fellow citizens, not only without trembling, but even encouraging the defenders on the walls to fire at the tower. Their names have come down to us to the greater glory of Crema and to the shame of tyranny and as a mark of the cruelty of that war: Codemaglio della Pusterla, Enrico de Landriano, Pagnerio de Lampugnano, the son of Azzo Cicerano and that of Bezo de

The stratagem of the tower of Barbarossa, to which were attached hostages in order to break the will of the defenders during the assault, is illustrated in this XIX century engraving, now in the Museum of Crema. This episode, one of the most famous in the struggle between the Empire and the Free Cities, has inspired many artists, among whom was Gaetano Previati (1852-1920), who painted the picture entitled The Hostages of Crema, also now in the same museum. Below: A coin of Barbarossa, coined in the mint of Cremona and found in the cathedral of Crema during excavations carried out it 1958. Crema was founded, according to tradition, in A.D. 570 when the overflow of the inhabitants of neighboring cities settled on its hills.

Sancto Bladore, Presbitero de Calusco, Turrico de Bonate, Aimo de Galliano. The Milanese chronicler of the period, Sire Raul, who together with Acerbo Morena of Lodi, represents the most authoritive Italian source of these events, has recorded the encouragement shouted to the victims from the walls of Crema, in order to soften the torture of the eight who were about to die.

Six months of desperate heroism and an incident like the above were not able to save Crema. On January 26, 1160, Barbarossa reduced the city through famine and then ordered its destruction. The walls were knocked down and the houses were given over to the flames. Thus died, after six centuries of life, one of the most lively communities of ancient Italy. Like Venice, Crema grew in the post-Roman period (tradition has established the date at around A.D. 570) following the flight of the population from surrounding centers, in search of safety from the fury of the advancing barbarians. At first a few mud huts among the swamps, then more solid houses, and finally the Commune, strong enough to defy the Emperor rather than betray its given word to its ally, Milan. In 1182 Frederick himself ordered its reconstruction, having established its new boundaries.

MILAN (1162)

A happy Easter in Saint Ambrose

The long struggle between Frederick Barbarossa and Milan witnessed its first bloody phase of the siege, already mentioned, of 1158. When, during the summer of that year, the imperial forces blockaded the city, they were reinforced on their flanks by contingents from many Italian cities.

The Emperor established his camp near the Roman Gate, the King of Bohemia near the present Venetian Gate, and the Archbishop of Cologne near San Celso. Milan had, at that time, a population of about 40,000. The besiegers could not have many more. Ragevinus speaks of 100,000 men, but that is certainly an exaggeration.

Frederick's main effort was directed against a fortified advance position of the Milanese, based on a tower raised on an arch in the present area of the Vigentine Gate. The garrison resisted for eight days and then surrendered because of thirst, and to escape the danger of the imminent collapse of the tower, mined at the base by German engineers. Actually, the tower must have still been firm inasmuch as Frederick was able to install a war machine on top of it which launched projectiles over the zone of San Nazaro.

Meanwhile, the Emperor's Italian "allies" scoured the countryside, falling like furies upon farms and people. The contingents from Cremona and Pavia especially distinguished themselves in this work of blind destruction, the violence of which so shocked Ragevinus. On October 7, 1158, Milan ceased its resistance.

On the following day the Bishop and the Consuls, barefoot, with their swords hanging around their necks like the crosses worn by penitents, followed by the citizenry, went to kneel at the feet of Frederick. Milan had

to recognize the independence of Como and Lodi, pay nine thousand silver marks, give over three hundred hostages, and accept the condition that the election of consuls would be effective only after imperial ratification. The conditions were harsh but, nevertheless, they left a slight hope of autonomy and liberty. Evidently the Emperor had not yet composed a document that would settle relations between Commune and Empire.

He attempted to do so two months later, on the occasion of a new diet at Roncaglia, inaugurated on November 11, 1158. The Emperor convoked the city consuls, the lay and ecclesiastic feudal lords, and four professors from the University of Bologna: Bulgaro, Martino, Jacopo, and Ugo. With their support, the Emperor established that it was his right to have absolute control of the fiefdoms and the city officials. The former were not to be sold or divided without his consent. The latter could be selected only by administrators under his control and trust. Control of finance, customs, tolls, taxes on water, and on use of state lands (which we would call property taxes today), all were to belong henceforth to the Emperor. He desired in this manner to reestablish the Roman law and this was what was done, without consideration of the fact that the Communes, through their own institutions, had founded a new law. Their world had moved away from out-dated judicial norms. The speech made by the Archbishop of Milan to Frederick sounds incredibly servile today. As he declared the City's acceptance of the diet's decrees, he burst out in exclamations such as the following: "This is the day of the Lord, let us be joyful for living it! It is the day of thanks and happiness, on which the peaceful conqueror deigns to stand amidst his people dictating laws

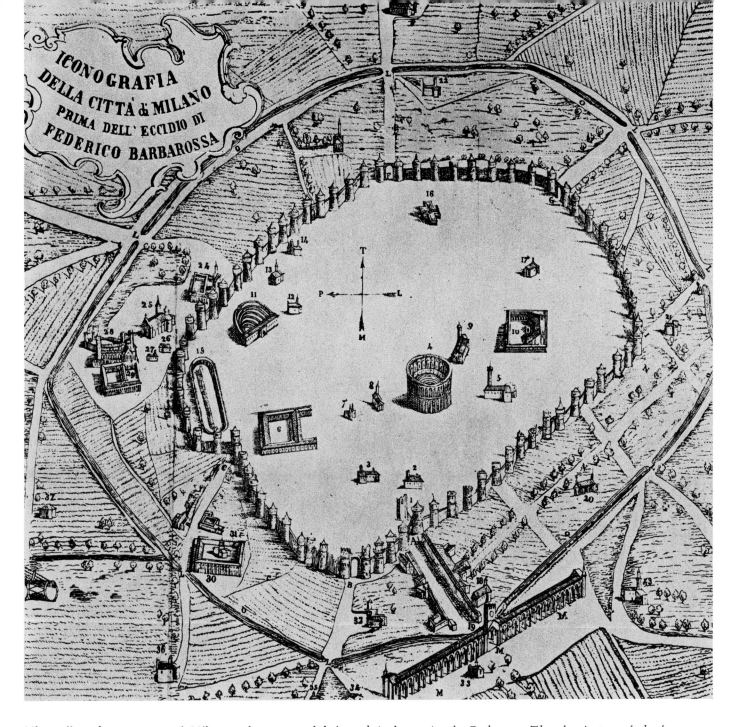

The walls and monuments of Milan as they appeared before their destruction by Barbarossa. The plan is part of the famous Memories of Milan in the Early Ages of *Count Giorgio Giulini (1717-1780)*. Below: *Milanese and their war chariot, from a drawing by Marco Cromosanto in* The Gallery of Prints, Arms and Insignia *(Milan, State Archives)*.

instead of menacing them with wars or tyranny ... O, august Emperor, your wish is law, since what is pleasing to the prince possesses the power of law!"

But the changing times were not long in making themselves felt. When Frederick sent messengers to establish his power among the Italian cities, many revolted. Milan was among the rebels. At the beginning of 1159, Ronald of Dassel, the chancellor of Frederick and his right arm, was obliged to leave the city by a tumultuous crowd. Milan and its allies were again put under the ban. The Archbishop of Piacenza in his exaltation compared Milan to Satan and prophesied its certain destruction.

The martyrdom of Crema, as we have seen, was the first act of this new drama. The second was another siege of Milan.

Frederick's increasing demands had alarmed Pope Hadrian IV, who encouraged the resistance of the city and its allies. At the same time he attempted to obtain the alliance of the Normans of Sicily and even that of Constantinople. On September 7, 1159, Hadrian was succeeded by Alexander III. The latter was much opposed to Frederick, who set up a counter Pope against him, Victor IV, and forced Alexander III to flee to France.

On February 28, 1160, under the haven of the cathedral of Milan, the voice of a papal legate of the fugitive pope was raised in a pronouncement of excommunication against Barbarossa. Among the accompanying "amens"

was heard that of the same archbishop who had made the servile exaltation of Barbarossa at Roncaglia. Words would now make place for arms.

While the city was making its preparations, a great fire devastated the zone near the Roman, Ticinese and Comasine Gates. Along with the buildings, the supplies which had been gathered for the imminent war were also destroyed. This serious blow, however, did not discourage the Milanese, who began a series of offensive actions and the establishment of forward bases at Lodi, Varese, Induno, Olona, Biandronno and elsewhere. They were even laying siege to the feudal rock fortress of Castiglione Olona, when, in April of 1161, Frederick reappeared in the Alpine passes. By June 1st the Milanese were again shut up within their walls and the Emperor was engaged in establishing his camp near the monastery of San Dionigi, where the remains of the great Ariberto d'Intimiano were interred. This was the archbishop who had introduced the use of the Carroccio, the war chariot which served as a rallyng point for the troops in combat.

Barbarossa was not long in giving evidence of his own personal anger. He ordered that the area surrounding the city be converted into a desert. A ring of desolation and terror was subsequently drawn around Milan.

Meanwhile, the city was experiencing the trials of the black market. And, as a final blow, treason was making itself felt. Reports began to circulate concerning

secret agreements between the more important citizens and the Emperor – concerning surrender. Quarrels broke out between those who supported this policy and those who wanted to resist to the end.

In the autumn of 1161 the Milanese were successful in making a raid in the countryside near Lodi, resulting in the bringing in of some supplies to the city. It is reported that the defenders ostentatiously exhibited sacks of wheat on the walls. Actually, they were sacks of sand.

In February, 1162, Milan informed Frederick that it was ready to destroy its own walls and towers, to receive an empowered imperial administrator, to pay a tribute, and to banish the partisans of last ditch resistance, who numbered, it appears, about three thousand. Frederick replied that the surrender had to be unconditional. The nobles of his entourage could give no other advice to the Milanese than to surrender.

On March 1, 1162, eight tired horses carried to Lodi the Milanese consuls. All these kneeled before Barbarossa and proclaimed that they were ready, in the name of the entire city, to carry out his wishes.

The Emperor, however, required a more elaborate ceremonial. On March 4, a Sunday, three hundred Milanese soldiers came to Lodi with the three hundred standards of the city. The standard bearers kissed the victor's feet, and placed before him, one by one, the standards they were carrying. After that Master Guintelmo, or Guintellino, the engineer in charge of the fortifications, gave over the keys of the city.

But it was not yet enough. Barbarossa demanded the homage of all those who had been consuls for the last three years, then that of the soldiers, and then that of the people. On March 6, 1162, the Milanese from three quarters paraded before him. Another ninety-four standards, those of the parishes, were piled at his feet, together with trumpets and weapons. But Barbarossa wanted to have within his grasp the most beautiful standard, and the one dearest to the hearts of the Milanese: the banner carried on the Carroccio, always straight into the wind, the halyard being arranged in such a way that the edges of the flag would be lifted by the breeze.

On the following day the scene was repeated so that the Empress could enjoy it too. And finally the Emperor spoke. He demanded four hundred hostages of rank, from among the consuls, captains, doctors and merchants; and demanded as well that the walls be taken down to their foundations so that the army could enter with ranks deployed.

But it was not yet over. On March 17th the Milanese received the order that they most feared. They had eight days in which to abandon the city. They were to take with them only their possessions that they could carry on their backs. All the rest was to be destroyed.

On the 18th the Archbishop took the road for Genoa, where he had met Pope Alexander III. Then there began the agonizing exodus of the refugees.

On March 26th the destruction of Milan began. In a sardonically clever move, the charge of razing the city to the ground was entrusted by Frederick to his Italian allies. Thus the Roman Gate was destroyed by the allies from Cremona, the Eastern Gate by the troops from Lodi, the Ticinese Gate by the Pavians, and the Comasine Gate by the Comasine contingent. The feudal levies from Seprio and Martesana would take care of the rest. Their long pent up hatred multiplied the force of the avengers and, after seven days, not one stone in Milan was left standing on another. The bell tower was cut off from the cathedral, and fell in on the building, ruining it. However, the monastery of Saint Ambrose was saved, a monastery where the monks were all ardent admirers of the Empire. Frederick even deigned to pay them a visit on April 1st and, while the fierce soldiery were still raging through the streets, bent on the complete destruction of Milan, the Emperor was smiling amiably at the Abbot who, in an access of devotion, offered him the Easter palms, blessed with holy water.

ALESSANDRIA (1174-1175)

"The Alessandrines will not surrender."

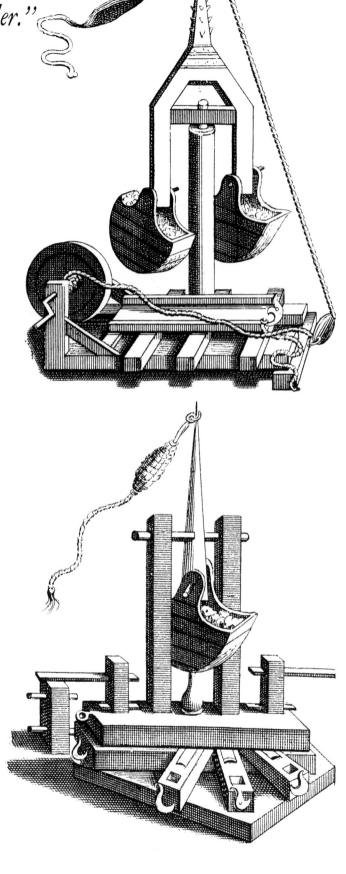

Having settled accounts with Milan, Barbarossa thought that he had solved the Italian question. But instead, it became more complicated. The communal movement, from this point uncontainable, found itself supported by the Papacy and the Norman Kingdom, preoccupied as they were by the increasing power of the Empire, as well as Venice and Byzantium. For this reason the coalitions of the League of Verona (1163) were formed and later the League of Lombardy, sanctified by the legendary "Oath of Pontida" (which was never pronounced) or, historically speaking, by a sworn and signed alliance between Milan, Cremona, and Bergamo, made on April 4, 1167, and later joined by other cities of Lombardy and Venetia. Pope Alexander III, conscious of the advantages which might accrue to him from this movement, gave his own support to the League, which, as a first concrete action, provided for the reconstruction of Milan (April 27, 1167) and the strengthening of an urban settlement in Piedmont which, in honor of the Pope, was named Alessandria (1168).

Alessandria was formed, in effect, from two original nuclei, Rovereto and Bergoglio, one on each side of the Tanaro. When moats were dug and embankments were raised for defense against the arrogance of the Marquis of Monferrat, the two towns were brought together, forming a new urban center. The population increased with the arrivals of inhabitants from Gamondio and Marengo, who formed themselves into separate districts, each with their own characteristics and privileges. Many other refugees came, victims of an era plagued by ruthless struggle, accompanied by sieges and the destruction of cities by one warring group or another. Alessandria, although described as having been "built of straw," because of the unpretentious buildings erected at the time it was first constructed, quickly prospered and undertook preparations to defend its liberty.

The first acts of the Commune indicate the rapid rise of Alessandria: in 1169 Alessandria had a council of credit with one hundred members, in March of 1169 it increased its territory by conquering the commune of Castelletto d'Orba, and on October 25 of the same year it concluded an alliance with Asti.

When Barbarossa descended again on Italy in September 1174, the Lombard League had thirty-six member cities and Alessandria was already prepared to attempt a military resistance. It might have been possible, in effect, for the city and the Emperor to arrive at a peaceful settlement. Actually Alessandria declared that she was willing to recognize the imperial authority (a formula used in the documents of the League as well). But Pavia and the Marquis of Monferrat prevailed on Fred-

Two medieval siege machines: the upper one has two counterweights, the lower one has a single counterweight but is maneuverable by means of a system of pins and grooves on its moveable base. The two weapons are depicted in the same engraving now in the Museum of the Army in Paris.

A XIX century print (Alessandria, Gabey Collection) illustrating the legendary episode of Gagliaudo, the peasant who in order to make Barbarossa stop the siege presented him with a cow filled up with grain, saying that that was the food the Alessandrines gave to their cattle, since they had an oversupply of it.

erick, convincing him to demand that the inhabitants of Alessandria should agree to the destruction of their new city and return to their towns of origin.

This attempt at intimidation aroused the disdain of the Alessandrines who replied by shutting themselves up within the walls and declaring themselves ready for last ditch resistance. At the end of September of 1174 the imperial forces began the siege. While within the city, according to reliable sources, there were only eight thousand inhabitants, reinforced by contingents of soldiers from Piacenza and Milan, the besieging army numbered about ten thousand men, endowed with a considerable supply of war machines.

The Alessandrines, governed by Rodolfo Concesio, empowered as governor in 1173, assembled a force of about three thousand men and placed it under the orders of the governor and of Anselmo Medico, the commander of the contingent from Piacenza. They resisted valiantly, notwithstanding the rigors of winter which were now upon them. Since every attempt on the part of the imperialists to open a breach in the defenses of Alessandria failed miserably because of the stubborn defense of the besieged, Barbarossa undertook an ancient and spectacular stratagem. On Palm Sunday (April 1st, 1175), a day by custom usually considered a day of truce, he sent a chosen detachment with orders to attempt

to enter the city through a secret tunnel, but the citizens were on guard and the detachment was routed. According to legend, the attack was thwarted with the aid of Saint Peter who, riding a white war horse, appeared in the sky over Alessandria and warned the besieged of the plot, and then guided them to victory. This proved decisive. On the 13th of April the Emperor raised the siege and went off toward new misfortunes. He was only thirteen months away from the disaster of Legnano.

Various legends have grown about the siege. One of the most pleasant concerns Gagliaudo Aulaci, one that also reflects the proverbial Alessandrine astuteness. Gagliaudo, after having fed his cow fine grain until she was filled to repletion, brought her to the enemy camp where, in front of Barbarossa, he slashed open the cow's stomach to show that grain was so abundant within the walls that it was used as the sole fodder for the cattle. Actually the Alessandrines were at the end of their forces and even at that moment were using up their last provisions. There has come down to us a version of this affair, based on the explanations of Gagliaudo to the Emperor: "For lack of hay and straw we will feed our cattle on grain. But I can tell you with pride, and swear it on my children, that even if the grain gives out, the Alessandrines will never give up."

ACRE (1189-1191) *The bishop's battering ram*

In 1187 Jerusalem again fell into the hands of the Moslems through the efforts of Salah-al-din, Sultan of Egypt, better known as Saladin. As in the case of the fall of Edessa, in 1147, which had been the cause of the Second Crusade, the fall of Jerusalem impelled the occident to organize the third Crusade. This new undertaking had as its principal episode the siege of Ptolemaïs of Phoenicia, called Akri by the Byzantines and, from 1229, Saint John of Acre.

In July of 1188, Saladin had set at liberty Guy of Lusignan, who had been King of Jerusalem from 1186 and Saladin's prisoner since 1187, after having made him swear that he would never take up arms again against the Moslems. However, after the king rejoined his wife, Sybelle of Anjou, at Tripoli in Syria, he suddenly set about finding a representative of the church who would free him from the oath made in prison. Thereupon he went off to Tyre to take up again the control of whatever was left to him of his kingdom after the battle of Hattin (1187) and the fall of Jerusalem. But there he found Conrad of Monferrat (one of the supporters of Barbarossa against the Lombard League) who had made a kingdom of his own in Tyre and who would not permit Guy to pass through the gates of the city. Guy renewed his attempt in April 1189, but encountered the same determination on Conrad's part. He thereupon made his camp in the vicinity and, in the second half of August, he joined the Pisans, who had arrived under the command of their Archbishop, Ubaldo, and, with the support as well of the Sicilian auxiliaries, he turned south with the intention of capturing Acre.

On August 28, he pitched his camp on the hills of

The surrender of Acre is illustrated in the print reproduced on the facing page (Milan, collection of the author). The conquered are depositing their weapons at the feet of the two conquerors, Richard the Lion Hearted (left) and Philip Augustus. The color picture represents Saladin.

Turon next to the Belus River. Some days afterward, after the first assault on the city had failed, he sent a request for reinforcements from the West.

In September a great fleet of Danish ships arrived. These were immediately employed to blockade the city from the sea. They were afterwards joined by French, Italian and German squadrons. Conrad of Monferrat himself offered Guy the support of his own army.

On the 4th of October, after having fortified their camp and given command to Godfrey of Lusignan, the brother of Guy, the Christians attacked Saladin's forces. The battle was bitter, with serious losses suffered by both groups and the outcome uncertain. Conrad escaped capture thanks to the generous intervention of his rival, King Guy. Many nobles last their lives on the field of battle. At the decisive moment of the battle the garrison of Acre had attempted a sortie, but the fortifications of the Christian camp had been sufficient to repel them.

The arrival of new reinforcements from all the lands of the West enabled the Crusaders completely to block Acre from the land side. When news came of the imminent arrival of the Emperor Frederick Barbarossa, Saladin too asked for reinforcements from all his vassals in Asia, Africa, and even in Spain. He received them and with these new forces his army was ready to surround the besiegers. At the end of October, and then again in December, Moslem ships crossed the blockade of the Frankish fleet and brought provisions to the city, which could therefore face the coming winter with a certain equanimity.

Life in the Christian camp was still made difficult by the lack of food. Meanwhile, Guy and Conrad arrived at a political agreement and Conrad left the camp in March of 1190 for the purpose of returning to Tyre to come back with ships loaded with arms and supplies. The attempt of the Saracen fleet to interrupt this expedition to obtain reinforcements was unsuccessful. After sharp combat Saladin's ships had to retire to Acre while the ships of Conrad unloaded their precious cargo.

With the material they had received the Crusaders constructed various towers. Using these towers, they made an assault on the city on May 1st 1190. But the towers were nearly all destroyed and the assault was repulsed. On May 11th Saladin, in turn, attacked the Christian camp in force and was also repulsed after bitter and long combat.

During the summer many French nobles and eminent prelates joined Guy's army: the most outstanding was Henry of Troyes, Count of Champagne, to whom was entrusted the command of the siege operations. In the first part of October the remains of the army of Barbarossa arrived. Barbarossa himself had been drowned in June in the Salef River, in Cilicia. Soon after the arrival of the Germans, still another assault was attempted against the city walls but this attack was once more repelled. No more successful was the attempt of the Archbishop of Besançon, who had designed a new type of battering ram.

Finally, in November, the Crusaders succeeded in opening a supply route after having forced Saladin to abandon some of his positions.

Meanwhile, sickness claimed many victims within the camps. Among these were Queen Sybelle and her daughters. Their deaths reopened the dynastic quarrel between Guy and Conrad and caused the formation of two parties, favorable to one pretender or the other.

In the winter, thanks to new reinforcements, Saladin once more was able to shut the Christian camp within a vise with no exit. The supplies of the Crusaders were rapidly exhausted.

In the winter of 1191 many of the Christians died of sickness. In March, with the arrival of good weather, Christian ships appeared with reinforcements which revived the forces of the Crusaders. Their hopes were lifted even higher when they received the news that the kings of France and England were already in the eastern waters of the Mediterranean.

The first one, Philip Augustus, arrived in the Crusader camp at Acre on April 20, 1191, and was greeted with great joy by the soldiers. He immediately undertook patiently to reorganize the besiegers' matériel and to construct new towers with a view to a new attempt to scale the walls. The second king, Richard the Lion Hearted, arrived in camp on June 8th and his arrival was greeted with no lesser manifestations of joy. A wave of energy and vitality seemed to flow through the ranks of the tired besiegers of Acre.

Richard had had outstanding experience in sieges. On his way by Messina he undertook a siege of a truly unique type. According to the report of the chronicler Richard de Devizes, a monk from Winchester, he gave orders that no counterfire be made to the storm of arrows from Messina until the enemy ran out of arrows. Thereupon the English fired their own arrows and no one could show his face on the wall from that point on without receiving an arrow in his eye. The final assault against Messina was launched with the aid of a tower which Richard brought to Acre, together with a great supply of boulders for the mangonels.

The attacks on Acre were directed especially toward one tower, called "The Accursed." The Moslems, repeating the stratagem employed at Plataea, had erected this tower on the walls in order to oppose a tower raised by the Crusaders. Richard, extremely active in spite of an attack of malaria which struck him shortly after his arrival, ceaselessly launched one attack after the other, although constantly harassed by Saladin from outside.

On July 3rd, 1191, a nephew of Saladin attempted to enter the city with supplies and help but was repulsed. Acre had no further recourse than capitulation. Its siege had cost the lives of one hundred and twenty thousand Crusaders. Among the surrender conditions imposed by Richard was the payment of a large ransom for the two thousand seven hundred prisoners he had in his power. Since the payment was delayed in arriving, Richard brought them all together in an area in full view of Saladin's camp and there had them all killed on the spot, by lance thrusts.

A hundred years after their victory over Saladin and the conquest of Acre, the Crusaders had to defend the city themselves against a siege by the Moslems. In these circumstances George de Clermont, seen here in action in a painting of the last century now in the Versailles Museum, especially distinguished himself. The city fell on May 19, 1291. In order to make the ruin of the city, the last bulwark of Christian arms in Palestine, more complete, the Turks filled in the harbor.

BAGHDAD (1257-1258)

Triumph and tragedy of the Abbasid caliphs

A Kirghiz of the Golden Horde according to a XVII century print (Paris, Library of the Museum of the Army). Below: An ancient oriental miniature showing the Mongol cavalry of Hulagu, strengthened by a contingent from the Golden Horde under the command of Baiku, and with Georgian horsemen, in bivouac under the walls of Baghdad, awaiting entry into the city through the breach.

The Mongols, who, under the leadership of Temujin, commonly called Genghis Khan, had extended their domain over Western Asia between 1206 and 1227, by the middle of the XIII century had not yet exhausted their drive to conquer. They were rather tolerant of the Christian and Moslem religions, but they were inflexibly against the Moslem sect of Assassins, either because of their extremist beliefs or because they were guilty of the killing of Jagatai, the second son of Genghis Khan. In 1256, a great Mongol army under the command of Hulagu, the brother of Mongka, the Great Khan, attacked Persia, a stronghold of the Assassins, and vanquished it after a year of warfare.

The Mongols then turned toward Baghdad, capital of the Abbasid Caliphate, where al-Mustasim was then reigning, a sovereign of feudal qualities dominated by his vizier, Aiberg, who, in effect, held the reins of power. The Caliph would have been able to mobilize an enormous army (the cavalry alone numbered one hundred and twenty thousand horsemen ready for action), but he preferred not to mobilize, offering instead a tribute to the Mongols equivalent to the amount that mobilization would have cost.

Hulagu would not accept the tribute and demanded the granting of sovereign rights over the Caliphate. As his demand was refused, Hulagu without further delay decided to make war on the Caliph, even though he knew that many of his own Moslem vassals were ready to betray him and that Baghdad had received many reinforcements. On his own side, the Mongol chieftain received the support of a contingent from the Golden Horde under the command of Baiku and a body of Georgian cavalry, plus a detachment of Chinese archers.

At the end of 1257, Mongol units crossed the Tigris at Mosul and proceeded along the western bank: these were the right wing, commanded by Baiku. The left wing, under the command of Kitbuqa, entered the plain of Iraq, to the east of Baghdad, while Hulagu approached the capital from the center of the advancing armies. Aiberg, who had taken command of the Caliph's army, left to meet the Mongols of Hulagu and engage them in a decisive battle. When he was informed that Baiku's army was approaching from the other direction, he

A medieval helmet and, below, a field forge, reproduced in the first half of the last century from Chinese originals, giving an approximate idea of the means of combat and of the arms which were available to Eastern armies around the middle of the XIII century.

crossed the Tigris again and made contact with the Mongols on January 11, 1258. Baiku then broke off contact and began a slow retreat in order to lure the Arabs onto a swampy area while he gave orders to his engineers to cut the dikes of the Euphrates.

On January 12 the Mongols took the offensive and the Arabs were forced to retire on a scattered front sixty miles from Baghdad. It was a complete disaster: only Aiberg and a few soldiers were able to return to the city: the rest were drowned or forced to save their lives by disordered flight.

On January 18 Hulagu, with his army, was already in front of the walls of Baghdad. The city was located on two branches of the Tigris River. This important watercourse was conquered by a series of bridges made of boats, quickly constructed by Mongol engineers. On the 22nd the city was completely surrounded and Hulagu began the siege by intensifying the attacks especially toward the eastern sector.

At the end of January, the Caliph sent his vizier, accompanied by the Nestorian Patriarch, to discuss surrender with Hulagu: they were sent back without being accorded an audience. The Mongol chieftain was more than ever determined to destroy the city and to this end he was only waiting for the arrival of new machines which were being prepared in far off China.

Finally, in the first week of February, Hulagu was able to subject Baghdad to a terrible bombardment of boulders. The eastern walls collapsed in large sections and spearheads of Georgian cavalry were ready to enter the city through the breach.

On February 10th, the Caliph al-Mustasim, accompanied by his staff and by the highest civil and religious leaders, gave himself up to Hulagu. They were all killed except the Caliph. He was slaughtered on the 15th of February, after having been forced to reveal to the conqueror the hiding place of his immense treasure. This was the end of the dynasty of the Abbasid, founded by Abbas, the uncle of Mohammed. It had reigned for five hundred years, having succeeded the Omayyad family in the leadership of the Islamic Empire. In the general massacre, only the Christians, who had taken refuge in their churches, were able to save their lives.

The carnage lasted for more than a month and it has been estimated that more than eighty thousand inhabitants of the city lost their lives. Men, women, and children met the same fate and even those who immediately surrendered were killed, the same as those who resisted. When, at the end of March, Hulagu ordered his soldiers to leave the city, Baghdad was to all purposes completely destroyed. The beautiful capital of the Caliphate was reduced to a mound of ruins and the stench of corpses poisoned the sky. Chroniclers have related that among the last sword blows dealt by the Mongols were those of a soldier who, when he found forty infants still alive in a street around their slain mothers, killed them one by one with the conviction that he was performing an act of mercy because, as he said, they had not any one who could give them milk.

NICOPOLIS OF BULGARIA (1396)

The sky falls on the barony of France

Above: *One of the first firearms of the XIV century, very different from those attributed to the Turks in the miniature reproduced* on the opposite page. *The latter comes from the H codex 1523 from the XVI century, now at the Topkapi Library in Istanbul, and represents the victorious entry of Bajazet into the city of Nicopolis of Bulgaria, then an important Turkish stronghold.*

The expansion of the Ottoman Turks, already notable under Murad I, founder of the Janizaries (1359-1389) was taken up with even more vigor by his successor, Bajazet I, who directed his fury particularly against Bulgaria, then a mosaic of small feudal states. One of the greater ones was the kingdom of Vidin, the vassal of Hungary, and this is the one that Bajazet conquered first. This made inevitable a conflict between the Sultan and Sigismund of Luxemburg, King of Hungary. But Pope Boniface IX also felt that the Turkish menace was becoming too dangerous and therefore he began to organize a new Crusade. Sigismund assumed command. His principal allies were the French of the Duke of Burgundy and Charles VI, but Venice also intervened, sending her ships to the mouths of the Danube. The French army, about ten thousand men strong, was concentrated, in April of 1396, at Dijon, from which it moved a short time later toward Germany and to arrive under the walls of Buda toward the end of July. The King of Hungary had readied an army of sixty thousand men, to which had been added German, English, and Wallachian forces.

The French were led by the twenty year old Jean de Nevers, by Philippe d'Ortois, Count of Eu and Constable of France, by Guy de la Tremouille, by the Admiral Jean de Vienne, and by Jean le Meingre, called Boucicaut. This was the undisciplined and headstrong nobility to which was attributed the saying: "If the sky fell, we would be able to hold it up with our lances." Sigismund, pressed by the French, crossed the Danube and approached Vidin. The commander of the Turkish garrison, a Bulgarian named John Srachmir, suddenly went over to the side of the Crusaders and opened the gates for them, thereby making it possible for the Turkish garrison to be massacred. The fortress of Rahova suffered a simi-

lar fate. In spite of determined resistance, the army of Sigismund conquered it in a short time. The pillage was followed by a useless massacre in which, besides the entire Turkish garrison, many Christian Bulgars also lost their lives. Only a few hundred persons were spared, those whose rank indicated the possibility of ransom.

Finally the Croatian army came in sight of Nicopolis, a famous Turkish stronghold located at a very important strategic position on the banks of the Danube. The city, garrisoned by a Turkish force under the command of the Governor, Dagon Bey, was situated on top of a steep hill and was defended by a double ring of strong walls. Several assaults against the city were repulsed. Since siege machines were lacking, recourse was made to mines and new ladders were constructed. But these efforts proved fruitless; the city resisted stoutly. A decision was then made to continue the siege by blockade.

On September 25, 1396, the Christians caught sight of the advance guard of a Turkish relief army, at the head of which Bajazet personally was leading his troops. Sigismund arrayed his army with a view to a defensive battle. But the French preferred to attack and, encouraged by their first success, fell into a mortal trap. They were surrounded by the Turkish cavalry and wiped out.

Others, who were taken prisoner, were killed. These numbered about three thousand and were executed in revenge for the massacres performed by the Crusaders at Vidin and Rahova. There were spared only certain nobles, among whom was Jean de Nevers. For his release Bajazet demanded a ransom of one hundred thousand ducats. When he liberated the Count de Nevers, the Sultan remarked: "You are young and perhaps thinking of revenge. I could demand your oath of never raising a weapon against me, but I will not do so: I disdain your oaths as much as I do your weapons."

L'AQUILA
(1423-1424)
"The valiant arm smashes one and all."

In 1423 Andrea Fortebracci, called "Braccio da Montone" (Mutton Arm), one of the most famous soldiers of fortune of the XV century, was in the service of Queen Giovanna II of Naples. After having been appointed by this sovereign governor of the Abruzzi, Fortebracci appeared before the chief city of this region, L'Aquila, and demanded passage for himself and his troops, comprising three thousand two hundred cavalry and one thousand infantry. But the gates did not open to him. The city made known to the adventurer that before receiving anyone within its walls, it first wanted to clarify his views on the dynastic conflict then taking place in Naples. Giovanna II, in effect, since she

lacked direct heirs and was menaced by Louis III, duke of Anjou and count of Provence, had first decreed that the throne of Naples would pass, upon her death, to Alfonso, King of Aragon, Sardinia, and Sicily. Then, suddenly, in the same year of 1423, Giovanna II changed her mind, revoking her adoption of Alfonso and transferring the designation to Louis III. This provoked a quarrel between Aragon and Anjou and gave rise to the formation of conflicting parties favoring one or the other.

Since Braccio stood for Aragon, Antonello Papacorda, suddenly arrived in L'Aquila, summoned by Louis III to stir the population of the city to resistance.

provisions. In the meantime, through frequent and sudden sorties they were often able to break through the circle of the besiegers and to procure new supplies. Toward the end of March, several fortified towns rebelled against Braccio, who concentrated his fury on Barisciano, where he caused the dwellings to be razed to the ground and the men slaughtered. The women were suspended nude under the walls of L'Aquila as a warning to the besieged.

In April the relief army was finally ready. The command was given to Jacopo Caldora, formerly a follower of Braccio and now in the service of the queen, Giovanna II.

On May 20th he arrived in the environs of L'Aquila and, on May 25th, made contact with the enemy. Braccio, against the advice of his captains, refused to take the opportunity of surprising the Anjou forces while they were traveling through the difficult passes of the Apennines, but preferred to seek a pitched battle, face to face with the enemy. On June 1st he ordered the dikes of the Aterno River to be broken in order to flood the

Left: *Illuminated eagle adorning the manuscript* Statura Civitatis Aquilae, *also referred to as* Capitula 1541 *from the date on the first document.* Right: *Portrait of Andrea Fortebraccio, called Braccio da Montone (Mutton Arm), from an already mentioned book by Paolo Giovio.*

Braccio, who had with him two other famous soldiers of fortune, Niccolò Piccinino and Gattamelata, attempted various attacks, but without success.

But Anjou was preparing an army of ten thousand men. While it was being readied, Braccio's great rival, Muzio Attendolo Sforza, in the service of Anjou, moved toward the Abruzzi. Braccio, from Chieti, followed his movements. The presence of Piccinino, with but a few troops, kept Sforza from crossing the Pescara, all through November and December. This river, with its swift and icy current, placed Sforza in a critical situation and finally decided his fate. He went to Ortona with part of his forces to cross the river, together with his son Francesco and with Micheletto. But Braccio guessed this move and by forced marches reached the besieged city, thus avoiding being trapped between two fires.

Finally Muzio Attendolo attempted to ford the Pescara. But he never reached the other side.

Meanwhile, the people of L'Aquila, sure of help, made ready for a last-ditch resistance and, through a voluntary tax, furnished Pietro Navarrino with four hundred horses. In addition, they sent out of the city the old, the weak, and the children, in order to prevent "useless mouths" from draining the already scanty supply of

countryside and prevent pack trains of supplies from reaching the beleaguered city. Braccio deployed three thousand infantry on the right of the Eterno and, while a company under Piccinino kept the Aquilans at bay, he himself confronted the enemy in the open field. The shock was tremendous. Braccio's ranks weakened after a pitched battle of seven hours and even the intervention of Piccinino aggravated rather than improved the situation. The besieged now made a sortie and assaulted the camp. Braccio was captured because, as immortalized by the anonymous poet of L'Aquila, he refused to flee: "Io non vo' fuggire, sotto il mio standardo prima vo' morire" (I do not wish to flee, I wish to die in front of my standard). While he was being led to Caldora's tent, he was struck on the head by a Perugian exile, a certain Lionello Micheletto. A short time afterwards a physician cleaned the wound with a probe. A slip of the surgeon's hand forced the instrument to penetrate too deeply. Thus, on June 5th, 1424, died he who was proclaimed, by a song of the time, to be invincible. In 1417, when Braccio had taken Perugia from Pope Martin V, the people sang:

(Pope Martin is not worth a cent;
the valiant arm smashes one and all.)

ORLÉANS (1428-1429) *France wins her first Verdun*

In the year 1428, while the so called Hundred Years War was going on, waged between the English and the French between 1337 and 1453, northern France was in the hands of the English and their allies, the Burgundians.

John of Lancaster, the Duke of Bedford, ruled in Paris in the name of Henry VI, King of England, while Charles, the Dauphin, had retired with his court to Chinon. The English were preparing for a last effort, aiming at Orléans, the last important obstacle to the spread of their forces into the southern regions. The English troops, whose command Bedford had given to Thomas of Montacute, Count of Salisbury, appeared under the walls of the stronghold on October 12, 1428.

The city was located on the northern bank of the Loire but, by this time, its southern suburbs had extended across the river and were connected to the center of the city by a fortified bridge. The end of the bridge was protected by defense works which extended along the southern bank: two towers, popularly called "Les Tourelles," rose from the bridge at a point where the bridge crossed an island. At this point the stonework of the bridge ceased and the island was connected with the bank by a drawbridge.

This remarkable defense system and the size of the garrison it could contain, gave to the inhabitants of Orléans a certain sense of safety, but the English commander, sensing the importance of the position, succeeded in winning possession of the bridgehead and the two "tourelles," after repeated and bloody assaults launched between October 13 and 23, 1428. He had therefore succeeded in cutting communications between the southern section, faithful to the Dauphin, and the people of Orléans.

The French, in order to prevent that position from being used for a direct assault on the city, demolished a part of the bridge constructed with defensive walls, but the English had already positioned a battery in the "tourelles" and the city was suddenly bombarded from that point.

The English decided to apply a blockade and to take the city by hunger. They built six "bastilles" around Orléans at regular intervals, one from the other, and connected them with trenches.

Artillery duels began. These were usually of a scope not so destructive to defense works as they were to men. The calibers of the guns used, in fact, were rather small. Such a shot, fired apparently by a boy, cost the life of the Count of Salisbury, commander in chief of the English camp. He was succeeded by William de la Pole, Count of Suffolk.

Even though the river route was still available for food supplies and munitions, the city very soon began to feel the lack of regular rations. But the besieging force also encountered the same problem, as they were so far from their bases. It was indeed a supply operation carried on by the English which brought about the first pitched battle.

In February, 1429, the French learned that a large convoy, principally bearing salted fish, was on its way to the English camp under an escort of one thousand archers and one thousand two hundred Burgundian in-

Facing page: *It is Mary 7, 1429. Joan of Arc is about to lead the assault on the bridge of the "Tourelles." The Maid is at the head of her troops, on her white horse, and lifts her famous standard. In the background, on the island of Saint-Aignan, the reserve army. In the foreground, behind Joan, can be seen the "assault" company, with ladders, and then the "attack" companies, with archers and slingers and, finally, the cavalry. On the river, at right, the barges which had transported the army to the left bank of the Loire.* Below: *Joan on her knees before Charles VII, in an engraving of the first part of the XIX century.*

The sword said to have belonged to Joan of Arc (Museum of Dijon). Below: *The siege of Orléans in the celebrated Kausler Collection of the most memorable battles (Karlsruhe, Herder, 1931).* Right: *Joan of Arc as she appears in a collection of prints published in Paris in 1655 under the title of* Les portraits des hommes illustres français qui sont dans la galérie du palais du Cardinal de Richelieu *(The portraits of illustrious Frenchmen which are in the gallery of the palace of Cardinal Richelieu) (Milan, Bertarelli Collection). She is the only female figure in the collection. As the Latin inscription says "nulli plus debet Gallia salva viro": France owes more to her than to any man.*

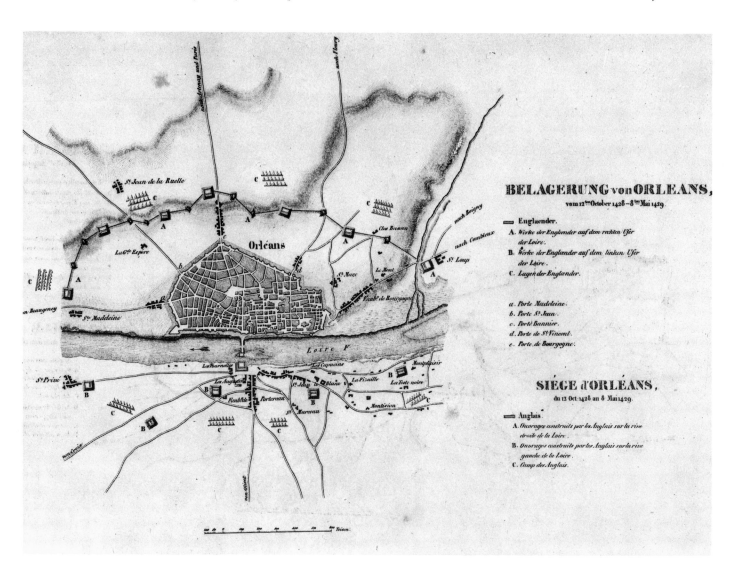

fantry, under the command of Sir John Falstolf. Thereupon the Count of Clermont, who was assembling an army near Blois, joined his forces with those of Jean de Dunois, called the Bastard of Orléans, and marched against the English with four thousand men. The encounter took place near Rouvai on February 12, 1429 and, because of the provisions that were being transported, it has passed into history as the "Battle of the Herring." The English forces put themselves on the defensive, using a tactic that the pioneers of the Old West would one day make famous; that is arranging the wagons in a circle and putting archers on top so that they could fire from an advantageous position. The fire of the French artillery and the furious French attacks could accomplish nothing against the improvised English fortress. On February 15th John Falstolf arrived in Suffolk's camp with his precious cargo of supplies.

This is the moment for a small insertion concerning the career of Joan of Arc, who would afterwards be called the "Maid of Orléans." As everybody knows, Joan was a young peasant girl of Domrémy, a village located in the valley of the Meuse. She was very devout

and "heard" celestial voices. When she heard the news of the serious sufferings inflicted by the English on the city of Orléans, Joan, in her ingenuousness, equated the enemies of religion with the enemy of her country. She convinced herself that she was chosen by heaven to accomplish the salvation of France, of the Crown, and of the very city of Orléans. In January of 1429 she had occasion to meet Captain Robert de Baudricourt, commander in charge of the town of Vaucoleurs and most faithful vassal of the Dauphin. It was he who, won by the ingenuous enthusiasm of the young girl (she was then seventeen), presented her at court. Joan journeyed to Chinon dressed as a man and there, on February 24th, the shepherdess of Domrémy was able to pick out Charles in the midst of a group of nobles. She asked him to entrust to her the neccessary men to raise the siege of Orléans and to open the way to the consecration, in the cathedral of Reims, of the King of liberated France. The Dauphin was convinced and since, at Blois, the survivors of so many misfortunes who were gathered there seemed to be galvanized by the promises and by the personality of Joan, he decided to send the girl to Orléans, with the same small army of survivors and with a convoy of food and munitions.

Joan appeared at Blois, riding a black horse and wearing splendid armor, a gift from the king. She wore a sword with a seal of five crosses discovered, according to her, in the church of Saint Catherine at Fierbois. Her ensign was a white banner of satin with lilies of gold and the names of Jesus and Mary. On April 27th she marched on Orléans, arriving in front of the walls of the city on the day of the 28th. In spite of some strife with her captains and a furious night storm, Joan was able, on the 29th, to enter Orléans with her following of soldiers, artillerists, and reinforcements, to the great joy of the population.

Before leaving Blois, Joan had sent several notes to the English, urging them to "Give up the keys of the French cities you have occupied, if you wish to avoid divine punishment." When she arrived in Orléans, she repeated the warnings to the commander of the garrison of the "tourelles," William Gladsdale, speaking from the top of the city wall. But she received in reply only lewd epithets and obscenities.

On May 4th a strong new convoy of food and munitions approached the besieged city and Joan, together with La Hire, a brave French officer, went out to meet it and escorted it back within the walls. They passed right through the line of *bastilles* established by the besiegers who, however, remained shut up within their fortifications without disturbing the French in any way.

On the same day Jean de Dunois attacked the English position of Saint-Loup, but the attack was bloodily repulsed. Joan, who was resting in Orléans, quickly armed herself and, jumping on a horse, rushed to meet the soldiers who were retreating in disorder after being repulsed by the English. They regained their courage, renewed the attack, and triumphed over the defenders.

On may 6th 1429 an attack was made on the English *bastilles* on the southern bank of the Loire. The troops from Orléans crossed the river in boats and unexpectedly assailed the forts of the Augustins and of Saint Jean de Blanc, which were captured after a bitter struggle.

Since there was talk of the imminent arrival of an English relief army under the command of Falstolf, the besieged, awaiting a favorable moment, decided to try also an attack against the key enemy position: the "tourelles." These towers were manned with five hundred archers and men-at-arms under the command, as has been noted, of William Gladsdale.

The following day, May 7th, Joan mounted her horse, shouting her famous war cry "He who loves me, follow me!" and approached the Burgundian Gate. Gancourt, the governor of Orléans, refused to open the gate, but the populace forced the gates and the sortie started. The stronghold's best soldiers crossed the river in boats and attacked the English position on the other bank of the Loire. The conflict was terrible. The English defended themselves with great fury. The Maid, at a certain point, planted her standard on the edge of the moat and after jumping down into it, placed a ladder against the wall and began to scale it. But an arrow between the neck and shoulder, put an end to Joan's action. Rescued by the soldiers who immediately came to her aid, she pulled out the arrow with her own hand.

The arms of Charles VII, Dauphin of France at the time of the siege of Orléans, from a collection of prints about the most famous persons in French history, now at the National Library of Paris.

Arbalétrier. Archer. Mangonneau. Bombarde. Fauconneau. Veuglaire sur son affut. Voulgier. Cranequinier.

Les remparts d'Orléans pendant le siège. (1er octobre 1428 - 8 mai 1429.)

It is reported that some soldiers suggested that the wound would be helped through the use of magic words, but this only aroused the Maid's scorn. From the records of her trial we know she then declared: "I prefer to die rather than to do anything against the will of God. I wish to be helped only if my wound may be cured without committing a sin." Then she made her confession and waited for death. But the "heavenly voices" came to comfort her. Again according to her declaration, Joan knew that her wound would be cured. "It was revealed to me. I was the first to place a ladder against the fortress of the bridge. But Saint Catherine gave me great comfort and I was cured in fifteen days."

Once more ready for the fray, she called Dunois and the other commander who, discouraged by the failure of their repeated attacks, had already given the order for retreat. She exhorted them not to despair and to continue the struggle. And, effectively, affairs soon began to improve. The garrison of Orléans, using planks joined together to make a platform, succeeded in repairing the missing parts of the bridge and assailed the "Tourelles" from the city side as well.

Gladsdale decided to concentrate all his forces at the "Tourelles." He crossed the drawbridge to rally his forces and Joan, who had already scaled the wall, called on him to surrender. The Englishman replied with his usual scorn, but at that very moment a cannon ball

On the bastion of Orléans during the siege according to a XIX century illustration (Rome, Central National Library). At the rear, a trebuchet, indicated in the commentary as a mangonneau. *Actually a distinction is usually made between a mangonel and a trebuchet because of the fact that the latter is equipped with a sling while the arm of the former ends in a fixed "spoon," into which the projectile is placed.*

knocked the drawbridge out from under his feet. The proud "Glacidas" (as he was called by the French) thus ended his days in the eddies of the river, along with many of his men. This was the end of the English possession of the "Tourelles." Three hundred men had lost their lives defending them, and two hundred were made prisoners. Joan reentered the city from the same bridge of which the passage had been barred for so long.

The entry of Joan of Arc was triumphant and the entire night between the 7th and 8th of May was passed in rejoicing, while all the city's bells rang in a festive outpouring of sound: the long nightmare was over.

In effect, within the *bastilles* that they still held, the English were deciding upon a retreat. The following morning, May 9, 1429, the people of Orléans noted great fires coming from the last English positions. They were blowing up the munitions and burning the provisions which were supposed to have been a guarantee of the fall of the city. France had won her first Verdun.

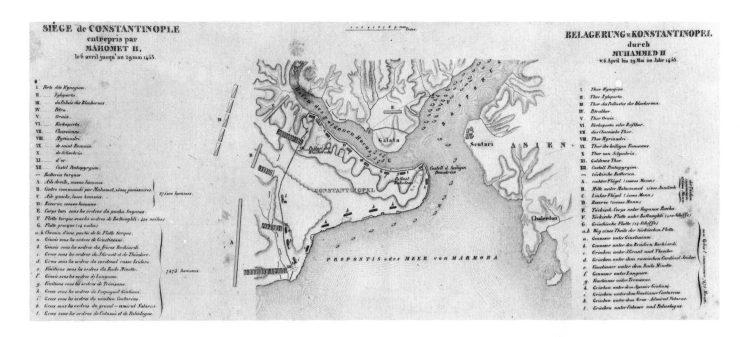

CONSTANTINOPLE (1453)

"The city has been taken and I am still alive."

Above: *Another picture from Kaustler's Atlas (see page 96) showing the plan of the siege of Constantinople.* Facing page: *Folio 207 of manuscript 9087 of the National Library of Paris (Le Siège du Grand Turc). On the top left can be noted the Turkish ships which, pulled by man power, were transported from the Sea of Marmara to the Golden Horn, thereby hastening the Byzantine collapse.*

At dawn, April 5, 1453, the inhabitants of Constantinople woke up to a deafening noise of trumpets and drums, accompanied by shouts and chants. From the Sea of Marmara to the Golden Horn, an enormous mass of Turkish soldiery extended from under the walls as far as the eye could reach. This was the army of the Crescent, two hundred thousand strong. Under the impetus of so many victories on European territory it was now about to attempt a decisive action against its secular enemy: the Roman Empire of the East. At its head stood an englightened and ruthless sovereign scarcely twenty-three years old, Mohammed II. Facing him, with eighty thousand Byzantines, was Constantine XI.

The few Imperial troops that were available were joined by Italians, either mercenaries or volunteers, who had come from Pisa, Venice and Genoa. The Genoese, who numbered seven hundred, were under the command of Giovanni Giustiniani and were among those who most distinguished themselves. The Byzantine fleet, now impotent, had been reduced to thirty ships in all.

The city, set on a triangular peninsula, between the Sea of Marmara and the bay called the Golden Horn, was defended by an imposing system of a series of encircling walls. The outer wall was constructed during the reign of Theodosius, in the V century. It enclosed the peninsula from the land side, was five miles long, had eight gates and was reinforced by fifty towers, large and small. Near the Golden Gate a castle, called Yedikule, meaning "of the seven towers," connected the above defense system with the wall which protected the city along the coast of the Sea of Marmara and the Golden Horn, and this too was strengthened by towers for the entire length of its seven and a half miles. It was a formidable system in medieval times and capable still of commanding respect at the middle of the XV century, if there had been, within the city, sufficient forces to garrison it. In reality, after taking into consideration the necessary personnel for guard and other duties, the Byzantines were able to place only one man for each eighteen foot section of wall. In addition, the Turkish artillery had to be faced. This artillery was composed entirely of pieces based on fire power, while the Byzantines still possessed mixed artillery, composed of modern cannons and of throwing weapons.

The fortification complex had suffered a decisive loss of efficiency one year before the siege when, in 1452, Mohammed II had been able to build, without opposition, the castle of Rumeli Hissar at the eastern outlet of the Bosphorus, on the European shore. It faced another castle, Amaduli Hissar, on the opposite bank. These two castles were able to keep ships coming from the Black Sea from reaching Constantinople, which found itself isolated. In addition, artillery stationed at Rumeli

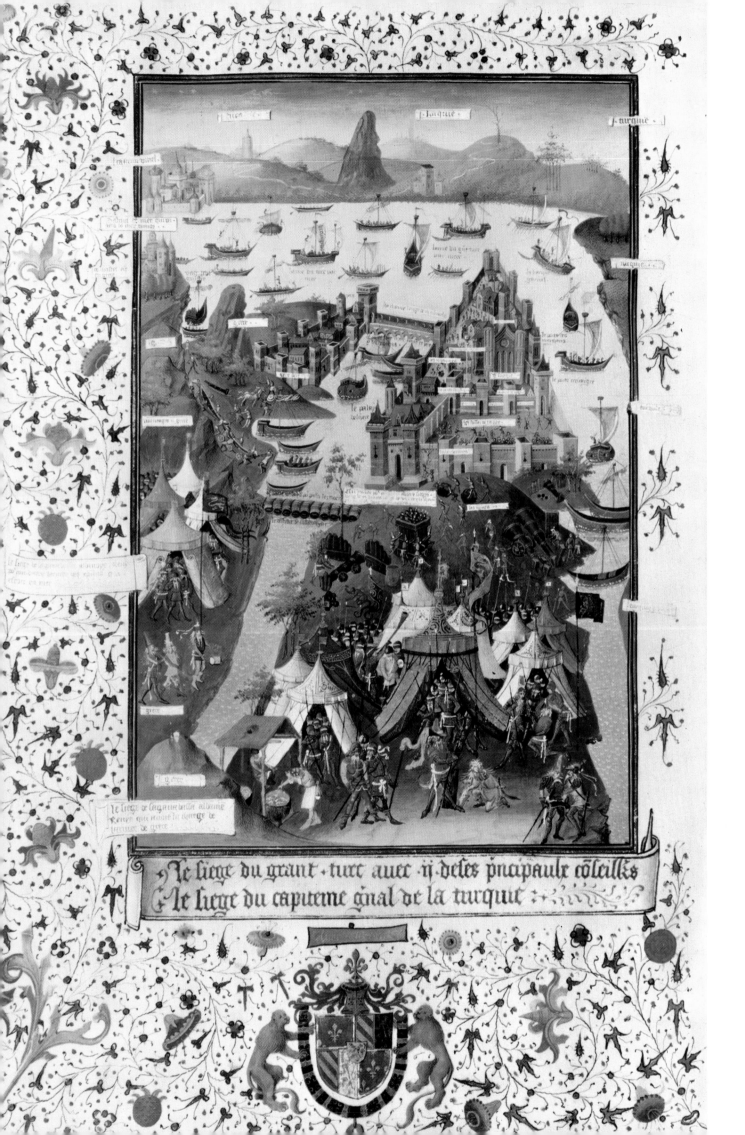

Le siege du grant turc auec ij defes pricipaulx coſeilles
Le siege du capiteine gñal de la turquie

Hissar was able to bombard the center of the city.

The city was guarded, on the side of the Golden Horn, by great chains stretched from the walls of the tower of Galata, effectively blocking the Turkish fleet.

Constantinople had at its disposition a great quantity of provisions. These had been requisitioned in abundance from the surrounding countryside; cattle, grain, and other provisions. Water, which in normal times flowed into Constantinople through an aquaduct constructed in the IV century by the Emperor Valens, had been stored in great quantities within the huge cisterns, some of which were extremely impressive constructions of considerable architectural value.

Some few citizens still enrolled in the defense of the city but these were improvised soldiers of little value in combat.

A miniature from the Book of Achievements *(manuscript 373 of the Topkapi Library of Istanbul) illustrating the decisive moment of the siege. After having transported their ships by land across the Galata Peninsula the Turks of Mohammed II attack the walls near the Edirna Gate. It is May 29, 1453. After three unsuccessful assaults the Turks found a hidden passage and penetrated within the city, putting an end to the Roman Empire of the East.*

The other decisive factor in the siege was the artillery; the lack of Byzantine artillery has already been noted. In describing the Turkish artillery, special mention is due to the great bombard, or early cannon, that Mohammed II put in the field and which remained, in a sense, without equal. It was a real monster made of bronze, twenty feet long, which fired projectiles weighing more than thirteen hundred pounds apiece with a diameter of thirty-two inches to a distance of well over five hundred yards. To transport this monster, fifty yokes of oxen were needed and four hundred and fifty men as well. Two months were taken to transport it from Adrianople to Constantinople. By the use of this artillery piece as well as the other cannons which he had at his command, Mohammed submitted Constantinople to a bombardment such as no city had ever before experienced and was able to open fearsome breaches in the walls. Through these he launched the Turkish infantry on the day of April 18th. Giovanni Giustiniani and his Genoese strongly repulsed this first attempt. Mohammed II, somewhat daunted, proposed a parley to Constantine XI. He proposed that the Emperor retire to the Peloponnesus and continue his reign. But the Basileus made it known to Mohammed that there would never be a surrender.

But the Sultan was determined to succed. Since his ships had not been able to pass over the chains which shut the Golden Horn, Mohammed caused to be built, across the Galata Peninsula, a road five miles long, whose exact course has never been successfully established. It was on this road, on April 23, 1453, with the help of greased wooden rollers, that thousands of men and hundreds of oxen dragged seventy Turkish galleys. When the Turkish sails appeared in the waters of the Golden Horn, the city understood that it was lost. On May 23rd, Mohammed II offered the Emperor new proposals for surrender. But once more the Emperor refused.

Meanwhile, within the city, religious quarrels between the Catholics and members of the Orthodox Church reached an absurd climax. Orthodox confessors denied absolution to combatants who had dealings with the Catholics or who had taken part in a Mass celebrated by a priest favorable to Rome.

The end was in the air. It came on May 29th, when Mohammed II ordered a general attack.

The first two assault waves were repulsed. But Giovanni Giustiniani, gravely wounded, had to leave the fight. It was an irreparable loss. Bitter fighting went on for another twenty-two hours and the outcome was still uncertain until a detachment of Janizaries discovered, near the Adrianople Gate, a passage that was unprotected. It was the *Kerkoporta*, the entrance to the circus, which had an opening on the bottom into a moat and led directly into the city. The defenders of the walls, who had also repulsed the third assault wave, suddenly saw the Turks appear in back of them, screaming and drunk with victory. In the Church of Santa Sophia the yells of the conquerors and the sounds of the battering in of the doors, drowned out the prayers of the faithful

Turkish armor, formerly the property of the Czar of Russia. Below: *A curious example of Turkish arms seen from the front and the side (Paris, Library of the Museum of the Army).*

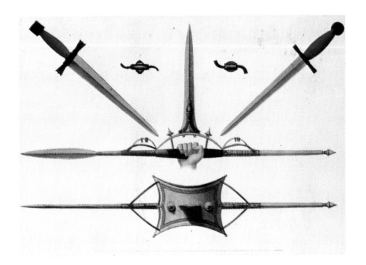

who had taken refuge there. Then, the massacre started. Constantine XI with his sword drawn, threw himself into the tumult shouting: "The city has been taken and I am still alive." A short time afterwards he was killed, one among many. His body, recognized by his red boots, a symbol of Imperial authority, was taken to Mohammed II. Mohammed ordered the head to be cut off and thereupon sent it to various points of his empire, attended by an escort of forty youths from among the Moslems and another forty chosen from among the Christians, so that the people might see to their satisfaction that Allah had indeed conquered.

BEAUVAIS (1472)

The city of the fortified gates humiliates Charles the Bold

When he distributed French territories to his own heirs, Jean II, called the Good, gave the duchy of Burgundy as a fief to his last-born son, Philip the Fearless. In the course of a few decades Philip and his successors were able to obtain possession of other fiefs from Flanders to Artois, from Picardy to the Franche Comté, from Brabant to Holland, to Luxemburg and other territories. This considerable extension of territory had the result of making the duchy of Burgundy one of the most prosperous among the European powers of the time and also resulted in Burgundy itself becoming a flourishing center of art and commerce. The Dutch historian, Jan

LA SAVLT. DE. BEAVVAIS.

national scale, Burgundy made alliances against France with England, Castile, and Aragon. The final aim of Charles the Bold was to effect the changing of his own title of Duke into that of King and to place the projected Kingdom of Burgundy under the sovereignty of the Empire.

It was suddenly clear that hostilities would break out because of the slightest pretext. In effect, when Louis XI refused to honor a certain promise he had made to turn over to Charles the Bold the cities of the Somme, Charles immediately took the field and occupied several of these cities. In addition, he gave definite indications of being about to invade Normandy. The route to Normandy passed through Beauvais.

The city, besides being protected by its own walls, had entrusted its defense to a garrison composed of fifty crossbowmen and thirty free archers. In addition, there was a kind of civic guard, raised by districts, and there was also a certain amount of artillery equipped with powder and ammunition. Charles the Bold, for his part, led an army whose composition has been reported differently by different sources. According to some he had eighty thousand men, while according to others he had only fifty thousand or even forty thousand. From this number of course, one must subtract all non-com-

Facing page: *Burgundians during the attack on Beauvais in a miniature of the School of Rouen (XVI century) from the* Mémoires de Philippe de Commines *now at Nantes, in the Palais Dobrée.* Above: *A marshal of France, according to a reconstruction by Philippoteaux (Paris, Library of the Museum of the Army). The rank of marshal, created in 1185 by Philip Augustus, became the highest in the French military hierarchy when Richelieu abolished the rank of constable.* Right, within the oval: *Jeanne Hachette, the heroine of Beauvais, from a lithograph in the National Library of Paris (Bureau of Prints), from a picture by N.H. Jacob. As is often the case with popular heroes, there is a question about the real name of this "wool carder." Her real name seems to have been Jeanne Layné, the daughter of Matthieu, although some of her contemporaries also called her Jeanne Forquet.*

Huizinga, considers Burgundy, perhaps rightly, to have been the nerve center of the Renaissance in Europe.

Philip the Fearless was succeeded by Jean without Fear and he in turn by his son Philip the Good (1419-1466). Philip's monarchical plans and the spread of his influence began to be a matter for preoccupation to Charles VII of France. Charles frequently had to bargain for the security of his own throne by making ever greater concessions to his Burgundian vassal. Charles the Bold, the son of Philip the Good, and Duke of Burgundy from the year 1467, was called on by destiny to settle accounts with the King of France by the sword.

Louis XI thus became the adversary of Charles the Bold. Louis perceived that within his realm he was attacked by the "League of Public Welfare," organized by Charles among the great feudal lords. On an inter-

batant forces such as, for example, carpenters, servants, merchants, vivandières, and the many "filles de joye" ("girls of joy") who at that time were a fixed institution in every army. In the army of the Duke of Burgundy these girls were assigned at the rate of thirty per company. The Burgundian army, therefore, lacked true and effective cohesion as it was composed of feudal units, the followers and dependents of local lords. Among the nobility in the cavalry of the Burgundian army, a company formed by one hundred Italian cavalrymen made an especially fine show.

The siege operations lasted from June 27th to July 22nd, 1472. At dawn on Saturday, June 27th, the laborers who were working on the roof of the city cathedral suddenly saw the advance guard of the Burgundian army advancing toward Beauvais. All the bells in the city sounded the alarm and Beauvais was on a war footing in just a few minutes.

At about eight o'clock a Burgundian herald rode up to the walls to make known the command of Philippe de Crèvecoeur, commander of the advance guard, to the citizens of Beauvais. It was to open the gates to the forces of Burgundy. The refusal was short and decisive. Crèvecoeur who, for some reason, thought he could take the city from the east and from the west, without waiting for the main body of the army, sent five hundred Burgundians to attack the west side of the city. The results seemed to prove him right. From that side, the advance points of the fortifications were held by about twenty soldiers equipped with arquebuses under the command of the city's captain, Louis Gomer, Lord of Balagny. The soldiers were not able to hold the position and he himself was wounded. The Burgundians were able to take possession of a suburb, but in twelve hours of attack they were not able to scale the walls nor to force the nearest gate, called the Stone Gate or the Limaçon Gate. To the east at the gate of Bresles, the combat was much fiercer. The citizens of Beauvais, helped by their women, defended themselves from the Burgundians, who were scaling the walls, by pelting them with boulders and pouring down boiling oil, water, and flaming projectiles on their assailants. The gate caught fire and the flames spread to the neighboring houses. To support and lift the morale of the defenders, the coffer containing the sacred relics of Saint Angadresma, especially venerated in Beauvais, was carried to the scene of combat. Jeanne Layné, popularly called Jeanne Hachette, was especially noteworthy among the defenders. She noted a Burgundian who was planting a standard on the bastion and, although she was unarmed, she approached him and forced it out of his hands. The flag was later offered by her to the "God of Battles" in the church where she worshipped.

On June 27th and on the following days, men, arms, and victuals arrived in support of the besieged city. In the early part of July the city was able to count about fifteen thousand defenders. From without, it could also count on the support of the royal army under the command of the Constable, Count de Saint-Paul, the highest military authority in France, after the King.

The Burgundian artillery, arrayed to the north of Beauvais, suddenly began a very heavy bombardment of an intensity never before experienced. Besides the colubrins and the serpentines, the Burgundians had enormous bombards, of which they were particularly proud. These great pieces were twenty feet long with a caliber of more than sixty centimeters and weighing up to thirty tons.

On July 9th, an attack was again made on the gate of Bresles. The Burgundians rushed across the moat over which they had previously constructed a passage under very difficult conditions, but this blew up in the very moment that it was crowded with the attackers. During the preceding night a page, named Bellot, had mined it and was able from within the city to light a long fuse which was sufficient to cause the disaster. That day the Burgundians suffered a loss of more than six hundred dead. A week later their losses were more than three thousand.

Charles' stubborn attack against the gates of Beauvais was almost unbelievable. But when they fell and the Burgundians passed through, they found themselves still caught in long and narrow passageways (such was the internal structure) that they had to penetrate under enemy fire as well as to deal with permanent or temporary barricades. The defenders had even built walls within the city leaving a passage to the outside only by the gate of Paris. Charles the Bold understood therefore that Beauvais could only fall through breaching the walls and to this end concentrated against these bastions the whole force of his artillery, under the command of Jacques d'Orson, the most famous artillerist of that time. Projectiles of stone or of iron of all calibers and weights bombarded the houses of Beauvais for fifteen consecutive nights and days and opened fearsome breaches in the walls. But the citizens of Beauvais took up the paving stones from the streets and filled in the breaches of the walls with them. While they were engaged in this work, they attempted to protect themselves from the English archers who were with the Burgundian army by letting down bolts of material from the top of the walls to form a screen. These archers enjoyed an enviable reputation within the army. As each of them had twelve arrows in his quiver, they used to say that their quiver held the destiny of twelve souls. Using their great bows which measured five feet in length, they could fire their mortal

Facing page and on the right: *Three pictures of Charles the Bold. The first is an alabaster sculpture from the XVI century, the others are oil paintings from the XVI century* (above) *and XVII century* (below). *This last painting is a modification of a painting originally representing Saint William* (Museum of Dijon). Above: *Jeanne Hachette in the center of the struggle in a painting by François Watteau* (Valenciennes, Museum of Fine Arts). *Charles the Bold was an extremely authoritative and violent character. His repulse at Beauvais made him furious. According to a contemporary report, he gave the order, before lifting the siege, for every one of his artillery pieces to aim at the city's cathedral and to send it a volley of farewell: "et lui envoya une volée d'adieu."*

arrows to a range of two hundred and thirty yards without ever missing a target.

The attack on July 9th was the most disastrous of all for Charles the Bold. His most valiant knights died on that day, run through while on the scaling ladders by the lances of the French. These lances, which the defenders used with great skill, were more than seventeen feet long.

The following day, four hundred of the French, under the leadership of Jean de Salezart, made a sortie from Beauvais and caused serious losses to the enemy ranks.

Charles the Bold still tried to encourage his men to new endeavors, claiming the city could be taken from the side of the gate of Paris. But he was the only one left to hold this opinion and finally he resigned himself to his defeat. On July 11th he made a proclamation to his troops stating that the army was called elsewhere, to accomplish more pressing matters than the capture of Beauvais. It was but an excuse to hide his discomfort. On the 22nd the Burgundian army struck camp. Beauvais had won not only its own battle, but that of all France. As the chronicler noted, Burgundy *"oncques puis ne prospéera"* (from then on would prosper no more).

GRANADA (1489-1492)

The sigh of the last King of the Moors

The Arab rule of Spain lasted for seven and a half centuries. It was a long intense period making, in comparison, the two and a half centuries they spent in Sicily a minor episode in the history of Arab conquests in the West. When the Arabs made their first penetrations from African bases in 710, Arab sway in Western Africa was not yet completely consolidated. But the Spain of that time was a land in crisis under the uncertain rule of a Visigoth Kingdom. A year later, in the spring of 711, it was not able to stop Tariq, a freed Berber slave, from carrying out the first real invasion operation, which resulted in the Moorish conquest of Spain.

Spain resumed the offensive less than three centuries later, under Alfonso VI and El Cid, a continuing offensive which liberated the greater part of Spain. Only toward the middle of the XIII century did the two opposing groups face each other in temporarily established positions. On one side stood liberated Spain, which seemed for the moment to have lost its impetus; on the other side stood the last Arab bastion in Spain, the Kingdom of Granada, now reduced to a political pawn in the power struggle between the various Christian states and further acting as a buffer between the Peninsula and Africa. In this way the throne of Granada continued to belong to the Moorish kings for another two centuries until, at the end of the XV century, a tragic epilogue took place. As the marriage of Ferdinand and Isabella sealed the union of Christian Spain, the Reconquista (as the crusading movement to win back Spain from the Moors was called) suddenly regained its vigor. The last King of Granada, Mohammed XI, usually referred to as Boabdil, paid the price. As he was hemmed in on all sides by the Christian forces, he made an unusual agreement with the Catholic monarchs, Ferdinand and Isabella. According to this agreement, he would give over Granada to the Spaniards if they were successful in conquering the cities of Baza, Cádiz, and Almería. The siege of Granada may therefore be said to have begun with other operations far from the capital of that Arab kingdom.

At the beginning of 1488 Ferdinand and Isabella had already occupied half of the western part of the kingdom of Granada. Early in June of that year, Ferdinand, who had established his headquarters at Loja, advanced with a small army to the town of Vera, which immediately gave up without fighting. The King then turned to the city of Almería where, according to agreements secretly made, the gates would be opened to him. The plan did not succeed however, and the King thought it safer to retreat. Operations started again in the spring of 1489. First Baza was laid siege to, with an army of thirteen thousand horsemen and forty thousand infantry. Baza defended itself vigorously. When the money to cover the expenses of the expedition began to give out, Queen Isabella herself did not hesitate to pawn all her own jewelry and to appear personally in the field.

The arrival of the Queen under the walls of Baza marked the beginning of parleys between the defenders and the besiegers. In Granada the inactivity of Boabdil was beginning to come under criticism and it was murmured that the loss of Baza would indicate the definite ruin of the Kingdom of Granada. The King of Granada thereupon arrested the critics and condemned them to death by decapitation. Opinions about his indecision seemed to change but this was not enough to stop the success of negotiations between the Catholic Monarchs and Prince Sidi Hiaya, on whom depended not only Baza, but also Almería and Cádiz.

After Baza was taken the monarchs turned toward Almería. The governor of the city went to meet them and symbolically turned over to them the gates and fortifications. Ferdinand and Isabella, together with the Cardinal of Spain, entered the gates of Almería where they received the oath of fealty from the inhabitants. A few days later similar manifestations took place in Cádiz.

As the conditions mentioned in the agreement had now been brought about, Ferdinand sent messengers to Boabdil requesting that the pact be fulfilled. The Moorish King, however, making use of several excuses, replied that it was impossible for him to fulfill these conditions right away. His intentions became more clearly evident when he occupied the fortress of Padul, near Granada, which was already held by the Christians. Evidently he intended to settle the decision by force of arms.

In the spring of 1490 Ferdinand accepted his challenge and ordered all the trees cut down and all the crops destroyed on the fertile plain or "vega" of Granada as a preparation for an assault on the city. The cavalry of Granada undertook a series of sorties which cost the lives of many Spanish soldiers, but this was not enough to interfere with the work of destruction which continued to create a zone of "scorched earth" around the beautiful and powerful city. As a reprisal, the forces of Granada laid siege to the fortress of Alhendin and forced its surrender. This victory was a signal for a revolt of all the Moors in the surrounding countryside. The King's governors were expelled from their castles, many losing their lives along with their possessions. The castle of Mondújar, in the absence of its governor, was defended by a noble and heroic lady, the wife of the governor, María de Acuña. The Moors also tried to capture the coastal city of Salobreña, important for its small port, which would have enabled them to communicate with the Kingdom of Barbary, in Africa. The garrison defend-

Left: *The sword of Isabella "la Católica" (the Catholic). Right: The royal hilt of the "Great Captain," Gonzalvo de Córdova. Above: A view of the Alhambra of Granada from the XVII century atlas by Braun (Genova-Pegli, the Civic Naval Museum). The three special inserts respectively depict the gate from which Boabdil left the city to surrender, the ditches where the Moors dropped their prisoners and, finally, the Algibe cistern, constructed in such a way as to accumulate rainwater.*

ed itself heroically and the Moors, even though they had penetrated within the city through the complicity of their fellow religionists within the walls, were not able to take the capital. When word was received that King Ferdinand was on his way with his army, they raised the siege and fled to Granada. King Ferdinand again entered on the plain before Granada. Since it was September and the grain was ripe be caused new destruction of the crops and then returned to Cordoba.

A short while later new alarms sounded: the Moors of Granada were stirring up to rebellion those of Baza, Cádiz, and Almería. The King suddenly appeared at Cádiz by forced marches and his presence there calmed the situation. But as he now understood the spirit of his Moorish subjects, continually apt to break out in revolts, the King ordered those who lived in fortified cities to leave them and to go to live in open cities or to emigrate to Barbary after having sold their property. After having brought about in this way a certain tranquility in his dominions, he resumed the preparation for the siege of Granada.

In the spring of 1491, the Catholic Monarchs marched on the Moorish capital. Ferdinand, arriving on the plain before Granada which he had ravaged so many times, detached a contingent of three thousand horsemen and ten thousand infrantrymen from his army and assigned them to the command of the Marquis of Villena. These were to enter the valley of Lecrino and to destroy all fortified points. A short time afterwards, however, he followed them with the rest of the army, fearing that the Moors, with their special knowledge of the difficult terrain, would surprise Villena's detachment by ambuscades or guerrilla warfare. Nevertheless, Villena's operations were successful. The fortified points were neutralized and the Spanish detachment returned to camp with much booty and many prisoners. The King, however, was not content. He ordered Villena to return to the scene of his past actions and to destroy absolutely everything, including any future harvest. It appeared that he would not be able to defeat Granada without making a desert around it.

This delay helped Boabdil who, having learned the timing of King Ferdinand's march, occupied the Tablate and Lanjarón passes, hoping to surprise the Christians at that point during their return march. But Ferdinand's commanders attacked the Moors from other directions and expelled them from the passes. The King passed through the mountains at Lanjarón, where he waited for the return of the detachments who were operating in the territory of Orgiba and the neighboring mountains. When he had finished his work of devastation, the King with his entire army again entered on the plain before Granada. On April 26th he established his general headquarters near some springs, called "Ojos de Huércal," and thereupon undertook to lay a true and final siege to Granada.

Queen Isabella, according to her usual custom, wished to be present, not only because she liked to witness events of great importance, but also because she consid-

ered that her presence would encourage the soldiers. She had with her her own children, Prince Juan, heir to the throne, and Princess Juana.

Through the carelessness of a serving maid who neglected to put out a candle, the tent of the Queen caught fire and burned along with many others. The monarchs thereupon had a masonry city constructed containing two principal streets in the form of a cross.

The city was called Santa Fé (Holy Faith) and not Isabella, as the soldiers had wished. It was surrounded by walls and protected by a deep moat, thereby protecting the royal quarters from fire and from eventual attacks by the enemies. The enemy, noting the new construction from the walls, realized that the sovereigns were now truly resolved to conquer Granada.

Within the Christian camp were the bearers of the

The moment of Boabdil's surrender to the Spanish Sovereign. The last Moorish King of Granada is about to surrender to Ferdinand the keys of the city under the proud and compassionate regard of the Queen. Afterward the King will embrace him and will not permit that Boabdil kiss his hand. Then the conquered King will go on his way, often turning to look sadly upon the city that, in the reproachful words of his mother "he was not able to defend." A painting by El Pradilla, The Surrender of Granada *(Madrid, Palacio Senado).*

A suit of armor said to have belonged to Abu Abdullah Muhammed, called Boabdil, the last Sovereign of the Arab Kingdom of Granada, now in the Royal Armory of Madrid, as represented in a XIX century drawing (Paris, Library of the Museum of the Army).

proudest names of Castile and Andalusia, the heroic knights who would vie with the twenty thousand warriors of Granada, furnishing material to the epic songs of the *reconquista* and to the last chapter in the history of the *Chansons de Geste* and of knighthood.

One day the Queen wished to see Granada more closely — the wonderful gray-rose colored city (of "deep grays and blotting-paper rose" as Federico García Lorca would one day describe it). She stopped in a village from which she could admire Granada and its Alhambra. The Marquis of Cádiz, assigned to protect the Queen, was on duty with a few men between the city and the village when suddenly horsemen made a sortie from the gates of Granada. The Marquis impetuously charged the enemy, putting him to flight and pursuing the enemy forces up to the gate of the city, inflicting many losses and taking numerous prisoners. In memory of this deed of valor Isabella founded at that very spot a monastery of the Franciscan Friars.

The summer passed by in encounters of little importance, often in skirmishes or even in individual duels. But by September, the Moors, who did not want to enter into negotiations for surrender, found themselves in difficult straits. The challenges to the Christian knights to single combat continued as well as an occasional sudden sortie, usually repulsed by the besiegers, but the ring of steel kept closing in and provisions, already scarce, diminished to a dangerously low supply.

The population of Granada within the walls had greatly increased because of the people who had fled to safety within the capital, under the slow but continuous pressure of the besiegers. This increase in population caused Boabdil considerable worry, not only because of the short supply of food, but above all because it brought about additional anxiety and possible revolts.

At a certain point, the King of Granada and his council realized the uselessness of prolonging a resistance which only caused additional suffering to the population and they resolved to initiate negotiations with the Catholic Monarchs. The negotiations were conducted in great secrecy so as not to anger those who favored a last ditch resistance. The latter still counted on aid from the Moslems of Africa and Asia. The negotiating plenipotentiaries met at night, secretly, in Granada or in a village not far from the capital. The Moors were represented by Boabdil's Vizier, Abu Kasim Abd-el-Malik, while Ferdinand and Isabella sent as their representatives their trusted counsellor Ferdinand de Zafra and Captain Gonzalo de Córdova. The articles of capitulation were ratified by Boabdil and by the Spanish sovereigns on November 25, 1491, and were (at least for the moment) of a generous nature. According to the terms of the agreement the Moors were allowed to continue freely to practice their religion, to keep their own ways and customs, to be judged according to their own laws, and to speak their own language. They would be able to keep and dispose of their own property as they wished and, if they wanted to leave, they could do so whenever they wished. Those who remained in Granada would not have to pay greater tribute than that which they habitually paid to their own King and, moreover, for the first three years they would be exempt from taxes. King Boabdil would be able to reign over the small territory of Alpujarras and would be a vassal of the Crown of Castile. The Moors would have to surrender to the Christians their fortresses and artillery. The city would be obliged to open its gates within sixty days from the date of the capitulation (December 14, 1491).

The court of King Ferdinand prepared to celebrate in sufficiently solemn manner a moment so glorious in the history of Spain; the end of Moslem dominion over the last vestige of Spanish territory seven hundred and eighty years after the beginning of the Moslem conquest. The royal family, which was in mourning because of the death of Alfonso the Infante of Portugal, suspended mourning. The monarchs, wearing their most splendid apparel, went to meet King Boabdil and embraced him (see the painting on page 111).

The Spanish have preserved relics of the reconquista *with veneration. This is the* armor of Ferdinand of Aragon who, when his kingdom and destiny were joined with those of Isabella the Catholic, unified Catholic Spain and led her to the victorious conquest of Granada. This ended the centuries-old struggle of the Iberians against the Moslem invaders. Below: *The King's stirrups reproduced from a XIX century drawing (as was the armor) which illustrated an old catalog of the Royal Madrid Armory to which we have already referred. (Paris, The Library of the Museum of the Army).*

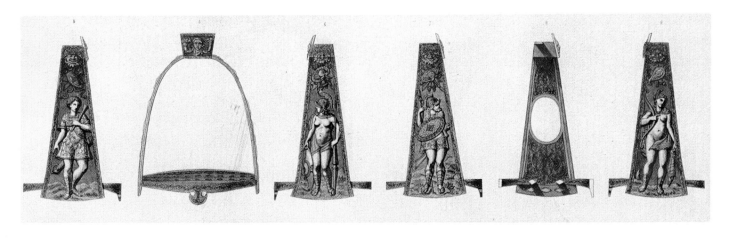

PADUA (1509)

"I wish there could be a little sirocco for six days, and half of them would vanish."

The Emperor Maximilian according to an English print of the early XIX century (Paris, Library of the Museum of the Army). On facing page: The frontispiece of a contemporary work on the siege of Padua preserved in the Trivulziana Library of Milan. The Andrea Gritti mentioned in the title was then superintendent general of San Marco and became Doge of Venice in 1523. Venice owes him her rescue from Charles V.

On May 4, 1509, after the battle of Agnadello against the French of Louis XII, the army of the Serene Republic of Venice, thrown into complete disorder, retreated to Mestre, where it tried to reorganize.

In June the French army of Louis XII began its withdrawal, but left garrisons in the different cities of the former Duchy of Milan. Meanwhile the first German forces of Louis' ally, the Emperor Maximilian, began their descent from the Alps following the various river valleys to the Adriatic. Cities such as Verona, Vicenza, and Padua, already occupied by the French, were forced to accept German governors and garrisons.

As they realized the sparse distribution of the imperial forces and counting on the basic loyalty of the citizenry, the Venetians suddenly revolted. On the night between the 16th and 17th of July, they undertook a sudden attack against Padua which routed the German infantry garrison and resulted in the capture of the city. This success was a signal for other cities to revolt which, freed from the German governors, returned to the banner of Saint Mark.

In the meantime, however, the Emperor had received reinforcements from Austria and from Louis XII and was able to reoccupy some of the cities on the Venetian mainland. Only Padua and Treviso were able to resist.

In Padua, the new Venetian garrison strengthened the inadequate fortifications of the city and prepared it to withstand an eventual siege. They did this with speed and were assisted by the local population who worked with them under the direction of Giovanni of Verona, a Dominican, better known by the name of "Brother Giocondo" (1433-1515). The walls and the bastions were reinforced and the moat was deepened and filled with water.

Within a few months, through the feverish activities of the Paduans, the city took on the aspect of an unassailable fortress. Among other things, it was able to muster more than a hundred and twenty artillery pieces. When Maximilian arrived on the scene, he was afraid to attack immediately, inasmuch as his forces lacked sufficient war

machines because of the understandable difficulty of transporting them through the valleys of the Alps. The Emperor therefore had to content himself with observing the labor of the Paduans without being able to disturb it.

The garrison was composed of about two thousand cavalry and eight thousand regular infantry in addition to ten thousand other combatants recruited for the occasion from among the more adventurous city dwellers and peasants. On August 19th the imperial army completed its own deployment but was not able to surround the city completely even with the arrival of other allied help. These reinforcements included three thousand from the Papal forces, Ferrara, and Mantua, and a contingent of five hundred French lancers under the command of Jacques II de Chabannes de La Palice, whom Sanudo calls "Monsieur Peliza." According to Marin Sanudo, the imperial forces numbered fifty to sixty thousand and included sixteen thousand regular infantry and fourteen thousand cavalry. The rest were composed of mercenaries and adventurers "and it is certain that if there were a little rain," observes the Venetian chronicler, "half of them would disappear. I wish there could be a little sirocco for six days."

The artillery convoy which was advancing toward Padua from Vicenza under escort of three hundred German cavalry was attacked by a column of Venetian crossbowmen issuing from the besieged city. Only the intervention of a detachment of French cavalry made it possible for this convoy to reach Maximilian's camp.

From the 3rd to the 10th of September the imperial forces made various raids on the territory around the city, not yet completely encircled, but were repulsed by the Venetian light cavalry. The walls of Padua were subjected to sporadic artillery fire which was effectively returned by the artillery within the city. Meanwhile attempts were made to alter the course of the Bacchilione River in order to stop the water supply to the city's mills.

On the 14th of September the siege began in earnest with the placing in position of the long awaited batteries. The defenders replied with great energy in attempting

La obfidione di Padua ne la quale fe tra
ctano tutte le cofe che fonno occorfe dal
giorno che per el preftantiffimo mefle
re Andrea Gritti Proueditore ge
nerale fu reacquiftata: che fu
adi.17. Luio.1509. per infi
no che Maximiliano
imperatore da quel
la fi leuo.

PADVA

to interfere with this positioning but on the evening of the 15th, the imperial forces were able to launch a great bombardment of the city, concentrating particularly on the bastion which protected the Codalunga Gate. The result of the artillery action was unsatisfactory and on the 20th the first assault by several Spanish infantry companies was also blunted. For the imperial forces it was a disaster: many attackers fell dead and the remainder, the majority of whom were wounded, had to retreat. Two new assaults, made on the 26th and 29th of September, were equally unsuccessful. The Emperor Maximilian, disheartened by these reverses, and embittered by the refusal of the French cavalry to support the Spanish-German infantry in their attacks, and now also short of supplies and ammunition, decided to abandon the undertaking. On the night of October 1, 1509, the imperial army retired toward Vicenza. The "little sirocco" was not needed after all.

TENOCHTITLÁN (1521)

The eagle and the rattlesnake in the "sad night" of Cortés

Hernán Cortés, the law student of Salamanca who gave Mexico to Spain, was thirty-four years old in 1519 when he received the order to explore "the mysterious land of the west." On November 8th of that year the Emperor of the Aztecs, Montezuma II, received him in the capital of Tenochtitlán (today Mexico City) with all possible honors. He considered him, in fact, to be the incarnation of a god. But the "white god" soon dropped his mask. Montezuma died soon afterwards in mysterious circumstances and the Spaniards, seized by the fever of conquest, gave themselves over to the excesses that the Aztecs could no longer tolerate. On the night between the 30th of June and the 1st of July, 1530, which would go down in history under the name of "la noche triste" (the sad night), Cortés and his followers were forced to abandon Tenochtitlán, escaping only after bitter struggle against the attacking Aztecs. Cortés and his men returned in April of 1521, thirsting for vengeance.

As the city was built in the middle of the lake of Texcoco, Cortés ordered the building of thirteen brigantines. On the 28th of April 1521, Father Almedo, after having celebrated mass, solemnly blessed them. Thereupon amid the music of the Te Deum and repeated salvos of artillery, the Spanish forces passed in review. They numbered one hundred and eighty-four arquebusiers, crossbowmen, and men-at-arm, eighty six horsemen, eighteen artillery pieces and a vast array of native allies, who were ex-allies or ex-vassals of Montezuma's successor, Cuauhtémoctzin or Cuauhtémoc. Cortés decided to attack the city from three sides and divided his forces into three groups, entrusting the command of each of these to his lieutenants, Pedro de Alvarado, Gonzalo de Sandoval, and Cristóbal de Oleda. For himself he kept the command of the flotilla of brigantines, each one of which carried twenty-five Spaniards and twelve native rowers.

On May 26th Sandoval and Alvarado destroyed the great acqueduct at Chapultepec. Thereafter not a single drop of water arrived from Chapultepec to the Aztec metropolis to supply its large population (a contemporary reported that the city contained more than sixty thousand buildings). On May 31st the Indians attacked with hundreds of canoes, filled with warriors, but a light breeze suddenly came to the help of the Spaniards, permitting Cortés' brigantines to raise their sails. They swiftly crossed over the lake and destroyed almost al the Aztec canoes with cannon fire. At dusk Cortés ordered his squadron to land at Toloc, a point where the two causeways met and which constituted the defense system. of Tenochtitlán.

After a brief advance along one of these causeways, the Spaniards found themselves faced by a rather long break which could not be crossed except by swimming. On the opposite side the Indians had constructed a

Facing page above title: *Spaniards within a stronghold defend themselves from attack by the Aztecs. This illustration, as well as the one represented above, was made by an artist who lived at the time of the events he illustrated. The artist was a native of Tlascala but a student of the Spanish school of painting. In his style may be glimpsed the artistic influences of Indian and European styles. The document is called the* Lienzo de Tlascala *(Bookroll of Tlascala), and illustrates the dramatic story of the conquest of Mexico. The episode reproduced here concerns the siege of Tenochtitlán.* Below: *Two horsemen with the armor and trappings typical of the age of Cortés, from* The Album of Spanish Chivalry. *Cortés was born in Medellín in Extremadura in 1485 and studied law at Salamanca between 1499 and 1501. He left Spain three years later and reached Santo Domingo probably in the function of* escribano *for a civil office. In 1511, under the orders of Diego Velásquez, he took part in the conquest of Cuba and, in 1518, began to prepare the undertaking which would make him famous: the exploration of Mexico. One year later, on March 23, 1519, he landed in the Empire of Montezuma and his undertaking changed from one of exploration to that of conquest.*

barricade of stones and earth, from behind which well-placed bowmen were able to fire clouds of arrows at their attackers. But a breach in the causeway permitted Cortés to move two brigantines into the other part of the lake. Thus the stronghold could be captured. Cortés now found himself in the outskirts of Tenochtitlán. Some rounds from the cannons opened a breach in the last wall which barred his advance and shortly thereafter the musketeers and crossbowmen of Spain were able to enter the great plaza of Tenochtitlán. They pillaged the sanctuary, tearing off the god's golden mask adorned with precious jewels. This provoked a furious reaction from the natives who attacked with such force that the invaders were compelled to retreat.

Alvarado and Sandoval were also in difficulties. They were not able to reach the outskirts because of other barricades on the causeways. Cortés sent half of his ships to help them out of their difficulties.

Many other attacks were made in the following days but they were unsuccessful. During the night the Indians broke new openings in the causeways and sent requests for help to tribes in the surrounding mountains by means of great drums. These were accompanied by the sounds of the great temple drums, with which the priests were also able to send messages in code from the top of the massive temple pyramid. During the daytime, the Spaniards could see a grim spectacle enacted on the level of the pyramid. There the priests sacrificed Spanish prisoners according to the usual ceremony of tearing the heart out from the breast of a living victim and offering it to Huitzilopochtli, the god of war, to whom rattlesnakes were sacred. The corpses were then thrown down the steps of the pyramid to be used as food by the hungry populace. Such horrible scenes served to strengthen the force of the Spanish attack, as they were ready to face any danger rather than to fall prisoner. They made a fresh attempt on the city, and succeeded in entering it and in advancing step by step in a long drawn out and bloody hand to hand struggle which lasted over three weeks. The final attack was made in the first half of August. A large part of the city was burned; the great plaza of the marketplace was occupied and a huge catapult was constructed which contributed to the destruction of the rest of the city by incendiary missiles.

Bernal Díaz, an eyewitness of the siege, reported that the unburied bodies were so many and so close together that it was impossible to walk without stepping on them. And Cortés, in describing the fury of his native allies during the last assault, wrote: "I have never known a race to be so pitiless, nor human beings to be so deprived of pity." A long-repressed hatred for the Aztecs found its expression in a general massacre. It was reported that a hundred and fifty thousand were killed.

On August 12, 1521, the Spaniards captured Cuauhtémoctzin. He requested Cortés personally to put him to death. The "black legend" concerning the cruelties of the conquest mentions torture, while others speak of direct punishment. In any case, he vanished along with the Aztec Empire and with Tenochtitlán.

RHODES (1522)

The first explosive grenades of history burst

After their first occupation of Rhodes, occurring in 1310 with the aid of the Genoese pirate, Vignolo dei Vignoli, the Knights of Saint John of Jerusalem, also referred to as the Hospitalers, undertook to transform their island capital into an unassailable bulwark. All the Grand Masters who successively followed each other in ruling the order brought their own contributions to the strengthening of the fortifications. At the same time they did not cease to oppose, with their own few ships, the maritime operations of the Turks (not those of the other Moslem states, however, with whom they had made commercial agreements). This openly anti-Turk policy on the part of the order was to lead to a fatal action against the island on the part of the Sultan. The first attack came in 1480 and was unsuccessful. After three months of siege the Turks were obliged to retire.

Conflict broke out again in 1522, when Suleiman (who was later known as "The Magnificent") decided to destroy the monastic republic of the Knights of Jerusalem. The news of the great preparations for war being carried out in the arsenal of Constantinople put the other Mediterranean powers in a state of alarm. However, each one thought that the Knights would be able to meet this challenge with their own forces alone. In May of 1522, when the Grand Master Philippe Villiers de l'Isle-Adam reviewed them, their ranks included six hundred Knights, four hundred mercenaries from Candia in Crete, five hundred Genoese, fifty Venetians, and four thousand men-at-arm from various other places. All measures were taken for the security of the stronghold, such as closing the port with great chains, demolishing all constructions which might interfere with artillery fire, and the stocking of necessary provisions.

The Knights were arrayed by "languages" as was customary within the Order: the French at the Gate of Filermo, then the Germans at the Gate of Saint George, and thereafter the "languages" of Auvergne and Spain, the English, the Provençals, and finally, the Italian Knights. As a reserve there was a contigent of Genoese, Venetian, and Sicilian sailors, chosen from the ships that were in port. Commanders for the defense of the different sectors were chosen and three great ensigns were distributed: that of the Crucifix, Religion, and the Grand Master.

On the morning of June 26th at daybreak, the entire Turkish fleet — about three hundred ships — appeared before the island. Sailing north, it dropped anchor at Parambolino where, protected from the winds, it could land the imposing expeditionary forces which counted two hundred thousand men. Mustafa was in command of the army. Achmet Pasha was General of Engineers and Piri

The Sultan in a decoration of a portolan map of 1561 preserved at the Civic Naval Museum of Genoa-Pegli which also has the painting reproduced on the following page. It is by an unknown author of the XVI century and represents the siege of Rhodes by the Turks.

Pasha was Chief of Staff. The landing was undisturbed (as was the case in 1480 as well) because of the lack of naval weapons capable of contesting it. The Turks carried on their offensive preparations with great care, digging trenches and arranging in batteries their many pieces of artillery of all calibers, among which were forty bombards and twelve large basilisks or columbrins. These launched over Rhodes the first explosive grenades recorded in history. The preparations of the Turks lasted about one month.

Meanwhile, during the night of June 22nd, the famous Gabriele Tadini di Martinengo, an engineer from Crema, landed at Rhodes. He had been in Candia, employed as superintendent of fortifications by the government of Venice. Desiring to be present at such an important trial of arms, he had risked the perils of a trip through the enemy blockade to join the Knights.

On July 28th the Turks began an artillery bombardment, probing for a weak point in the defenses. This proved to be in the southern wall, around the ghetto: the same point that was under fire by the artillery of Meshid Pasha for thirty-five consecutive days, albeit unsuccessfully.

At the end of August the enemy, who mustered about forty thousand engineer troops, was feverishly working in the preparation of mines. Martinengo, however, who had the artillery at his disposal, directed its fire with such precision on all sectors that the Turkish camp was thrown into dangerous disarray. Suleiman in person was forced to intervene with fifteen thousand arquebusiers, not only to encourage his troops, but to prevent a mutiny. The situation of the besieged, however, was already critical. Many bastions had been demolished, and it was only due to the sacrifices of the military and civilian population that the situation had not become even worse.

On September 4th the Janizaries made a violent attack on the bastion held by the "Language of England" but were repulsed by the Grand Master who arrived in person with fresh troops who, in turn, made a counterattack. The entire month of September went by characterized by mining operations and in violent sudden attacks by the Turks by which they attempted to take advantage of the momentary panic of the defenders. But these surprise attacks were not successful and the Knights could always launch effective counterattacks.

According to chronicles of the time, the Turks, in their attack on September 24th, sustained a loss of more than fifteen thousand dead and wounded while the Knights lost only two hundred. If help from the West had arrived perhaps the miracle of 1480 would have been repeated. But Charles V and François I were fighting each other, and the Pope was not in a position to

dislodge the Turks from the siege of Rhodes. The Turks recovered from their losses and continued their attacks.

During the month of October Suleiman was able to capture an advanced fortified point, but the Knights, by means of strong counterattacks, were able to recapture the position. On November 22nd the Italian Knights, in fierce hand to hand combat, expelled the enemy from the bastion of Italy. The Sultan, amazed by such boundless courage, offered surrender with honorable terms. The Council of the Order met, but no agreement was reached and the combat was renewed. On December 17th a new assault was repulsed. But this was the last effort. The Grand Master now informed Suleiman that he was ready to negotiate the surrender of the Knights under certain conditions. It was the eve of Christmas, 1522. The Knights were granted the right to leave the island in honor and with their arms, taking with them the sacred relics and the treasure of the Order on their own ships. The Janizaries then took possession of the stronghold and Suleiman entered on horseback, with great pomp. Before leaving, Philippe Villiers de l'Isle-Adam went to render homage to the conqueror. Then, on January 2nd, with all the members of the Order, as well as with five thousand inhabitants of Rhodes who wished to go with him, he gave order to weigh anchor.

PAVIA
(1524-1525)

"All is lost except honor."

One of the first results of the long struggle between François I and Charles V, which broke out in 1521, was the expulsion of the French from Lombardy, where they had firmly established themselves in 1515. A corps of the army of Charles V, under the command of the "traitor" Charles de Bourbon, Constable of France, who had gone over to the service of the Empire because of disagreements with François I, crossed over the Var and laid siege to Marseilles.

The King himself, with a strong army, took the field for the purpose of freeing the city and, on September

28th, after having forced the Constable to raise the siege, proceeded with rapid marches to within Italian territory. He took Milan, depopulated because of a recent epidemic, and then turned toward Pavia. This city was again called upon to play the decisive role as a key fortress of Northern Italy.

When he arrived beneath the city walls he experienced a pleasant surprise: there was no moat around the walls. Therefore, losing no time, he placed his artillery and started bombarding the walls in order to make a breach, without even digging trenches or protecting him-

A celebrated painting by Ilario Spolverini (1657-1734) illustrates the decisive moment of the battle in which Ferdinando Francisco d'Avalos, Marquis of Pescara, freed Pavia from siege by the French under François I. The King himself was taken prisoner by the imperial forces after having made all possible efforts to recover his forces from the surprise executed by Pescara. Among the imperial troops was the Constable of Bourbon. François, although he was advised by his generals to choose another spot for the conflict, replied: "On ne recule pas devant un traître" (One does not retreat from a traitor). After the encounter, his famous phrase would be: "Tout est perdu, hors l'honneur" (All is lost except honor).

self from the rear with the usual counterembankments. The walls did not long resist the infernal cannonade from the French guns and a breach was made. The French swarmed into the breach, now sure that they had the city within their grasp. Instead, they suddenly encountered a moat full of water cutting them off and leaving them exposed to the mercy of intense musket fire coming from the windows. The French retreated.

Pavia held a garrison of five thousand German mercenaries (the redoubtable "Lanzknecht") and a thousand French, Swiss and German infantry, as well Leyva. These forces were also supplemented by the population in general. François I was able to put twenty thousand French, Swiss and Germany infantry, as well as two thousand cavalry, against the imperial forces.

Instead of immediately initiating the necessary siege operations, the King undertook to change the course of the waters of the Ticino. But when the work of weeks was wiped out by a cloudburst, he decided to besiege Pavia by means of a blockade.

Meanwhile, an imperial army, camped near Adda, had reorganized and increased its forces with the return of Charles de Bourbon and his twelve thousand Lanzknecht. The army thereupon moved toward Lodi and made camp there. During January, 1525, it was joined by the Lanzknecht under the command of Georg von Frundsberg, famous for his victory in 1522 at la Bicocca.

The imperial forces moved from Lodi to Pavia on June 24th. They were under the supreme command of the Spanish Ferdinando Francisco d'Avalos, the Marquis of Pescara, who had already opposed Gaston de Foix at Ravenna in 1512 and also at la Bicocca in 1522. On the 29th they captured Sant'Angelo Lodigiano, taking great booty. The French strengthened their fortifications and intensified the blockade of the city. One of the strongpoints was the park of Mirabello, enclosed by a long wall. It would eventually prove to be a trap.

On Febraury 2nd, Pescara, marching on Pavia, advanced to within a mile and a half from the French camp.

The skirmishes between the forces of the two armies began at once and increased in frequency. The famous companies of Giovanni de' Medici, who was in the field with François I, especially distinguished themselves until de' Medici was wounded and had to abandon the struggle.

French soldiers from the time of François I according to a lithograph preserved in the Museum of the Army, Paris, as is the XIX century illustration on facing page, representing the sword of François I. Although he had to rely strongly on foreign levies the King did not neglect the French army. He divided the national territory into four military districts: Picardy and Champagne in the north, and Guyenne and Piedmont in the south. In this way the army was composed of four groups, with individual insignia and soon with special traditions, eventually giving rise to the regular French army. In 1534, he redeployed these units into seven legions, divided according to regions. These were: 1. Normandy; 2. Brittany; 3. Picardy; 4. Languedoc; 5. Guyenne; 6. Burgundy, Champagne, Nivernais; 7. Dauphiné, Auvergne, Lyonnais.

Thereupon his companies lost their fire and, at the decisive moment, collapsed completely. Another serious blow for François I was the defection of eight thousand Swiss, soon followed by other disasters. The King became increasingly wary, and remained within his positions awaiting developments. But Pescara could wait no longer. He lacked money to pay his soldiers and, according to the custom of the times, he had offered his troops the possibility of booty in lieu of pay. In other words, it was a necessity for him to start the battle. The Marquis of Pescara acted with some astuteness. The entrenched French camp was on the left bank of the Ticino, between the city and the Mirabello enclosure. The French, after having opened several breaches in the city walls had taken part of the enclosed park of Mirabello as a supply and pasture area for their horses.

On the eve of the battle Pescara had about thirty thousand men in his command, counting the besieged garrison in Pavia, and a total of seventeen cannon. The French, on the other hand, mustered thirty-one thousand men equipped with fifty-three cannon.

During the night of February 24th, 1525, the imperial troops began their operations in silence, leaving a strong guard within their own camp. First they marched north, then they executed a movement to the left, marching along the wall encircling the long enclosure. Passing through several breaches which had been silently opened by an advance party of sappers, the imperial army began its entry into Mirabello. First came the arquebusiers, then the cavalry, and finally the Lanzknecht mercenaries.

At the first light of dawn the French realized the situation and rushed to arms thinking that it was only a simple infiltration. Perhaps the fog, which at that season of the year was always extremely heavy, or perhaps even the heavily wooded terrain prevented them from realizing what had really happened. The imperial troops, on the other hand, as soon as they found themselves exposed to artillery fire, left in search of a protected zone.

François I, leaving the companies of Giovanni de'

One of the famous tapestries showing the siege battle of Pavia, preserved at Capodimonte. The city is in the background and its principal monuments can be identified. The scene depicted shows the critical moment of the struggle: the sortie of five thousand Lanzknecht German mercenaries from the garrison of Pavia resulting in the disastrous rout of the French. Only the companies of Giovanni de' Medici and the German Lanzknecht in the service of the King opposed a last ditch resistance.

Medici on guard within the camp, took the field at that moment with his personal guard, causing even more confusion in the French ranks. The entry of the heavy cavalry reestablished the situation for the moment, which now seemed to be turning in favor of the French. Pescara, however, advanced at the opportune time, one thousand five hundred arquebusiers, protected by cavalry. Their deadly fire opened fearsome holes in the French ranks. Thereupon the imperial cavalry charged the dismayed French with a result that seemed to be decisive.

The infantry was more steadfast. The five thousand Lanzknecht in the service of the King of France, against whom were thrown two squares of pikemen of the imperial forces (each square containing six thousand pikes) died at their posts without surrendering an inch of territory. Eight thousand Swiss formed for a time an immovable wall against Pescara's forces and, possibly, might have succeeded in changing the outcome if the five thousand Lanzknecht from the garrison of Pavia had not made an unexpected sortie. They were opposed, for a short time, by Giovanni de' Medici's adventurers, but they were overcome, and with this development the Swiss left the field, seeking safety in flight toward Milan.

Around Pavia, now freed from the siege by seven thousand French among whom was La Palisse, of the curious proverbial renown of being still alive "un quart d'heure avant sa mort" (a quarter of an hour before his death). It was a light note in the great tragedy of that day which saw the King of France fall prisoner, recognizing that everything was lost "except honor."

VIENNA (1529)

The bastion of the West stops the Crescent

Its natural geographic position has always given the city of Vienna a very important role in the exchanges or encounters between the Orient and the Occident, between the Roman Germanic world and that of the Slavs and Hungarians. Its strategic value did not escape the Romans. At the time of Augustus they made Vienna the base of their flotilla which operated on the Danube. When the menace of Barbarian invasions arose over the Roman Empire, the city became one of the principal objectives of the invaders. In the V century it suffered incursions from the Huns. Later, Germans and Magyars would fight for it (in 881 the name "Venia" was first applied to it). In 1137 it became the chief city of a "boundary march," underlining its character as a bastion of Germanic and Christian civilization, first against the Slavs and Magyars, and subsequently against the Turks.

In 1529 the latter, returning from their bloody triumph of Mohacs (1526), which had assured their control of Magyar territory, reentered Hungary in force for the purpose of putting down a rebellion and reestablishing on the throne one of their puppets, John Zapolya. After having overrun in Budapest the advanced posts of Ferdinand I, brother of Charles V (legitimate King of Hungary, Archduke of Austria and future Holy Ro-

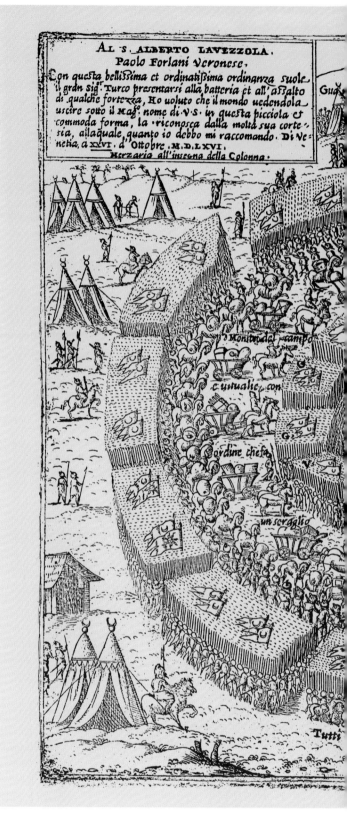

Left: *Artillerists from the first half of the XVI century (Paris, Library of the Museum of the Army).* Above: *A woodcut of the XVI century showing the "ordnance" mustered by the Turkish army for an attack on a fortress (Milan, Bertarelli Collection). In the background can be noted prisoners who have been impaled or stuck on pikes, clearly in view of the besieged, for the purpose of inspiring terror. The Turks were masters in this kind of operation and have been referred to by subsequent experts in more modern siege operations for the purpose of establishing the best method of attack and defense of an area under siege. See details on page 152 concerning the Turkish trenches of Candia.*

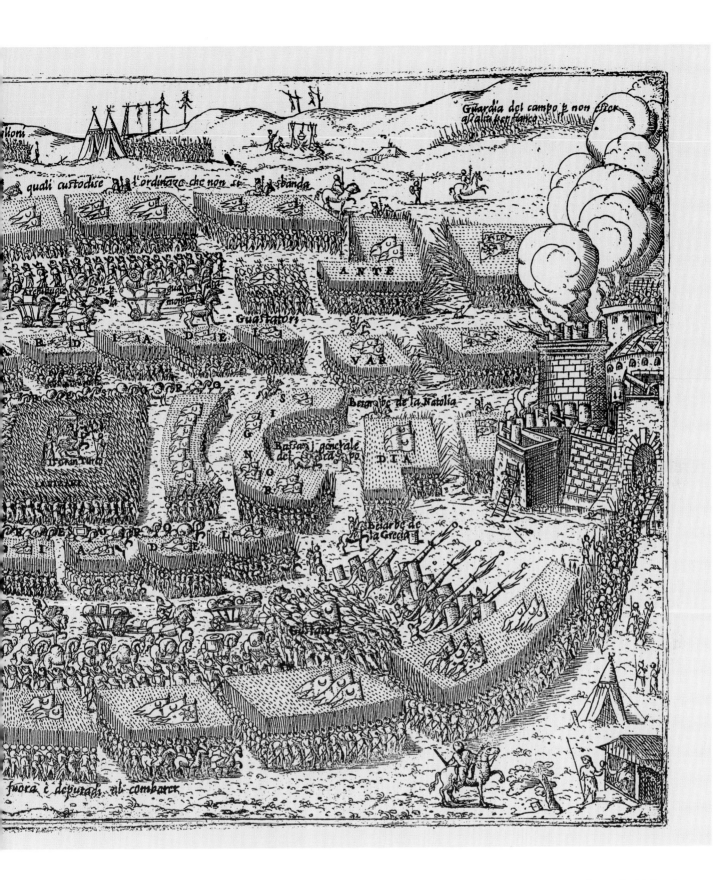

man Emperor), the Turks, under the command of Suleiman I, called "The Magnificent" (but called by the Turks "The Giver of Laws") marched on Vienna.

While the imperial army was assembling at Linz, although not in time to reach Vienna, the Palatine Count, Phillip of the Rhine, succeeded in entering the city with sixty horsemen before the pocket could be closed. This was a negligible force but it was nevertheless important because of Phillip's personality. The city entrusted him with the defense of the Totenterm Gate at the

Kärntertor. The supreme command was held by the seventy-year-old Count Nikolaus von Salm, aided by the Field Marshal Wilhelm von Roggendorf; by Max Beck von Leopoldsdorf, who was responsible for the services of supply; by Eck von Reischach and Leonard von Fels, chiefs of the Lanzknecht troops; by Abel von Holleneck, who commanded the infantry of Carinthia and Styria; by Ernst von Brandestein, commander of the Bohemian forces; by Luís de Avalos with the Spanish forces, included in which were the poets Garcilaso de la Vega and

Cristóbal de Castilejo. In all there were about twenty thousand men. Among other names that the Austrian defenders have not forgotten are those of Bishop Kolonitz and representatives of the noblest families, some of whom were destined to great military renown: Hardegg, Pappenheim, Berlichingen, Schwarzenberg, Starhernberg, Auersperg, Liechtenstein, Herberstein, Trauttmansdorff, Kinsky, Hoyos.

The walls of the city were, for the most part, not more than seven feet high and were not in especially good condition. The artillery which defended them comprised only seventy-two cannon.

The bulk of the Turkish army arrived under the walls of Vienna in September, 1529. It numbered a hundred thousand regular troops and other forces varying between a hundred and fifty and two hundred thousand men. These were deployed in a semicircle south of the city, with the right wing anchored on the Wien. A fleet of four hundred ships ranged the Danube, destroying bridges and preventing the arrival of relief forces from the north.

The immense Turkish army was divided into sixteen encampments, forming a huge city of tents. The artillery park included three hundred pieces, whose efficiency was somewhat reduced by bad weather.

Suleiman did not lose time. He sent a standard bearer among his prisoners to the Count of Salm with a demand for surrender within three days. When the reply was negative, he began the bombardment while his engineers excavated subterranean passages. According to legend, a baker's assistant had noted in the midnight silence noises which indicated the underground activities of the Turks and had given the alarm. In reality, the Turkish mines were revealed by deserters.

The Akindskis, Turkish light irregular troops, who served as the advance guard of the Turkish army, sacked Wiener Neustadt and devastated the surroundings over a radius of forty kilometers to the east and south of Vienna. They slaughtered about one hundred thousand persons, especially ravishing and burning the east section of the Wienerwald. They did less damage across the Danube, toward the north, since the people in that area were especially watchful for landings on the left bank of the river. Churches, monasteries and convents were transformed into small fortresses.

The military levies that garrisoned Vienna were, for the most part, unfamiliar with wars against the Turks. Eck von Reisach offered to instruct them and to lead them in small trial sorties. Finally, in the first part of October, a sortie in force was decided on. The operation, which was supposed to take place at night and employ eight thousand men, started late, in the morning. This was the fault of the Lanzknecht troops who, delayed by excessive drinking the night before (in spite of von Leopoldsdorf having rationed the wine), arrived late on the field, when the Janizaries had already been awakened. Now wide awake, the Janizaries immediately counterattacked, throwing the Bohemian infantry into confusion and overcoming the rest of the Hapsburg forces.

The pursuit ended under the walls of the city, providentially still capable of stopping the army. Five hundred of the defenders lost their lives, including Wolf Hagen.

The city now expected a Turkish attack in force. The psychosis of imminent danger provoked, during the same day, three false alarms, causing considerable discontent among the Lanzknechts.

At midnight, messengers arrived from King Ferdinand and from the Palatine Count Frederick. The army, which should have reached Vienna from Linz before the Turkish pincers closed, needed another eight days to come and set free the city. In an explosive frenzy of joy, the city gave the command for free fire to the artillery and lit up the night with brilliant fireworks. Suleiman, fearing perhaps a sortie in force, gave the ready command to his infantry, and kept his cavalry in the saddle for the entire night. Meanwhile, mining and countermining activities continued beneath the ground. In spite of the care exercised by the Viennese in neutralizing the Turkish mines, two of these exploded under the Gate of Carinthia, opening in the walls a breach through which not less than twenty-four men were able to pass shoulder to shoulder. Nevertheless, not a single Turk succeeded in passing through the breach in spite of three consecutive assaults. According to their custom, the Lanzknechts urged the Turks to attack. But the Turks only moved two days later, after other mines had exploded. At that

Powder holders of the XVI century preserved in the Royal Armory of Madrid.

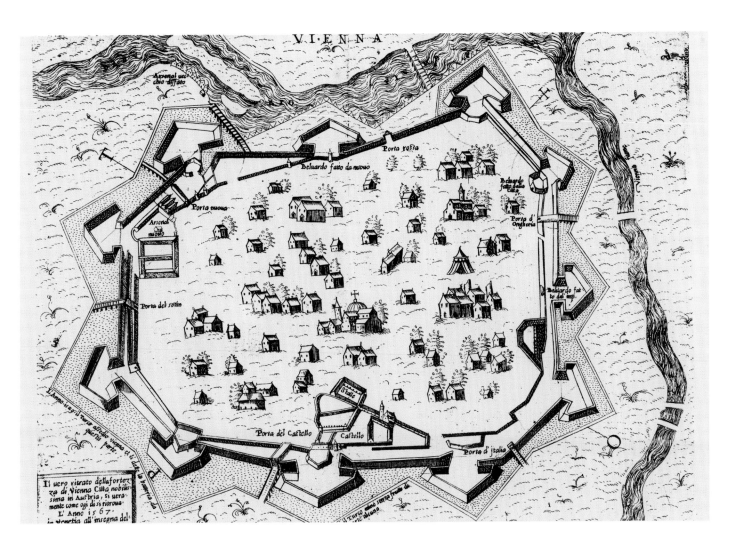

A drawing by Giulio Ballino, dated 1567, presents "the true picture of the fortress of Vienna, a most noble city in Austria." It is contained within the work Plans of the Most Illustrious Cities and Fortresses of the World *(Milan, Bertarelli Collection). On it are indicated assault points of the Turks and the fortifications manned by the defenders. The repulse inflicted by the latter on Suleiman under the walls of the city was decisive in stopping the Moslem wave of conquest in Europe.* Facing page: Powder holders of the XVI century preserved in the Royal Armory of Madrid.

point they launched three more desperate but unsuccessful attacks.

On the 12th of October the Turkish leaders met in council. Bad weather was not far off. In addition, supplies were running short, and the troops considered that they had already done everything possible to take the city. Retreat was discussed, but before taking such a step it was decided to make a final effort.

In the night between the 13th and 14th of October, heralds rode through the Turkish camp. They proclaimed that there would be a great reward for the first soldier to scale the walls of Vienna. At dawn, everything was ready, beginning with the Sultan, who rode inspection on horseback along the ranks of the three detachments chosen for the assault. These were respectively commanded by the Grand Vizier Ibrahim, the Begberbeg of Anatolia, and the Aga of the Janizaries. In case there

was any hesitation in the Turkish ranks, Ibrahim, the Grand Vizier, had established an efficient system of military police. The latter were quick to distribute stimulating whip lashes, blows from staves, or scimitar slashes among the Turks who might hold back.

Therefore, when another two mines blew up under the walls of Vienna, the great mass advanced toward the breaches and, for two hours, attempted to storm them unsuccessfully. Count Salm was gravely wounded, but the defenders held firm. Suleiman thereupon appeared out of the smoke-covered area and gave the signal for which his army was anxiously waiting. The drums sounded retreat and the noise of the battle soon faded.

On the following night the Turks struck their tents and on October 6th, the army of the Crescent took the road toward Adrianople. There an early as well as a tragic winter awaited it, between snow storms and sudden attacks of the imperial cavalry, which caused heavy losses.

The failure of the siege of Vienna is considered a decisive moment in the struggle between the West and Moslem expansionism. In effect, however, Suleiman never stopped fighting. Only in 1533 did he agree to end the war and to make a compromise with Ferdinand regarding Hungary. He continued, however, a war by sea against Charles V, as a result of the "impious alliance" which the France of François I made with the Sublime Porte, to the great scandal of the Christian West.

FLORENCE
(1529-1530)

In Italy's long night, the light of Gavinana

After the sack of Rome, Emperor Charles V and Pope Clement VII, in the world a Medici, made peace by means of the treaty of Barcelona, in 1529. The Emperor made some territorial concessions to the Pope and, above all, promised to reestablish the rule of the Medicis in Florence, from which they were ousted in 1527.

Florence resolved to defend its new republican government and took a firm stand against the return of the Medici family. The Florentines summoned the famous Michelangelo (his family name was Buonarroti) for the purpose of reinforcing existing fortifications and of constructing new ones, in accord with the most up-to-date developments of military art. The citizen's militia was reestablished and various men of arms were hired. Malatesta Baglione, from Perugia, was chosen as supreme captain, an unfortunate choice, as we shall see later.

The Imperial army, under the leadership of Philbert of Chalons, Prince of Orange, and about forty thousand strong, laid siege to Florence in October of 1529. Against these forces the republic was able to muster about twenty-one thousand men.

The besieging forces limited themselves at first to a blockade of the city from the left bank of the Arno. They started to bombard the city and, at the same time, engaged in a series of raids in order to deprive the besieged of any food supplies from the surrounding countryside. When confronted by the frequent and courageous sorties of the besieged Florentines, the Imperialists employed a somewhat elastic tactic, avoiding serious conflict. This tended to wear down the Florentines who were not able to count on reinforcements. In February, 1530, the Imperialists occupied Volterra. Francesco Ferrucci was dispatched to win it back and, having done so, held it fast against the subsequent assaults of the enemy. Ferrucci was the true hero of the defense of Florence, one may say its very incarnation. He had been elected commissioner by the Republic and had also defended Empoli, before being sent to reconquer Volterra. He also recaptured Castelfiorentino and San Miniato from the Germans. Ferrucci came from an old merchant family but was no stranger to arms. He had seved under Giovanni de' Medici of the Black Companies as, it was reported, his paymaster officer.

When Signa, Pistoia and Empoli fell to the Imperial forces, and, in Florence, hunger was joined by pestilence, the Florentines saw in Ferrucci their only hope. From then on the siege was tightened, despite frequent sorties. Two of these, on May 5th and on June 21st, brought the Imperial forces to the brink of a decisive defeat.

When Ferrucci started his march to the help of the city, he had under his command about three thousand infantry and four hundred cavalry. According to his detailed plan, he planned to establish a base at Pisa to await reinforcements and from there to reoccupy Pistoia, which had been abandoned, and then, passing through Fiesole, finally enter Florence, bringing soldiers and supplies and perhaps lift the siege forever. A sortie of the besieged was also projected in the planning. The maneuver was, however, betrayed to Orange by Malatesta Baglioni, who assured Orange that he, Baglioni, would remain inactive. With his plans known and now pursued by two Imperial columns, Ferrucci sought safety in Gavinana, a small town in the Apennines. He split his small army into two parts, keeping with himself the cavalry. In front of him were the troops of the Prince of Orange while, from the mountains on his left, he was menaced by Maramaldo's infantry.

On August 4th, 1530, at seven o'clock in the evening, the first encounter took place. The Imperial forces were repulsed. The Prince of Orange was fatally wounded in a cavalry charge. The Florentine arquebusiers, placed behind the chestnut trees of the woods, repulsed the attack with sustained and precise fire. While the Prince of Orange's forces, now deprived of their leader, fled, a furious combat raged in Gavinana between the infantry of Ferrucci and that of Maramaldo, the latter having descended from the mountains and entered the village from the other side. At first, this second combat also seemed to favor the Florentines. But when Maramaldo sent in the Lanzknecht reserves the fight started to go badly for the Florentine army. The heroic resistance of the troops served to put off the end only for a while, although they caused great losses in the Imperialist ranks. The end came on the 22nd, when even Ferrucci gave up, worn out and weakened by many wounds. At this point Maramaldo performed the deed which made

Above: *Spanish infantry of Charles V at the time of the siege of Florence (Paris, Library of the Museum of the Army).* Below: *Francesco Ferrucci forcing the surrender of the city of Volterra, occupied by the Imperial forces. This episode, reconstructed in a drawing of the early XIX century, the work of Luigi Sabatelli (Milan, Bertarelli Collection), is considered by many to have been decisive in the siege of Florence as well as in the life of Ferrucci himself. Ferrucci had caused to be hanged, at Volterra, a messenger of Fabrizio Maramaldo, captain of the Imperial army. When Ferrucci fell prisoner at Gavinana, Maramaldo avenged this "affront" by stabbing him. Volterra boasts a fortress of great historical and architectural interest.*

him forever infamous, and his name a synonym for cowardly injustice. He thrust his dagger twice into Ferrucci's throat. Ferrucci, before dying, had time to cry: "Coward, you have killed a dead man!" A letter of Ferrante Gonzaga, who succeeded Orange in the command of the Imperial army, contains this passage: "Fabrizio killed Ferrucci with his own hand, since they had some old account or other to settle."

The tragedy of Gavinana divided the Florentines into two groups: those who advocated an honorable surrender and those who wished to resist to the very last. The first party prevailed, principally because of a new and open act of betrayal on the part of Baglioni who surrendered a bastion to the enemy and re-aimed its cannon over the city.

On the morning of August 10th, four Florentine envoys presented themselves at the Imperial camp in order to negotiate with Gonzaga. The conditions were honorable and, most important, Florence was spared the horrors of pillage by the Lanzknecht troops.

The resistance of Florence and the bravery of Ferrucci proved a good seed for the future of Italy, inspiring writers like Francesco Domenico Guerrazzi and Massimo d'Azeglio when, at the time of the *Risorgimento* (the national revival), it was necessary to demonstrate that the Italians have always been ready to do battle and to die, even in the dark hours of their country.

NICE (1543)
The "unholy alliance" misses the target

In October 1535, with the death of Francesco II of Sforza, the Spanish took possession of the Duchy of Milan. François I of France, who wished to put a member of the Orléans family on the throne, invaded Piedmont for the purpose of preparing bases from which to attack the Milanese. Within a few days Charles II of Savoy retained only Nice and Vercelli.

Sometime after this, in the first part of July, 1541, Antonio Rincon, the French Ambassador to Constantinople, was assassinated by Imperial soldiers near Pavia, in the territory of the Duchy of Milan. François I thereupon requested that Suleiman I put into operation the secret treaty that France and Turkey had made in 1536 (the famous "unholy alliance" that had scandalized Europe). He asked Suleiman to move his fleet against the common enemy, the Empire, and to attack Nice forthwith. Suleiman hesitated for some time. Finally, however, in 1543, he sent the King of France a letter which stated that his Admiral Kayr-ed-Din had received orders from Suleiman to put to sea and to place himself at the orders of the King and of Rincon's successor. This latter was a certain Antoine Paulin, so-called "baron de la Guarde," popularly known as Paolino or Polino, a rather shady and adventurous person.

Kayr-ed-Din sailed to Marseilles with one hundred and ten galleys and fourteen thousand men. There he

The polychrome statuette of Caterina Segurana, reproduced here, and the print on the facing page are preserved at the Massena Museum of Nice together with other relics of the siege conducted against Nice in 1543 by the French of François I and his allies the Turks of Kayr-ed-Din Barbarossa. At that time the city presented the aspect seen on the print reproduced below. The incident concerning Caterina Segurana is commonly supposed by tradition to have taken place near the Pairoliera Gate, which faced the river near the bastion but was located nearer the mountain.

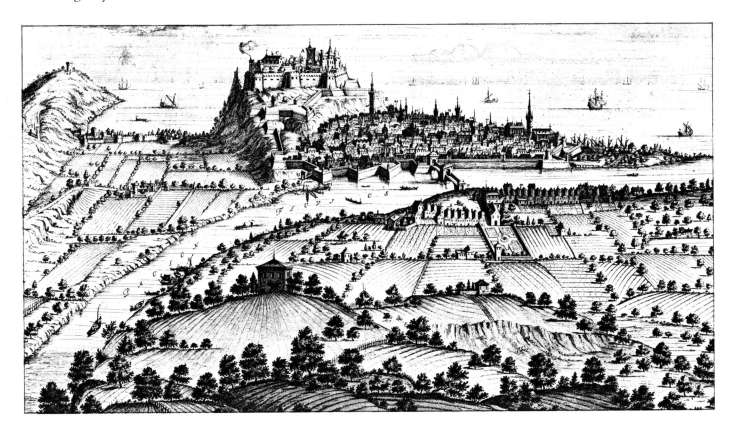

joined the French fleet, forty galleys and seven thousand men strong, under the command of Paulin.

When the people of Nice saw the Turkish fleet appear before their city, in June, 1543, with their prows turned toward Marseilles, they understood that affairs had became serious. However, they were not very surprised. On June 16th of that year several French galleys under the command of Count Louis de Grigan, Lieutenant General of Provence, and that of a traitor from Nice, a certain Benedetto Grimaldi (called Oliva), had attempted a landing near a site known as Lympia (where the port of Nice is located today) in order to take the city by surprise. Giannettino Doria captured them and took them to Genoa. A Frenchman named Magdalon who was badly wounded revealed, before his death, that the Turkish fleet would soon come to Provence.

The city was garrisoned by six companies of arquebusiers and was protected by relatively strong walls.

The defense of the city and of the walls was entrusted to a hero, André Odinet, Count of Monfort. For the protection of the castle, garrisoned by a small detachment of men, the arrival was expected of a veteran of several wars against the Moslems, the Knight of Saint John of Malta, Paolo Simeoni de' Balbi, of Chieri.

The forces of Nice were faced in front by the fleet of Barbarossa, with his fourteen thousand men; Paulin's

French fleet had seven thousand and, from August 11th, could count on another twelve thousand French soldiers on land, the army which the King had placed under the command of François de Bourbon-Vendôme, Count of Enghien. In addition, there were also arrayed against Nice a company of Tuscans under Leone Strozzi, and a volunteer corps from Provence, attached to Paulin. Among others considered traitors who had gone over to the French was another Grimaldi, Giovanni Battista di Beuil, Lord of Ascros, a bitter enemy of Savoy.

On August 7th, the Turks, after having dropped anchor in the neighboring bay of Villefranche, landed in force and attacked the city with determination. A bitter conflict followed, lasting an hour, during which Paolo Simeoni de' Balbi, at the head of fifty resolute men, was able to take advantage of the confusion and enter the city and then the castle. Here, as we have noted, he was anxiously awaited. The Turks were repulsed and the inhabitants of Nice realized that they could resist with some hope of success.

On Saturday the 11th, after the defenders of Nice had refused various offers to surrender, there arrived on the field the forces of the Count of Enghien. Giambattista Grimaldi was given the order to deliver another ultimatum. This was entrusted to a French herald and to Benedetto Grimaldi, called Oliva, the same Oliva

A sketch of a painting by Massimo d'Azeglio of the siege of Nice, presently in Turin, at the Art Gallery. The painting is also in Turin at the Royal Palace. In the background the castle can be seen. This was the last bastion of resistance by the forces of Nice and a place where the enemy was unable to set foot. Today the castle of Nice no longer exists.

mentioned in the action of June 16th. He presented himself before Nice at the Sant'Alodio gate, sure of being treated as a saviour. Instead, he was immediately arrested, while the herald, respected by custom and the rules of war, returned to the enemy camp with the emphatic "No" of Nice. Oliva was whipped for three hours and afterward strangled and hanged head downward in view of the enemy.

On August 15th, at dawn, a hundred and twenty galleys left the harbor of Villefranche, sailed past Mount Boron and arrayed themselves in front of the city. At eight o'clock in the morning all their cannon opened fire, in an immense din.

A breach was soon opened in the vicinity of the Pairoliera Gate (also called the Saint Sebastian Gate) which guarded the city from the north. Turks and French rushed pell-mell toward this breach, carrying ladders for scaling the walls. But the defenders resisted with vigor. The defense was equally determined on the Sincaire tower or bastion (from Sinq-Quayre, meaning "pentagonal"), against which Barbarossa hurled the Janizaries of his guard, under the command of the famous pirate Dragut, together with Strozzi's Tuscans and the Provençal forces of Paulin. At one point, a Turkish standard bearer succeeded in reaching the top of the breach and in planting there the red flag bearing the white crescent and star. A certain washerwoman, with other women of Nice, was on the wall right behind the defenders. This washerwoman, armed only with a paddle stick, a mark of her trade at that time, attacked the Turk, knocked him down, and tore the standard from his hands. At her cry of victory, the defenders were inspired by new vigor and successfully expelled the invaders from the breach. Her action, reminding one of the deeds of Jeanne Hachette at Beauvais, is of the stuff that legends are made, and there are some who claim that her deed contains more elements of fantasy than of historical reality. Nevertheless, her episode marked the end of a heroic day for the soldiers of Nice and gave a new impetus to the war and a firm resolve to the defenders of the city.

The Turks and the French left three hundred dead

French costume from the middle of the XVI century according to a XIX century print, showing François I between two ladies of the court. The King had been most anxious to take Nice from Charles II (to whom, moreover, he was related). This city, and even more important, its castle, would by useul for bases or the campaign that he wished to wage in Italy, against his eternal rival Charles V, for the purpose of taking Milan away from him.

and many wounded on the field and returned to their bases. Meanwhile, the artillery duel continued. On that day no less than nine hundred and seventy-five cannon shots were fired against Nice. The walls collapsed at some points and Monfort realized that continued resistance would condemn the city to destruction. He therefore dispatched an envoy to negotiate with the Duke of Enghien and, on August 23rd, the French were finally able to set foot within Nice, together with Strozzi's Tuscans and the Provençal troops under Paulin, assigned to Giambattista Grimaldi. Barbarossa was requested not to enter with his Turks and he reluctantly agreed not to. He recalled his soldiers to Villefranche.

The castle still remained to be captured. The French, however, were short of ammunition and had to request some from the Turks. But Barbarossa, already angered by the lack of booty, took the occasion to goad Paulin, observing that the French, during their stay in Marseilles, did nothing other than load casks of wine instead of powder. The great Moslem Admiral also threatened to abandon the allies and to set sail for Turkish ports. Only at the insistance of the Duke of Enghien himself did he agree to stay.

On September 6th news arrived that an Imperial army was on the way and only a two-day march from Nice. In addition, it started to rain incessantly. The Turks and the French abandoned their land positions and retreated in disorder to their ships. On September 7th the artillery was removed. On the 8th the Turks landed again and indulged in unrestrained pillage. Enghien and the French set fire to the city, then they retired across the river Var, which marked the French boundary, while the Turkish fleet set sail for Toulon.

SIENA (1547-1559) *"Not a single one was afraid."*

At the close of 1547 Charles V, having settled accounts with the Protestants in Germany, could now turn to Italy and take care of the problem of Siena. Siena was the last gap in the line being prepared by the Hispano-Imperial power along the Tyrrhenian Sea.

To this effect, the Emperor entrusted the administration of Siena to Don Diego Hurtado de Mendoza, a true celebrity of the XVI century. He was a bibliophile, an eminent scholar of Greek studies, translator of Aristotle, reputed author of *Lazarillo de Tormes*, an outstanding figure in Spanish literature, a veteran of the sieges of Pavia and Tunis, and an inflexible servant of the Spanish crown. Mendoza arrived in Siena in October, 1574, and took over the administration, sustained by the arms of a greedy soldiery which the populace called, with a certain charm, "the needy ones." He therefore made ready to construct a fortress which would serve to keep the city under control. He chose a location on the hill called San Prospero, in back of the walls. In 1550 work on this project was begun amid the hostility of the Sienese. The latter dispatched an embassy to make a protest to Charles V. But the envoys, who presented themselves dressed in mourning, were told that if they continued to be insistent, the fortress could become two instead of one.

The Sienese resistance then prepared a revolt. A conspiracy supported by the Papal Court permitted the Sienese to form an army of liberation. Under the command of Enea Piccolomini, this army attacked Siena at ten in the evening of June 27th, 1552, while

Mendoza, who had been obliged to go to Rome, had left the command of the city to Francisco de Avila.

The Spanish sought refuge within the fortress, but on August 3rd they had to surrender this too, as French reinforcements had arrived in the meantime under the command of the Florentine Pietro Strozzi, Marshal of France. After he had captured the fortress he turned it over to the Sienese who, in turn, tore it down.

This seemed to have resolved the matter. But Charles V, who had been distracted from the question of Italy by new difficulties with the Protestants, solved his problems with the latter by the Treaty of Passau and now was able once more to take up the question of Italy and of Siena. The Turks, by menacing Naples, kept him from taking definite action for the entire year of 1553. But on January 26th, 1554, Gian Giacomo Medici, Marquis of Marignano, called "the Milanese," a man of arms from Milan, with tendencies of a brigand, obtained from Charles V the command of the Imperial forces against Siena. He thereupon began a siege that was destined to be memorable.

Within Siena were Pietro Strozzi and the legendary Biagio di Monluc, who would later write: "Fortunate are the Sienese, among whom I have not known one to be afraid." Strozzi, in spite of the opposition of Monluc, forced the blockade in July, 1554, through the Valley of Chiana, and continued to Florence to face his mortal enemy, Cosimo de' Medici, first Grand Duke of Tuscany, the son of Giovanni of the Black Companies.

On August 2nd he was bloodily beaten at Mar-

A painting by Pietro Aldi (1852-1888) in Rome, in the Capitoline Gallery, near the Gallery of Modern Art. It is entitled The Last Hours of Sienese Liberty. *Aldi is one of the most valued Italian painters of historical subjects. He studied in Siena and his frescoes are preserved in the Palazzo Comunale of Siena.* Above: *The Hapsburg eagle which appeared on the Imperial banners at the time of the so-called "Sienese War" of which the siege described here was the final episode.* Below: *A view of Siena and its fortifications, which Charles V considered that he could easily destroy with his artillery. However, the cannon that he brought onto the field for this purpose were neutralized by the counterfire of the Sienese batteries.*

ciano. It was a grave hour for Siena, where Monluc, who had fallen ill, was not in condition to mount an immediate counterattack. The enemy, in a knightly gesture, sent him medicines for which they had sent to Florence. But the siege itself was tightened and intensified and despite a new effort by Strozzi, the city's situation became precarious.

On Christmas eve, 1554, Monluc received gifts from the enemy consisting of capons, partridges, and good wine. Then, during the night, Marignano attacked in force both the citadel and the fortress of Camollia. This was temporarily taken by the Imperial troops but the Sienese, under Monluc's leadership, took it back.

At the end of January, to prove to the Emperor that Siena could not hold out against artillery fire, Marignano established batteries, between the Ovile Gate and the Grande Osservanza, of twenty-seven cannon that he had received from Florence. Six were put out of commission by fire from the Sienese batteries. The others had practically no effect on the defenses.

Every Sienese, including women, was actively engaged in the city's defense. The names of Vittoria Piccolomini, of Laudomia Forteguerri and of Livia Fausti will never be erased from the memory of Siena. The city would surrender solely because of famine on April 17th, 1555, after having essayed every means and made every possible sacrifice, including that of sending away from the city the "useless mouths," who were subsequently the victims of the ignoble Marignano.

Resistance continued for another four years with the epic defense of Montalcino, under the leadership of Strozzi, until, on July 15th, 1559, three months after the peace of Cateau-Cambrésis, the last bastion of Italian liberty also crumbled and the entire peninsula fell under Spanish dominion.

MALTA (1565)

Parisot de la Vallette's rings of fire

The Knights of Jerusalem were expelled from Rhodes in 1522. Eight years later they received the island of Malta as a feudal domain from Charles V. Thereupon they proceeded to disturb the sea traffic between Alexandria and Constantinople. The Turks decided to take action only in 1562, after a meticulous preparation that extended over three years.

Through information that French agents had sent Charles IX from Constantinople, it was known throughout the West that by spring of 1565 the Sublime Porte would be able to muster one hundred and fifty galleys, besides those which would come to join the Sultan's fleet from the sea forces of the Algerian pirates, under the command of the doughty Dragut.

At Malta, the Knights of Jerusalem prepared their defense with diligence, under the energetic leadership of the Grand Master of the Order, Giovanni Parisot de la Vallette, a veteran of the defense of Rhodes with an extensive knowledge of the Turks. Knights of the Order who were living away from the island were recalled and the fortifications were strengthened.

On May 18th, 1565, the Turks, under the command of Piali Pasha, a Croat, landed at Marsa-Muse.

The besieging forces, commanded by Mustapha Pasha, were composed of twenty-eight thousand men, among them seven thousand Janizaries belonging to his bodyguard as well as six thousand Spahis. The artillery, which the Sultan had personally assembled, was formidable. He had caused to be cast, especially for this undertaking, three special pieces of heavy artillery. One monstrous piece weighed almost forty tons and fired balls weighing more than two hundred pounds. The other two were mortars weighing twenty tons, which fired iron balls weighing ninety pounds. There were other pieces of all calibers. It is said that the Turks had brought with them one hundred thousand iron cannon balls and almost a hundred and seventy thousand tons of powder.

At Malta, on May 7th, the galley *San Michele* had placed a thick blocking chain across the entrance to the port, while the Fort of Saint Elmo was reinforced by ravelin earthworks. The men of arms, mainly Spanish, numbered about five thousand. The Knights, as usual, were divided into "languages" and each "language" unit had its own post. It is interesting to note that the Genoese also had their own post assigned, held by Girolamo Villavecchia and the crew of his vessel.

The Turks began the bombardment of the Fort of Saint Elmo while the Knights attempted various sorties, with the aim of disturbing the work on the trenches which was being carried out by the Turks. On the 28th the Knights killed all the dogs within the walls; their barking had confused the sentries.

The Turks captured the ravelin entrenchment of Saint Elmo, but the fort continued to resist. The defenders improvised a new weapon. Large circular iron bands, like those of barrels, were wrapped with tow, then immersed in boiling pitch and again treated with tow, then lit and thrown at the enemy.

On June 10th the Turks placed Saint Elmo under assault that continued night and day. They finally conquered the fortress and found fifteen hundred bodies inside. Five days before this a flying stone chip had caused the death of Dragut, a serious loss to the Turks. Twenty years previous to this he had been chained to an oar of a Genoese galley and la Vallette himself had urged Doria to accept the ransom offered by Kayr-ed-Din so that Dragut might be set free.

At the end of June the Turks began their attack on the fort of Saint Elmo against an almost superhuman resistance. Everything now depended on the

Finely worked armor of the XVI century, such as that worn by the defenders of Malta. In the XVI century extremely heavy siege armor would come into use.

arrival of reinforcements.

In the first part of August, while Malta was at the end of her forces, a council of war was held at Syracuse which finally decided to bring the "Great Relief Force" of about nine thousand men to the Knights' help. But a gale forced the squadron back to Syracuse. When the storm was over, on September 6th, the fleet took to sea again and, while the entire Turkish fleet was in front of the port of Malta, the landing forces disembarked in the bay of Melacca. The Turks, seized with panic, embarked their artillery and lifted the siege.

The Knights of Malta cruising before the fortifications of Valletta in a tempera print by an unknown artist (Genoa-Pegli, the Civic Naval Museum). The Maltese fleet was well trained and effective. The Grand Master sailed in a galley painted black.

SZIGETVAR (1566)

Suleiman the Magnificent flies to the shadow of the swords

The city fortress of Szigeth, or Szigetvár, was located about one hundred and seventy miles northwest of Budapest, in a strong position, surrounded by swamps. It was entered by two drawbridges, one leading to the west and the other to the east. The fortress was divided into three main sections and was dominated by a castle: it formed a truly impregnable complex.

In 1566 the Turkish army was marching on this masterpiece of military architecture in the course of one of its repeated attacks on Hungary, the key to Europe. Suleiman in person was in command, though already old and in ill health. After the unfortunate Malta expedition, Suleiman the Magnificent had become convinced that no undertaking could succeed without his personal presence. For this reason, toward the end of April, 1566, he left Constantinople for the Danubian plain. His departure was a solemn one: in the midst of four hundred crossbowmen of his private guard, equipped with quivers of gold, and preceded by three hundred chamberlains and twelve thousand Janizaries, Suleiman, mounted on his horse, gave to Constantinople and his people what would prove to be his last salute.

Almost as soon as he had passed through the gates of the city, he found a golden carriage awaiting him for the next part of the journey: the horseback ride through the city had worn him out. He summoned up the necessary force to leave for Semlin, again on horseback. Semlin was near Belgrade and Suleiman wished to make a triumphant entry there to increase fear and respect on the part of the subject people and of the enemy as well. He had his tents erected by the castle of Hunyardi, the glory of the Magyars and the symbol of hatred for the Turks. Here he received the governors of the province with much pomp. This was merely a pause before resuming the march toward Erlau, the first objective of the campaign. But a disturbing piece of news came to upset his plans. The proud lord of the castle of Szigeth, Miklós Zriny, had defeated the Pasha of Buda and killed the Sanjak, Mohammed Bey. It is reported that Suleiman swore on the Koran that he would be revenged on Zriny. Thereupon he gave orders to start the march to Szigetvár, after having first made an example of the defeated Pasha of Buda, by having him strangled.

To reach Szigetvár it was necessary to cross the Drava, which was at flood tide. Twenty-five thousand men, soldiers and engineers, were sent ahead to build a bridge. When the commander of engineers attempted

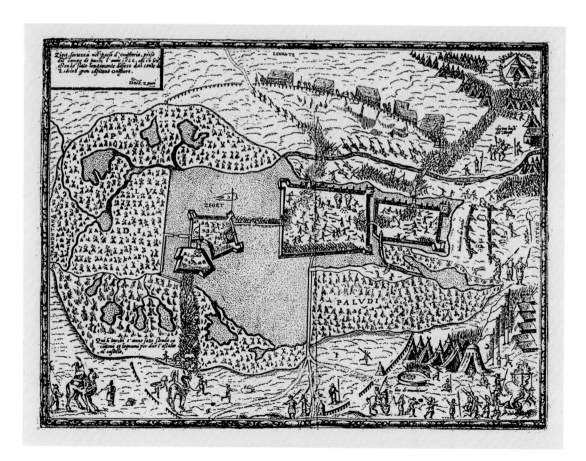

Ziget, or Zighet in Hungary, seen from the Turkish camp, from an engraving by M. Giulio Ballino, the artist of the collection of the XVI century already mentioned on page 127 (Milan, Bertarelli Collection). Facing page: The levies of Ferdinand of Hapsburg occupy a Hungarian village and deport all the inhabitants. Suleiman the Magnificent would intervene in the campaign of 1566 and besiege Szigetvár. In this illustration, from manuscript number H 1517 from the Topkapi Library in Istanbul, Suleiman can be seen at the bottom left, seated on a horse.

to obtain permission to meet a later date than that previously set for the finished construction, Suleiman threatened him with hanging if the bridge were not ready by the date he had established. The former date was honored and the bridge held well under the passage of the Spahi cavalry and the Janizaries, as well as the pack trains, camels carrying food supplies, and the oxen dragging the great siege cannon.

Count Zriny awaited the storm with firm resolve. Emperor Maximilian II, who succeeded Ferdinand I in 1564, had sent him a thousand Hungarian infantry. Adding this to the forces he already had, he could now muster about three thousand men and fifty cannon.

The Turkish army arrayed against him was quite another matter. On July 30th, 1566, the Beglerbeg of Rumania encamped within a mile of Szigetvár with a force of about ninety thousand men; almost as many more arrived with Suleiman on August 6th. The Turks erected their many-colored tents over an enormous area. On the most elevated position of the camp rose

Methods of supplying the Turkish army with water by the use of pack trains, showing the means of filling and carrying water on the horses' backs. From a XVII century print, Central Military Library, Ministry of Defense, Rome.

the pavilion of the Sultan, in a luxurious display of silk and surrounded by glittering standards.

The besieged, not to be left behind in this display, flew scarlet banners from the bastions and, as a sinister reminder, raised a gallows where the enemy could see it.

On August 5th siege operations began. The Turks installed their light batteries but they were unable to position the heavy mortars because of the swampy terrain. Nor were they able to fill in soft spots, as the besieged had burned off all the trees in the vicinity.

The Janizaries attempted a general assault on August 7th but were easily repulsed. The defenders, however, retired within the nucleus of the new city where they would be less exposed to the continuous artillery fire.

On August 29th the Sultan wished to mount his horse again to give the order for a fresh assault. This attack lasted twenty-four hours and was repulsed by the Magyars who, through prodigious feats of valor, inflicted immense losses on the enemy. It is reported that, because of the stench of the great number of corpses scattered on all sides, Suleiman had to move his camp to a point four miles off. The besieged, who, because of losses, were now reduced to about six hundred, set fire to the new city and retired to within the citadel.

Meanwhile, about fifty thousand men had been employed to construct canals to divert the water from the swamps, filling in later with stones, earth, and logs. It was then possible to press more closely in on the citadel. But the Sultan had other ideas for obtaining surrender, as he wished to avoid the loss of more men. He offered a kingdom to Zriny, and tried to foment discord among the defenders. He also threatened to kill his alleged prisoner, the son of Count Zriny, although Zriny's son was actually serving elsewhere.

The cohesion that continued to exist among the defending forces at Szigetvár has been immortalized at the end of the second act of the tragedy of *Zriny* by the famous German poet Theodor Körner, who died young while serving in the Prussian Schwarze Jäger units against Napoleon. Körner, famous for his *Song of the Sword*, portrays the final moments of the falling fortress, still held by Zriny and his troops, with the Count urging the defenders to take an oath together, in the following terms: "May heaven forsake me if I ever abandon you and if I ever fail to share like a brother with my Hungarians my fate, be it victory or death."

Seeing all his attempts fail, Suleiman, suffering terribly from dysentery, turned his anger on his Janizaries: if they did not succeed in crossing the moat into the citadel he would fill in the moat with their testicles. But on September 4th, 1566, the Sultan died. The campaign had proved too much for his seventy-two years.

His adviser, the Vizier Mohammed Sokolli, considering the importance of the moment and the dangers of succession (Selim, the son and heir of Suleiman, was hated by the Janizaries), decided to conceal the event from the army. With the aid of a Jewish physician, the Sultan was embalmed and placed on this throne in the center of his great tent. All others who knew of his death

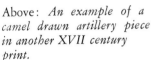

Above: *An example of a camel drawn artillery piece in another XVII century print.*
Right: *Section of the Ottoman miniature of the XVII century showing Turkish artillery in action against the fortress of Szigetvár. In the background can be seen the tents of the Turkish camp, where Suleiman is living the last hours of his life. He died on the night of September 5th, 1566, only a short time before the citadel fell into the hands of his vizier.*

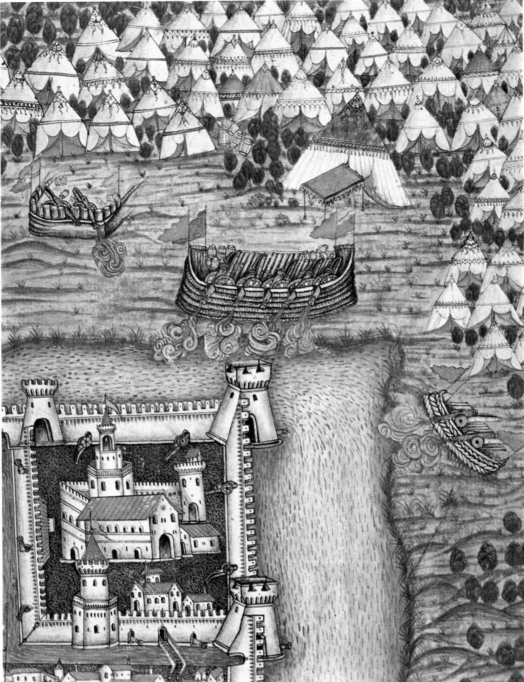

were strangled, it is said, by killers who were also mutes.

The Grand Vizier thereupon assembled the Sanjaks and announced to them that the Sultan, discouraged by the fact that his army was being held at bay by a few hundred Christians, wanted them to prove their loyalty to himself. The speech had a decided effect and the Janizaries renewed their continuous and savage attacks. When a shot from a cannon struck the tower it collapsed and spread destruction throughout the citadel. Count Zriny embraced all the defenders who now were reduced to less than three hundred. He put on his most splendid armor and, sword in hand, prepared to die with his men. Although wounded, he continued to fight on his knees until he was slain. His corpse was decapitated and tied to a gun carriage. His head, stuck on a pole, after being exhibited for three days for the pleasure of the army, was sent to the Count of Salm.

Szigetvár was wiped out but its ruins would have the last bloody jest. Since they were convinced that they would find a treasure among the ruins, the Turks burst in, among other places, to the powder magazine. Suddenly there was an unexpected terrible explosion, killing three thousand men instantly. All tod, the siege of Szigetvár cost the Turks thirty thousand soldiers.

Meanwhile, within the Imperial Pavilion, the Grand Vizier continued to play out his macabre comedy. Having installed the body of the Sultan in a litter as if he were alive, he started the march back with the army, arriving on October 9th in the neighborhood of Belgrade.

On October 24th, with the rising of the sun, the Grand Vizier raised a special prayer, following which he told the assembled troops that the great Suleiman had made his journey to the Paradise of the Houris, in the shadow of their swords.

ANTWERP (1584-1585)

The Archimedes from Mantua strikes and fades away

In the long struggle which the Netherlands waged against Spain for their independence from 1566 to 1648, one chapter concerns the city of Antwerp on one side, and, on the other, Alessandro Farnese, Duke of Parma and Piacenza, successor to John of Austria, and head of the Spanish forces charged to subject Holland once more to the rule of Phillip II.

Toward the end of 1584, Alessandro Farnese decided to lay siege to Antwerp with ten thousand infantry and one thousand seven hundred horsemen, against, however, the counsel of the greater part of his officers. It was known that Antwerp possessed a garrison of twenty thousand men led by Philippe de Marnix, Lord of Sainte-Aldegonde, Calvinist theologist, and able soldier.

But Farnese had an astute plan. Since he could not take the city by attack or surround it, he planned to shut off the means of supplying the city from the sea by establishing a blockade bridge across the Schelde River.

General view of Antwerp, from the already mentioned Atlas by Braun. In the foreground is the citadel.

This work, designed by Farnese himself, was carried out by Italian engineers, Giambattista Piatti, a Milanese, and Properzio Boracci, a Tuscan. When it was finished, on February 25th, 1585, the bridge was eight hundred yards long. The middle part (four hundred and thirty yards) was supported by thirty-two barges chained together and anchored to the bottom of the river. The two wings (one hundred and eighty yards each) rested on piles and, at the banks, were protected by two forts. A roadway extended the entire length of the bridge over covered beams, ten feet long. Two parapets made of wood and beaten earth protected the bridge traffic from musket fire. Each barge was armed with a cannon at the stern and another at the prow. The two forts, called Santa Maria and San Felice, had ten cannon each. The pile structure was protected by three pontoons per pylon, equipped with beams sharpened into points. A flotilla of twenty galleys made up the bridge's mobile defense.

The Dutch put ingenious devices into action against this formidable work. Another Italian worked on their construction — Federico Giambelli (or Gianibelli of Mantua, whom Schiller called the "Archimedes of Ant-

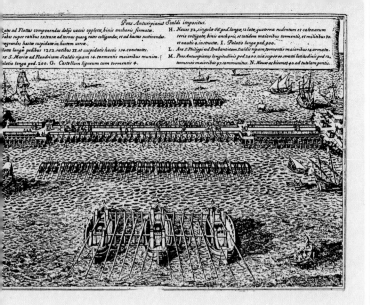

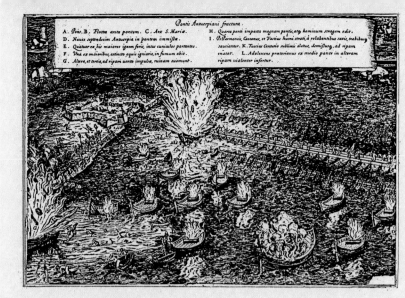

werp") — and a Fleming named den Bosche.

First casks, called "porcupines," with sharpened iron points on the outside and inflammable material within, were launched against the bridge. Then canvas sails were directed against the bridge under water so that the pylons would catch the canvas and the current, pressing on the sails, would "bring the bridge down." When these measures proved unsuccessful, den Bosche launched a raft charged with powder that could be ignited from the bank as soon as it hit the bridge. But the raft missed the target and was thrust against the other bank by the current. The Flemish engineer then formed the idea of constructing an armed pontoon, capable of carrying a thousand arquebusiers and numerous cannon. It never reached the bridge. Farnese's artillery caused it to run on to the shallows and there destroyed it.

April of 1585 arrived, and with it the unusual inventions of Giambelli: four flat-bottomed barges reinforced at the base with a walling about fourteen inches high, with a small channel full of powder running through the middle. At the bottom there were bombs, millstones, marble chips, gravestones, chains, nails, and cutting blades. All this was pressed together by boulders which were connected by iron bolts and the whole mass was covered with wood treated with pitch and strewn with sulphur so that it would appear to be an ordinary incendiary device. The explosion was to be set off at the proper time by clockwork mechanisms.

On April 5th the four floating bombs moved toward the bridge. Everything worked as it should—or almost. Three barges remained silent, but the fourth exploded with an enormous noise, shaking the earth within a radius of more than three miles and destroying about two hundred and sixty feet of the bridge. Eight hundred men died and Farnese was saved only by a miracle.

But the Dutch were unable to take advantage of the surprise. They allowed Farnese to repair the damage, and even to perfect the system of chained barges, such as being able to unhook them in case of necessity in order to let eventual new incendiary barges pass through.

The siege lasted for another four and a half months. The increasing difficulty of getting food into the city impelled the Dutch to seek a solution in a sortie, in

Above: *Two views of the bridge of Farnese, before and during the attack by Giambelli's explosive barges, pictured* below *(from De Bello Belgico {Concerning the Belgian Wars} by F. Strada).*

combination with forces from the outside. But Farnese blocked these attempts and then went over to a counter attack, and, early in August, 1585, launched an assault on the walls. On August 17th the citadel fell into the hands of Capizucchi, one of Farnese's loyal captains. Antwerp surrendered.

A three-day banquet ensued on the contested bridge. But without Giambelli, of whom there was no further news whatever.

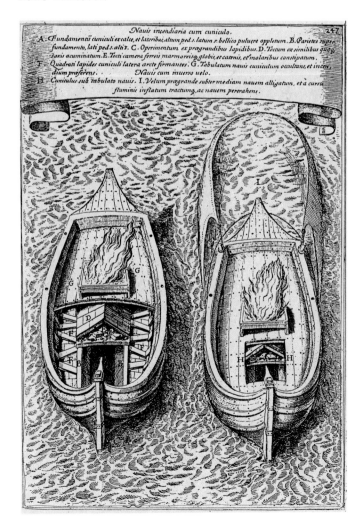

BREDA (1624-1625)

A court intrigue for the brush of Velásquez

In 1622 the long struggle for the independence of the Netherlands (Dutch subjects against the Spanish Hapsburgs) became entwined with the developments of the Thirty Years War in its Bohemian-Palatinate phase (German subjects against the Austrian Hapsburgs). In July of the above year the Marquis Ambrogio Spinola, at the apex of a brilliant military career, laid siege to Bergen-op-Zoom in the name of Spain, but an unexpected attack by Dutch forces and German Protestants under Maurice of Nassau raised the siege.

This partial setback offered an opportunity to the court clique who surrounded the Spanish King, Philip IV, an opportunity of presenting the Genovese soldier of fortune in a bad light. Spanish military circles and Gaspar Guzmán himself, Duke of Sanlucar and Count of Olivares, the all powerful Prime Minister of Philip IV, jealous of the power and glory of Spinola, intrigued against him. They persuaded Philip IV to order him to return to the Dutch city of Breda. This was a stronghold of northern Brabante, considered unassailable.

Spinola, somewhat worried but also stimulated by the difficulty of the undertaking, started his campaign in the spring of 1624, with about sixty thousand men.

Count Maurice of Nassau (son of William the Silent, Prince of Orange and then stadtholder of Holland), took early steps to provide all measures for the defense of Breda. He garrisoned it with nine thousand infantry, equipped it with a good artillery defense, stocked it with supplies and munitions and strengthened its defenses with moats, trenches, towers, and embankments.

Spinola had installed numerous batteries set up on specially constructed raised platforms so as to obtain the maximum result from bombardment. He had ordered the construction of a number of barricades to be carried out at points corresponding to possible points of egress from the outer city so that a small complement of men

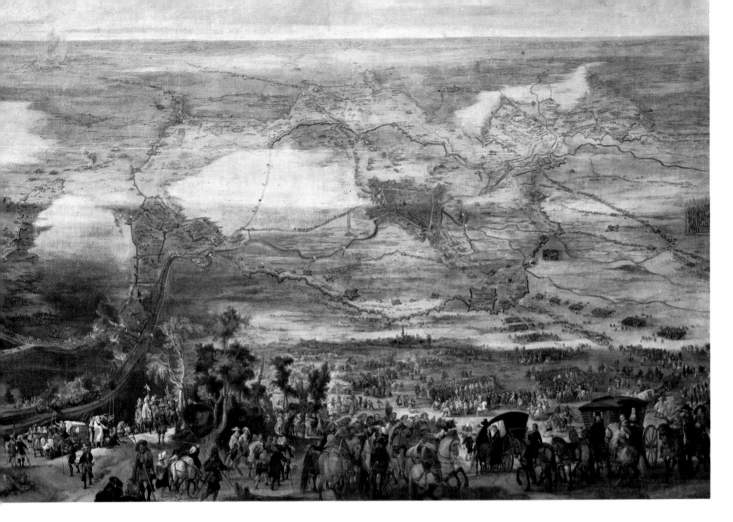

Facing page: *The famous painting by Diego Velásquez (1599-1660), entitled* The Lances, *or* The Surrender of Breda. *Above: According to a custom of the times, the nobility would attend siege operations as if the siege were a sort of spectacle or entertainment, as shown in this painting by Peter Snayers (1592-1667)* Isabel Clara Eugenia during the Siege of Breda *(Madrid, Prado Museum).*

could stop any sorties of the besieged. This permitted him to have at his disposal a large and mobile mass of light infantry and cavalry with which he could guard his rear against enemy relief armies.

The siege operations were, in effect, frequently disturbed by vigorous sorties by the besieged as well as by constant maneuvering on the part of Nassau. The latter had stayed outside of Breda and had placed his camp not far from the city. Spinola tried to entice him into a pitched battle, but Nassau refused the challenge and allowed Peter Ernst von Mansfeld, a German mercenary of noble blood, who was attempting to get provisions within the besieged city, to be defeated several times in his relief operations.

The winter of 1624-25 arrived. As it was very severe, both sides felt their hopes lift. But just as snow, ice, pestilence, and hunger did not force the defenders to their knees, neither did the freezing wind which continually blew through the Spanish tents cause the besiegers to give up their blockade.

With the return of good weather the Dutch received considerable reinforcements of German troops. With the aid of these they resumed their efforts to break the siege which, however, were unsuccessful. Maurice, who

died on April 23rd, was succeeded as stadtholder of Holland by his younger brother, Frederick Henry. The latter continued to employ the prudent strategy of his predecessor; that is, avoiding a direct encounter. The Count of Mansfeld, for the fifth time, tried to relieve Breda with a supply convoy escorted by an army of twelve thousand men. According to plan, two thousand Dutch issued from Breda on May 12th, 1625, and attacked the besiegers in the sector supposed to be the weakest, that held by Italian forces. Meanwhile, the relief forces tried to enter the city from the opposite side.

The sortie was carried out, but the Italian sector proved to be quite otherwise than what had been supposed. Few Hollanders escaped. Even diversionary action failed: Mansfeld was thrown back with great losses.

On June 1st, 1625, Spinola, who, in the meantime, had increased his own artillery and silenced the fortress batteries with his large caliber batteries "for dismantling," now brought up his "breaching" batteries to the counterscarp of the moat. After an effective bombardment the city was taken by assault and conquered.

With the change of fortune the very defensive works of the city were turned around for the purpose of attacking the second line of defenses. These too were bombarded until breaches were made for a fresh attack.

On June 5th the city surrendered under honorable conditions. The vanquished were allowed to take from the city four pieces of artillery, their own weapons and as much property as each one could carry. Only four thousand men left Breda. Five thousand had died in its defense, together with eight thousand women and children dead of hunger and privation.

LA ROCHELLE (1627-1628)

Taking a suggestion of Alexander the Great, Richelieu storms the "Synagogue of Satan"

On June 27th, 1627, when the English fleet left Portsmouth under the command of George Villiers, Duke of Buckingham, the eight or ten thousand men who crowded his ships knew that they were going to war but did not know which enemy they were going to face. It was certain that they were heading toward France but, since war had not been declared, the objective could also be Spain. Discussions on this subject ceased only when, on July 10th, the beaches of the Isle of Ré appeared before their prows, and Buckingham ordered the troops to disembark. Beyond the Isle of Ré, quiet under the summer sun, was La Rochelle, the Calvinist stronghold of the most Catholic land of France. The city was menaced by the threat of losing its communal and commercial privileges because of Catholic resentment against it. This resentment was well interpreted in favor of religion and the King by Cardinal Armand du Plessis, Duke of Richelieu, and then Prime Minister of King Louis XIII. In Rome, Pope Urban VII spoke of the city as a "synagogue of Satan."

As a royal army twenty thousand men strong was advancing on La Rochelle, Charles I of England had thought to send the city reinforcements, under the command of his favorite, the Duke of Buckingham.

On July 21st, a short time after the landing, a bloody encounter took place. There were many dead, principally on the French side. Marshal Toiras, who commanded the Ré garrison, then shut himself and his men inside the fortress of Saint-Martin, which was the only stronghold of the island.

Saint-Martin held out until the first part of October, at which point Toiras informed the Cardinal that if he did not receive reinforcements by the evening of October 8th he would have to cease resistance. The Cardinal lost no time. He personally selected ships and men, entrusting them to an officer of great courage, named Beaulieu-Persac, and on October 7th Toiras received his reinforcements. Richelieu then gave orders to one of his best commanders, Henri de Schomberg, to gather together a contingent of determined men, to have them make their confessions, and then to take them to Ré, under the cover of darkness. At dusk a furious hurricane hit Ré. Schomberg was able to move on Ré in silence. The following morning he was established on the island with four thousand men. Buckingham could only sound retreat.

While the English were hurrying to their ships, leaving everything, even their wounded, in their haste to depart, Toiras rode out of Saint-Martin on a white horse to meet Schomberg. His first words were: "How is His Majesty?" He then took part in the pursuit, during which almost all the English officers and one thousand eight hundred soldiers lost their lives. Buckingham barely escaped. He abandoned the island, sword in hand, at the very last. On November 12th he returned to an England boiling with popular fury.

Facing page, above title: *Cardinal Richelieu presents to Louis XIII the dike erected to blockade the bay in the back of which lies La Rochelle. In the center the opening can be seen, guarded on the inside by a flotilla of boats fastened together by chains and cables. On the outside, toward the Atlantic, there was a strong palisade. In spite of the stylized treatment, the drawing clearly illustrates the construction of the dike, which so impressed some of its contemporary admirers that it was suggested that a pyramid be raised over it in honor of the King, bearing a Latin inscription, saying, in part: "Sta, viator, ubi stetit Oceanus. Hanc specta molem quam mundus stupuit. Vidit Britannus et fugit..." ("Stop, oh passerby, where the ocean also has stopped. Gaze upon this great work which has astonished the world. The Briton saw it and fled...").* Right: *The portrait of François de Bassompierre of Lorraine (Paris, Print Section of the National Library), one of the commanders of the French army at the siege of La Rochelle. Apart from his military activities, Bassompierre is noted for* Le journal de ma vie *(The Record of My Life) which he wrote within the walls of the Bastille, where he was imprisoned from 1631 to 1643 by order of Richelieu, after Bassompierre had become an opponent of the Cardinal.* Below: *A view of the siege according to a painting by A. van der Kabel (La Rochelle, Orbigny Museum).*

FRANCISCVS DE BASSOMPIERRE
MARCHIO D'HAROVEL GAL-... LIARVM POLEMARCHVS
GENERALIS HELVETIORVM ... T RHÆTORVM PRÆFECTVS

SIEGE DE LA ROCHELLE 1628

Now Richelieu could concentrate all his forces against La Rochelle. His army, very well deployed, blockaded the city from the land. But the fleet was not large enough to blockade the city from the sea. This was the reason that impelled the Cardinal to construct the famous dike at the entrance to the long and narrow bay at the end of which lay the city. The idea, in reality, was not new. It had been suggested in 1621, on the occasion of another siege and the Italian, Pompeo Targone, had suggested blocking the bay with a system of boats. Now Targone was called back and his plan was reexamined. But he was not lucky. At the beginning of his project another Italian contributed his ideas in a much more decisive manner. This was the Marquis Ambrogio Spinola, who had arrived in La Rochelle on a courtesy visit to the King and the Cardinal. It therefore fell to the lot of two Frenchmen, Clément Métezeau, architect to the King, and his master builder Jean Thiriot, to plan the dike which would eventually force the surrender of La Rochelle. It was constructed with a system of pilings, strengthened by stone material loaded on boats which were sunk on the spot. In the middle, a narrow passage permitted the waves and tides to pass through without too much pressure on the two wings of the dike. It is necessary to add that the depth of the bay was such that the dike could be built outside of the range of the Huguenot artillery. The operation was begun in October and continued without pause throughout the winter. In January of 1628 the blockade was practically already in effect.

In February Richelieu became ill. He continued to direct the operations from his bed.

The months passed. The King became bored and returned to Versailles to hunt deer, promising to return for Easter. In the early part of March a Catholic from La Rochelle betrayed his own city and showed the royal troops where there was a secret passage. On the night of April 12th Richelieu in person, accompanied by five thousand men, established himself near the Maubec Gate and waited for the advance party of sappers who had penetrated the city through the secret passage to open the gate. But, at dawn, it was learned that no one had gone into the city. The sappers had got lost in the deep darkness and spent the night in the swamps.

The besieged reacted to the fear that they experienced at their narrow escape by making various sorties. These were the last indications of a vitality that hunger and hardship was rapidly diminishing. At the end of March a British ship succeeded in running the blockade and in passing through the narrow passage in the center of the dike. The ship's captain brought to the people of La Rochelle a letter from Charles I of England with a promise of help and encouragement to hold on. The defenders of La Rochelle regained their spirits. At that time they chose a new burgomaster, in the person of Jean Guiton who, according to legend, took over his duties with a passionate and romantic gesture: that of thrusting his own dagger into the wood of the table around which the councillors were sitting, and swearing

Above: *The arms of Cardinal Richelieu, from the collection of crests in the Section of Prints in the National Library of Paris.* Below: *The trumpeters of the famous Cardinal's Guard, made popular by the novel* The Three Musketeers *by Alexander Dumas. The Cardinal's Guard, composed of outstanding men of arms, was particularly favored by the great statesman, whom we see* on the facing page, *triumphing over the enemies of France, symbolized by the eagle and the lion, representing Austria and Spain. In the center, cared for by a solicitous Richelieu, stands the lily, symbol of France. This print, preserved as well as the former, in the Print Section of the National Library of Paris, underlines one of the principal aspects of Louis XIII's famous and mysterious minister. What is definitely known about Richelieu is that he was a great political figure to whom France and Europe owe much. His true personality is yet to be discovered.*

that, in the same way, he would stab it into the heart of anyone who dared to speak of surrender. In the middle of May, finally, English sails appeared off the island of Ré. On May 18th the fleet set its prows to sea and departed, after having fired a ridiculous volley against the dike. The Admiral in command, Lord Denbigh, had learned that a Spanish fleet had put to sea, sailing to the north, and he did not want to run any risks. He sent a message to the defenders of La Rochelle that it would be better for them surrender to Louis XIII, and then turned toward England under full sail.

Now, in truth, the people of La Rochelle had to gather together all their forces and to die fighting. There were desertions in great numbers, a black market, and hoarding of food. It was also reported that women of La Rochelle would, at night, go over to the French lines and sell themselves to soldiers for bread. When Richelieu learned of this he threatened soldiers who took part in such transactions with death on the wheel.

The burgomaster Guiton sent still another letter to the King of England, and Charles I did not spare his promises. Buckingham, in fact, was occupied in equipping a new fleet which would wash away the shame staining the reputation of the English fleet through the actions of the cowardly Denbigh. But Felton's dagger stopped Buckingham's heart before he could do so, and

the fleet left without him. On September 28th the English ships were in front of the dike, under the command of a determined man, Count Lindsey, the godson of the great Elizabeth. The ships carried eleven regiments and food for many months. But the supplies never left the holds and the regiments never set foot on land. The English were infiltrated by sedition, and Lindsey's resolution faded before the open revolt of his troops. Now for Guiton there was no further doubt: this time everything was really over. On October 27th four of the five thousand survivors of La Rochelle presented themselves before the Cardinal offering surrender. Two days later a deputation was received by the King on his throne, who implored his pardon. The gates were then opened and in the semi-deserted streets there echoed the heavy tread of the musketeers. Richelieu entered the city. Guiton went to meet him, surrounded by the municipal halberdiers. The burgomaster prepared to make a speech, but the Cardinal shut him off with a gesture and dryly informed him that he should consider himself deprived of their arms. Guiton bowed his head and prepared for the worst. A few days later he was banished from the city. He left with the sound of the walls and towers falling under the pickaxes of the soldiers and the laments of the people who continued to die of privation and pestilence.

PEVT on asses loüer cét excellant Ministre,
Qui soubs l'authorité du plus Iuste des Rois;
Chassant bien loin de nous tout Presage sinistre,
Par ses illustres soins donne vigueur aux Loix·

O qu'à nostre Repos ses Trauaux sont vtiles!
Par eux de toutes parts on voit enseuelis
Ces Insectes puans, et ces vilains Reptiles
Qui tâchent de ternir la beauté de nos LIS.

POVR conseruer ces Fleurs Royales et Duuines,
(Tresor cher aux François, et Gage precieux,)
Il ne se lasse point d'arracher les espines,
Que sement dans nos Champs les mains des Factieux.

MAIS tous nos Ennemis trop foibles pour nous nuir,
Sont en vain contre nous de rage forcenez:
Car le lion d'Espagne, et L'Aigle de l'Empire,
Tremblent soubs RICHELIEV qui les tient enchein

MAGDEBURG (1631)

In the name of religion a sea of flames and blood

On March 6th, 1629, Emperor Ferdinand II proclaimed the Edict of Restitution, according to which the Protestants would have to restore to the Catholics all the lands occupied at the time of the so-called pacification of Augusta. The Lutheran city of Magdeburg, one of the richest centers of northern Germany, obtained the support of Gustavus Adolphus, King of Sweden, and prepared to face the Imperial troops.

Gustavus Adolphus sent to Magdeburg Dietrich von Falkenberg, a clever German officer, who assumed command of the city. A short time afterwards the Imperial army, under the command of Count Gottfried Heinrich Pappenheim, summoned the city to fulfill the terms of the Imperial order. To this they received a sarcastic " no," and the troops of Ferdinand II immediately started siege

operations. On March 30th, 1631, Tilly, the Commander in Chief of Ferdinand's forces, was also on the field. Having captured the outer fortifications, he forced von Falkenberg's garrison, composed of some squadrons of cavalry and a few more than two thousand infantrymen, to enclose themselves within the fortress itself. This edification was so enormous, however, that in order to garrison it, it was necessary to have recourse to civilian levies.

While the Imperial troops set fire to the outlying cities of Sudenburg and Neustadt, Falkenberg was demolishing the bridge over the Elbe River. Pappenheim, however, crossed over the river some distance upstream and completed the encirclement. The hardship of the attack as well as Falkenberg's severity caused some dissatisfac-

MAGDEBURG.

tion among the citizens. But the determination of the Magdeburgers not to surrender triumphed and was underscored by their deeds. When Tilly sent them a summons to surrender they replied with a vigorous sortie.

On April 14th news reached Tilly that Gustavus Adolphus, in pursuit of the Imperial army that used to belong to Wallenstein, had attacked and captured Frankfurt-on-the-Oder the day before and was now within one hundred and twenty miles of Magdeburg.

Tilly redoubled his efforts and by May 18th he had overcome every obstacle and was ready to carry the city by assault. The savage struggle lasted two days. On the morning of the 20th the Protestant defense collapsed and the Imperial troops rushed into the city. Falkenberg fell slain while the soldiers let themselves go in a terrible massacre. At noon a series of great fires broke out, which soon transformed the city into a huge funeral pyre. Only five thousand Magdeburgers survived although they had numbered thirty thousand at the beginning of the siege. Six thousand corpses were thrown into the Elbe for the sole purpose of clearing the streets that Tilly planned to ride through while making his solemn entrance into Magdeburg.

This event horrified Europe. For the Protestants Magdeburg became a byword for vengeance at any cost. For Tilly, Magdeburg proved a pyrrhic victory: its destruction deprived him of a strategic base against Gustavus Adolphus, who was now joined by the Elector of Brandenburg, George William, the United Provinces of Holland, and Richelieu's France. Only the battle of Lutzen and the death of Gustavus Adolphus in the field (November 16th, 1632) would restore strength to the two-headed eagle of the House of Hapsburg.

Iohan. Com. de Tilly.

A portrait of Jan Tserclaes, Count of Tilly, Marshal of the Austrian Empire (1539-1632). The conquest of Magdeburg was his last great undertaking. He died the following year as a result of three wounds received at Breitenfeld, in a memorable battle against Gustavus Adolphus of Sweden.

151

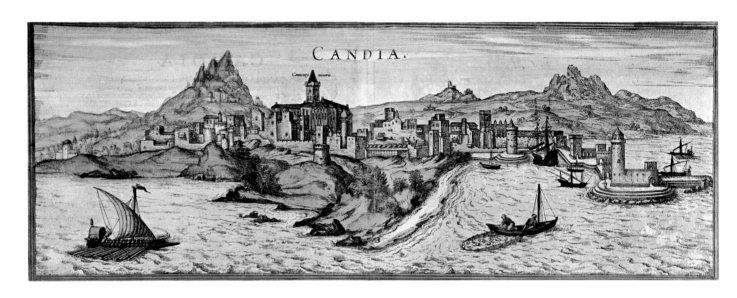

CANDIA
(1666-1669)

The Lion of Saint Mark trumples on his own hero

The celebrated siege set by the Turks in 1646 to the city of Candia, capital of Crete (then also called Candia), was part of the twenty year war waged by the Venetians, with much bravery and much honor, against the Turks, in order to retain possession of the island, which they had conquered in 1204.

Francesco Morosini, captain of Candia, was in Venice in 1666, as his term of command had recently expired. It was at this point that the Turks gave signs of attempting a final attack to resolve the conflict. Morosini was speedily appointed to an office of overall control and furnished with ten thousand men. Morosini set sail in January, 1667, and, despite a stormy sea, quickly arrived at Candia, where he had the pleasant surprise of finding two Piedmontese regiments of the Marquis Villa, sent by the Duke of Savoy. The stronghold possessed an artillery force of about four hundred heavy caliber bronze cannon and a garrison of six thousand regular troops, in addition to the two regiments already mentioned. On May 22nd, 1667, the Turks began offensive operations which continued until far into November.

Within this period there were thirty-two assaults on the city, seventeen Venetian sorties, and six hundred and eighteen mine explosions. There were twenty thousand Moslem victims of these hostilities and three thousand two hundred on the Venetian side.

When the hostilities were resumed, the Grand Vizier decided that it was useless to concentrate on a frontal assault against the city's impregnable defenses. He therefore essayed a blow using twenty galleys and two thousand picked infantry. Under the command of the famous pirate, Durak Pasha, these forces were to effect a landing at a place known as Santa Pelagia, during the night between the 8th and 9th of May. Morosini found out about the plan and went to meet the enemy in the dark of night, and after three hours of the most severe fighting boarded the galley. Durak died in the struggle and five ships fell into the hands of the Venetians.

The defeat irritated the vizier, who went back to artillery bombardment of one stronghold or the other, and launched one assault after another, day after day. By August of 1668 the garrison of Candia had been reduced to five thousand men. The hospitals no longer had space for the wounded, and there was not enough land to bury the dead. Morosini was forced to use sailors from the ships as reinforcements. On November 2nd, while he and the Marquis Alexander de Puy, who was in command of the infantry, were inspecting the "pincers" of Sant' Andrea, Morosini narrowly escaped death from an enemy mine.

In December of 1668 an expedition landed at Candia, composed of five hundred French nobles, under the command of the Duke de la Feuillade. These wished to carry out a sudden sortie, against the opinion of Morosini and the customs of war (which usually observed a truce during the winter months). At first they had an easy success, but a furious Turkish counterattack overwhelmed them and forced them to leave the island without delay. Then Louis XIV decided to send twelve regiments to Candia under the command of the Duke de Noailles. Pope Clement IX also prepared an expedition, under the command of Prince Rospigliosi, which included also Maltese contingents. These reinforcements arrived in Candia on July 3rd, 1669. On the 25th a French sortie almost turned into a disaster: the Turks would have been able to enter the city if Morosini had not come out to stop them. On August 9th, in a general council of war, an attempt was made to agree upon an operation which afterwards, because of dissension, never took place. On August 20th the French began to reembark.

On August 23rd, when the defenders were now reduced to one thousand six hundred, the Turks attacked

Sant' Andrea again for two endless hours: and once more they were forced to retreat by Morosini. When the Maltese and Papal troops started to leave, a council of war authorized the commander to negotiate with the Turks for surrender. The attempts lasted ten days, accompanied by effective sorties and mine explosions, in order not to let the Turks know about the weak state of the defenders. Thus was Morosini able to save what coud be saved, including honor. During September 26th-27th, 1669, the Venetian galleys left Candia, carrying with them all their artillery, the remains of the army, and the sacred vestments. The last galley to leave the port was that of Morosini. But when the great soldier of fortune debarked in Venice, the Senate of the Most Serene Republic imprisoned him. The accusation, later withdrawn, was that of treason.

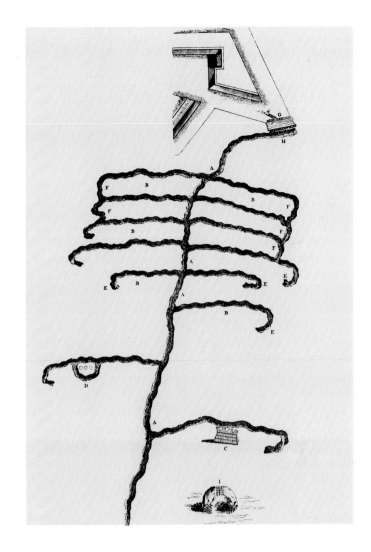

Facing page, above title: *A view of Candia, capital of Crete.* Right: *The "parallels" dug by Italian engineers in the service of the Turks during the siege, for the successive gradual approach to the spot chosen for the attack (Rome, Central Military Library). Soon this system would be developed by the great master of siege warfare, Vauban, who would use it in the siege of Maastricht.* Below: *The desperate defense of Morosini, in a drawing by Giuseppe Gatteri from the already mentioned* Venetian History *(Venice 1867). Typical of this siege was the war of mining and countermining conducted spasmodically. The opposing forces search for each other underground in an intricate and ever closer system of passageways. Morosini himself almost died because of the mine near the "pincers" of Sant' Andrea.*

MAASTRICHT (1673)

D'Artagnan, the Gascon, dies on the parallels of Vauban

The siege of Maastricht opened the second great war conducted by Louis XIV, the war he waged against Holland, who defended herself by flooding a great part of her territory. Louis, stopped in his advance on Amsterdam, decided to take Maastricht, then one of the strongest fortified cities in the world. He attacked it on June 13th, 1673, and conquered it within thirteen days. This was mainly due to the work of Sebastien Le Preste, Marquis de Vauban, one of the most famous engineers of all time. He was born in Paris in 1633 and was appointed "the king's engineer" by Mazarin at the end of 1655, when he was only twenty-two years old. Following the theories of a great predecessor, Blaise François Pagan, Vauban developed one of his theories on the means of taking a stronghold. This theory is worth a short description since it was the basis for siege operations essayed during the following centuries.

The operation was to begin with cavalry action intended to sweep the surrounding zone and to block all means of access. Thereupon, while the infantry was establishing camp in the most suitable place, the engineers would start operations of circumvallation and countervallation, that is, two lines of concentric fortifications, which we have already noticed in use in the wars of antiquity and which were designed to protect the besiegers either from sorties on the part of the besieged or from attacks on their own rear by eventual relief forces.

The five phases of assault then followed. The first consisted of digging a trench parallel (after meticulous investigations) to the front chosen for the final assault and outside of the circumvallation line, at about six hundred and fifty yards distance from the enemy. Here long-range cannon were placed in position and thereafter, advancing under the protection of other trenches arranged in a zigzag pattern, a new trench was prepared (second phase), parallel to the first one at a distance of three hundred and eighty yards from the enemy fort. Here were placed other mortars and howitzers to keep the enemy under control while the sappers were ready to put in the third phase of the operation: opening other small zigzag trenches enabling the attackers to establish themselves at a point one hundred and seventy yards from the enemy and there to dig a third trench parallel to the first two. From this trench, which was outside of easy range of enemy muskets, the work of mining was begun. The fourth phase was as follows: while the batteries of the first two trenches dismantled the enemy defenses, the infantry attacked (in daylight, in order to avoid confusion). The infantry made its attack from the third trench and burst in through the breaches made by the artillery or mining. This was the decisive moment.

A cavalry drum of the XVII century preserved in Dijon in the Small Hall of Arms of the City Museum. Below: An infantry officer and two soldiers (on horseback) of the corps of the King's Musketeers, who distinguished themselves particularly at Maastricht under the leadership of their commander, d'Artagnan, who died leading an assault on the enemy fortifications. He would later become the main character of The Three Musketeers by Dumas. Facing page: A model of Maastricht constructed in the time of Louis XIV, a part of a marvellous series of reconstructions of strongholds which form the collection of the Museum of Plans and Reliefs from the Royal Collection created by Louvois in 1668. It is preserved in Paris at the Hôtel des Invalides.

The fifth phase anticipated the final destruction of the bastion. But this last phase was one that was less and less frequently encountered. The custom of the time, in effect, permitted an honorable surrender to the besieging forces, once this point had been reached, considering that a battle within the city would be a useless and cruel ordeal. It even became possible to establish in figures what constituted an honorable surrender. According to some, a garrison could give up and save its honor if, at the moment of surrender, half of its effectives were still standing. Vauban, with more severity, claimed that resistance should continue until two-thirds of the defenders were hors de combat.

On the night of June 11th Louis XIV slept for the first time in bivouac under the walls of Maastricht. The city was guarded by four thousand five hundred infantry and one thousand two hundred Spanish cavalry. The French numbered forty thousand, including sixteen thousand horses. The King gave orders to Vauban to proceed speedily but not precipitously.

Trenches were dug in the section of the route to Namur along a pond made by waters overflowing from the Meuse and another small river. On June 18th twenty-six French cannon, divided into three batteries, bombarded Maastricht for some time, without any response from the city until late afternoon. However, during the following days the resistance was magnificent.

The 24th was the feast day of Saint John the Baptist. The King announced that he wished to attend Mass in Maastricht at all costs. Since the trenches were finished and the attackers had no longer anything in front of them except the enemy embankments, the counterscarp and the so-called "covered way," that is, the outside defenses of the moat, the last phase of the "Vauban style" siege could be said to be at hand. To finish it and make the King happy the infantry of the King's Regiment and the Company of Gray Musketeers, under the command of Charles de Batz de Castelmore, Count d'Artagnan, rushed into battle. D'Artagnan had already been the King's provost of Lille and recently named field marshal. Alexander Dumas would make him the immortal hero of The Three Musketeers, modifying the time of his deeds by half a century.

The severe fighting extended into the night when, after two counterscarps had been taken and they had penetrated into the moat the French entered into a "crescent," one of the advanced fortifications of Maastricht. The Spanish submitted them to an intense fire but succeeded in dislodging them from only a section. Thirty soldiers, under the leadership of the old Marquis de Vignory, remained there until the morning. Among them was Claude-Louis-Hector, Marquis de Villars, future duke and marshal of France. The operation was conducted by Duke James Scott of Monmouth, the natural son of Charles I of England, who was lieutenant-general "of the day" and who had proposed as his objective the conquest of the covered road. When the morning of June 25th arrived he sent word to the king that the objective was about to be taken at the price of one hundred men dead and wounded and that he was awaiting the order to proceed. The order was given for the Dauphin's regiment to advance. But du Montal, who was in command, hurled his men forward without protection, losing three hundred men, and had to retreat.

At noon the besieged were successful in exploding a mine under the crescent held by Vignory and recapturing it. But the Duke of Monmouth led the French to retake it. D'Artagnan, who was on the flank, was hit at that moment by a bullet in the throat and fell dead.

Maastricht fell on July 2nd and the garrison marched out with the governor at their head. He had been menaced with death on several occasions by the people and he had only a few troops still capable of resistance. The French were especially struck by the fine appearance of two regiments of dismounted Spanish cavalry and the Neapolitan infantry.

The Marquis of San Maurizio, Ambassador of the Duke of Savoy to the French court, witnessed the events. In a letter he wrote to his sovereign, dated July 4th, 1673, from the Camp of Maastricht, he observed: "I do not think that there has ever been so much earth moved around in thirteen days, nor finer works than those constructed for the assault as far as safety and usefulness. Monsieur de Vauban was in charge of the works and the King was so satisfied that he gave him as a reward four thousand *pistoles*."

Sebastien Le Preste, Marquis de Vauban (1633-1707), the greatest military engineer of modern times. Right: *The siege of Maastricht according to a painting by Jean-Paul de Marly (Museum of Versailles). Here Vauban, hardly forty years of age, applied his doctrine of systematic siege warfare, having derived it from the study of Turkish activities at Candia, during the siege of 1666-1669.*

VIENNA (1683)

The Sun King bows to the miracle of Charles of Lorraine

Towards the end of 1680, while Louis XIV of France, called the Sun King, was engaged in his agressive policy of expansion, which was then creating in Europe a serious unbalanced situation, other perils were making themselves felt on the Danube. In 1678 the Hungarians rose against the Empire and allied themselves with the Turks. The Turks then had a pretext once again for invading Hapsburg Hungary, thereby breaking the truce of Vasvar, to which they were bound in 1664; and in March of 1683 they moved on Vienna.

The Ottoman army started its advance on March 31 from Adrianople (or Edirne), where it had been assembled. The unwarlike Sultan Mohammed IV, with all his court (the harem alone was contained in one hundred vehicles), accompanied his army as far as Belgrade. The army was composed of contingents from all the peoples from the East and West, Spahi cavalry and Janizaries, Turkish bozniaks, Slavs and Tartars, making altogether a total of two hundred and forty thousand men, at the head of which marched the ambitious grand vizier Kara Mustapha. The allied forces contained another seventy thousand men among whom were the rebel Hungarians under the command of Count Emmerich Tököly. Their orders indicated their destinations: Vienna, Prague and then the Rhine and the Tiber. In Rome, according to the sworn promise of the Turkish minister Köprülü, the cavalry horses would enjoy a most luxurious stable: Saint Peter's Cathedral.

Faced with such a situation, the various states of Europe were anything but ready to undertake a united defense action. Quite the contrary, for the diplomats of the Sun King maneuvered to support the Turks against the House of Austria. When the Empereor Leopold looked for allies, the Pope, Spain, Portugal and the Italian states offered him money. Armed support was assured only by the King of Poland, John Sobieski, and from a group of German princes, among those all the princes of Bavaria, Saxony and Franconia. But many other Western rulers, among the most important of which was the Elector of Brandenburg, kept well away from the war.

A certain period of time was necessary to coordinate these heterogeneous units who altogether made a fighting force about eighty thousand men strong. But time was what was lacking. Therefore the designated commander, Duke Karl von Lothringen, or Charles V of Lorraine, who had been deprived of his territories by Louis XIV and was now in the service of the Empire, found himself forced to confront, with only twenty four thousand men, an enemy ten times stronger. Since it was impossible to face the enemy in the open field, he decided to leave ten thousand assorted infantry and artillery in Vienna along with six hundred cuirassiers and to take to the countryside with his cavalry troops while awaiting the above mentioned aid.

When the Turkish advanced guard reached the Wienerwald, the celebrated "Vienna woods" (this was July 1683) Emperor Leopold I left the city with his court. Vienna, with all possible haste, began to prepare for the siege under the command of Count Ernst Rüdiger von Starhemberg. Meantine, the Turkish army entered into the woods and gradually occupied the territory. The

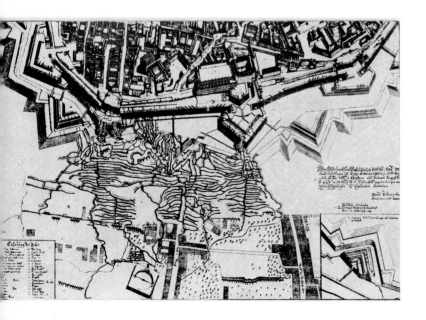

die Belögerüng Wien von Türgn
16 83

fires rose around the city, the first acts of pillage began, as well as the first deeds of valor.

A firm resolution gripped the people of Vienna. The imposing fortifications which had fallen into a state of ruin were repaired with feverish haste: the courageous and untiring burgomaster Andreas Liebenberg was an example to the citizens. Count Starhemberg assumed supreme command of the forces, within the fortified city. The defense could count on, besides eleven thousand regular troops left by the Duke of Lorraine, another five thousand citizen volunteers. The university students formed themselves into an armed company under the command of their rector, and even the guilds formed their own volunteer companies. There even came into being female auxiliary contingents, particularly active in the construction of trenches.

On July 14th the main part of the Turkish army appeared before Vienna and began to deploy for the siege. An endless city of tents was established in a semicircular shape between Laaerberg and Heiligenstadt. It would be there for two months. The main enemy offensives would take place against the strongest part of the fortifications, between Burgbastei and Löwelbastei, which were also the most favorable for the assault, since mine galleries could be dug there without being endangered by underground waters. Here the Janizaries were camped and other Turkish elite troops. Their Balkan allies were arrayed to the northwest near Heiligenstadt, while the Asiatic and African levies were established near Laaerberg.

While Kara Mustapha passed the time pleasantly at the Baden springs, Charles of Lorraine met Tököly and his Hungarian rebels at Pressburg and routed them. He thereupon marched on Bisamberg, while leaving a contingent to guard the bridge at Krems, on the Danube, with orders to defend it at any cost. Mustapha, who understood the strategic importance of this bridge, sent a column of fifteen thousand men to conquer it. But they were unable to stand against the cuirassiers of Charles of Lorraine, commanded by the intrepid Count Johann Heinrich Dünewald, formerly a common soldier during the Thirty Years War. His charge overwhelmed the Turks, forcing them to retreat leaving a thousand fallen.

Meanwhile, after these first days of attack, the grand vizier realized that the city could not be taken by a sudden attack. Not even a continuous artillery bombardment could force the city to surrender, either because the Turks, for some reason, had not brought enough heavy artillery to the siege or because the three hundred cannon which the Viennese had put into position on the walls was sufficient to oppose the enemy with an efficient counterfire and to keep the assault infantry at a distance. It was therefore necessary to capture the city slowly and laboriously, through the usual work of mining and blockade. Vienna was to fall by starvation.

Dysentery and illnesses of all kinds considerably weakened the capacity of the besieged to defend themselves. The mines which the Turks, under the guidance of French engineers, were digging under the walls and

bastions of the city, were demolishing the fortifications bit by bit. The lack of provisions soon made itself felt and became increasingly serious. Under the savage attacks of the Janizaries, the defending forces became smaller in number day by day. Bodies no longer were buried and lay scattered about the streets.

With all this, however, the garrison of Vienna continued to fight on with high spirits, including the six hundred cuirassiers, forced to fight on foot because of the circumstances and also because the horses were weak from lack of forage. Sixty of these, however, were still able to participate in a cavalry raid when their colonel, Dupigny, led them against an open Turkish trench at the place where Parliament now stands. The action succeeded but thirty cuirassiers were killed, including the colonel,

Facing page: *A section of the great painting by John Matejco dedicated to the triumph of Sobieski at Vienna (Vatican Gallery).* Center: *A young man who will soon make himself heard: Eugene of Savoy.* Right: *Charles of Lorraine, who would have to undertake the entire responsibility for organizing operations for the relief of Vienna, while Sobieski, because of his rank (he was King of Poland) held the supreme command. Behind Sobieski can be seen a contingent of the winged hussars, the famous Polish cavalry corps.* Below: *The Turkish cavalry camp (Paris, Library of the Museum of the Army).*

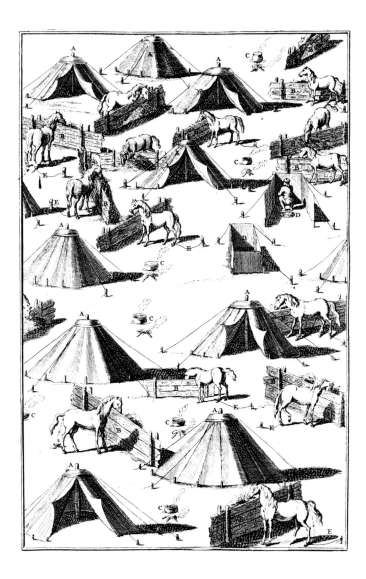

whose breast was pierced by a musket ball.

On September 4th the Turkish camp was alerted to the news that a relief army of seventy thousand men was on the march from Hollabrunn towards Vienna. Kara Mustapha sent the Khan of Crimea against it, with the order to not let it cross the Danube. But the army crossed nevertheless. It was part of twenty-seven thousand Austrians under Charles of Lorraine, and twenty thousand Poles under Sobieski, in addition to still another twenty thousand Saxons, Bavarians and Swedes. The general command was given to Sobieski, for reason of rank, but the burden of strategic planning remained the responsibility of the Duke of Lorraine.

The latter received from a courier, on the night of September 9th, a message from Sobieski begging him to hurry. In effect, the Turks had succeeded in opening several breaches in the walls. They were now near the Burg and the city's fall seemed inevitable.

On the following night, Lorraine established his camp at Kahlenberg, among the burned walls of the Carmelite convent. From Hermannskogel there arose three star bursts that were a signal that relief was imminent. Three joyful blasts replied from the Mölker bastion. On September 11th the incredulous eyes of Kara Mustapha, who had always discounted the possibility of a relief army, observed the united liberation forces deployed in the Wienerwald.

According to contemporary reports, the night of September 11th was warm and pleasant. At sunrise of the 12th, the army prepared for battle. Kara Mustapha who, against the advice of his general staff, had not been able to prevent the arrival of a relief army at the siege of the city, found himself forced to fight two fronts in an unfavorable position.

Sobieski deployed his own army on the right. The German forces took the center, and the Austrians, under Charles of Lorraine, established themselves on the left.

To the latter belongs the honor of winning the first significant success in what has passed into history as the battle of Kahlenberg. He took Nussdorf by assault. Thereupon, three squadrons of Italian cuirassiers stopped and scattered a body of Spahis, the flower of the Turkish cavalry, launched on a desperate charge. This operation opened the Heiligenstadt road to the liberators and convinced Kara Mustapha that the game was lost.

Meanwhile, Sobieski had successfully attacked the main body of the Turkish army. His legendary "winged hussars" charged in a wild attack, found themselves surrounded, broke the encirclement, and, supported by German infantry, rushed on to victory.

Vienna greeted her liberators, Kara Mustapha fled toward Belgrade and to his death. There, in fact, he would be strangled by orders of the Sultan.

Among the many congratulations that arrived at the Hapsburg court were those, necessary by royal courtesy, of the King of France. Referring to the unexpected liberators of Vienna, Louis XIV deigned to employ a special word: a "miracle."

NAMUR (1692 and 1695)

The white plume of the Sun King is seen for the last time in the field

When the so-called English revolution of 1688 offered the chance of assuming the crown of England to William III of Orange, Stadtholder of Holland, the France of Louis XIV found herself deprived not only of British support in her policy of expansion at the expense of the Netherlands, but even under attack by her English ex-ally. This was the beginning of a long struggle between France and England which would only finish at Waterloo.

At its inception this struggle first took concrete form with the nine years' war between Louis XIV's France, at the very height of the her power, and the forces of the so-called League of Augusta or Grand Alliance, that is Holland, the Empire, Sweden, Spain, the Electors of Brandenburg, of Bavaria, of the Palatinate, and later, the Duchy of Savoy.

The city of Namur, an important strategic position of the Brabant on the left bank of the Meuse, was involved in the events of this war on two occasions and each time the object of direct siege.

The first siege started on May 26, 1692. Louis XIV entrusted the conquest of the city to the already famous Vauban, who applied himself with his customary scrupulous zeal, both because the stronghold was important and he wished later to fortify it in his own way, and because another master of siege warfare was defending it. This was The Dutch Baron Menno of Coehoorn, the inventor of a special mortar and a supporter of artillery as the principal siege weapon, and perhaps the chief of the "Dutch school" of the art of fortifications.

The Sun King, as was his custom, went to the field of battle. But this was the last time that he would be in command of the operations of the French army. Among his followers was Jean Racine, the great tragic poet, who from 1677 had held the office of court historiographer, together with the not less famous Nicolas Boileau-Despréaux. Racine kept the latter informed of events by letters which Boileau used to compose his *Ode sur la prise de Namur* (Ode on the Capture of Namur). The above, while certainly not among Boileau's best works, is nevertheless a valuable document concerning the customs and tastes of the time. It includes verses such as:

"Consider in the storm / Arising from these ways / The plume which on his head / Of all attracts the gaze."

The city of Namur, whose governor, the Lord of Vimbergue, was more than eighty years old, resisted this "Vauban" siege for only eight days. But the citadel held out until the end of the month. French losses reached a total of two thousand six hundred men dead and wounded, and twice as many for the besieged.

The taking of Namur consoled the King for a recent unsuccessful exploit of his fleet which, on May 19th, had suffered a serious and decisive defeat at The Hague, causing plans which he had cherished for some time for the invasion of England to vanish into smoke. But the adulation of the court and his own conceit contributed to making the victory of Namur a true hour of glory. The Duke de Noailles, in command of the army on the Spanish front, received on July 7th a letter from the King dated June 30th informing him of the fall of Namur. He lost no time in replying: "This conquest is truly worthy of Your Majesty, and its honor belongs only to you. I praise God with all my heart that Your Majesty has been preserved."

New good tidings reached the King on July 31st from Steenkerke, in Hainaut. François-Henry de Montmorency, Duke of Luxemburg, had beaten William III of Orange in person, inflicting on his troops losses of eight thousand men of which half were English.

LOUIS LE GRAND ROY DE FRANCE ET DE NAVARRE.   L'HERCULE FRANÇOIS.   MONSEIGNEUR LE DAUPHIN.

Left: Two unusual pictures of Louis XIV and the Dauphin, taken from the frontispiece of an atlas of the time (Milan, Bertarelli Collection). Facing page: The King, the Dauphin, and Vauban at the siege of Namur in 1692. This is a painting by J. B. Martin now at Versailles. In the two consecutive sieges suffered by Namur in 1692 and 1695 the two most important "schools" of the siege warfare of the time met in confrontation: that of Vauban and that of the Dutch Baron Menno of Coehoorn.

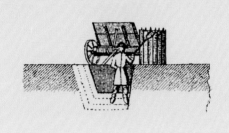

1° Zappatore   2° Zappatore   3° Zappatore   4° Zappatore

One year later, on July 29th, 1693, the Duke of Luxemburg again defeated the forces of the Grand Alliance at Neerwinden near Liège, while the navy, in a running campaign under leaders like Jean Bart, Duguay-Trouin and Torville himself, previously defeated at the Hague, passed from victory to victory. But a mortal fatigue was affecting France which, according to Fénelon, had become nothing other than a huge hospital. And Voltaire, with more mordant irony, observed that in France one could listen to the Te Deum of thanksgiving for military victories while dying of hunger. The idea was suggested that the King, in order to save France, should restore to his enemies places that, again from an observation of Fénelon, could not continue to be held "sans injustice" (without injustice). Without waiting for Louis to let himself be convinced (if he ever had that intention), his enemies did it by themselves. It was in this campaign of reconquest, in effect, that William of Orange set siege to Namur in the first part of 1695.

Duke Louis François de Bouflers, marshal of France for about a year, was scarcely able to shut himself within the city in time with seven regiments of dragoons. This brought the garrison to a strength of about seventeen thousand men with one hundred and twenty cannon, eight mortars, one hundred thousand crowns in cash and provisions for six months.

The Marquis de Villeroy, in heading the French army, remained in the campaign. The allies were deployed in three sectors along the rivers Sambre and Meuse over which three pontoons were constructed. William of Orange was beyond the Sambre toward Brabant, the Elector of Bavaria in the center between the Sambre and the Meuse (with a sector entrusted to General Coehoorn, who had come to take his revenge); while on the right, along the Meuse and under Namur, the forces of Brandenburg were deployed under the command of Baron Heyden.

On July 12, while the work of circumvallation was being performed, Bouflers carried out two disruptive sorties which were notably successful. On the 18th, Orange hurled ten thousand men into the attack. Four thousand were left on the battlefield. Right after this Villeroy, or rather his generals Montal and Feuquierë, took the two enemy towns of Dixmude and Deinse, capturing the first one, although it was well fortified, from General Hellemberg with ridiculous ease (Hellemberg was subsequently condemned to death by William of Orange), and the second town, much less fortified, less easily. Thinking that Villeroy was aiming at Namur, William sent reinforcements to Prince de Vaudemont, who was charged with delaying him.

Meanwhile, Coehoorn's engineers, digging like moles, brought their passages within close proximity to the edge of the Namur fortifications and the artillery opened breach after breach. On August 4th Bouflers retired to the citadel. Since there was no room in the citadel for the wounded he offered surrender of the city itself on condition that the wounded receive all possible aid. Two days' truce was given for the completion of the operation.

On the 6th, Coehoorn resumed his digging and the opposing artillery forces recommenced their duels. The Allied artillery, now able to concentrate its fire on a smaller area, unleashed an inferno of uninterrupted fire which, besides taking an ever increasing number of victims, prevented the besieged from working to repair the breaches. The general assault was launched on August 30th. Thousands of men on both sides were lost in a desperate struggle. The Allies conquered the covered entrenchments from the Sambre to the Meuse at a cost of three thousand dead and two thousand wounded. On September 1st they asked for a two hour truce to clear the terrain of the fallen. Bouflers accepted the truce and took the occasion to call a council of war. The council

rofilo di una batteria di mortai alla Vauban.

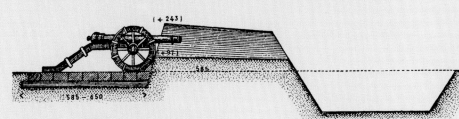

Profilo di una batteria di cannoni alla Vauban.

Profilo di una piazza d'arme (parallela) d'onde i granatieri procedono all'assalto.

decided for capitulation. The Allies accepted and conceded a surrender with the honors of war. But Bouflers was set apart from his dragoons and arrested. Indignant at such a serious violation of the rules of war, he demanded to know why. He was told that it was a reprisal since the French at Dixmude and Deinse had held the garrisons of the two strongholds as prisoners. When Bouflers demurred saying, "If that is how things are, you should have arrested the garrison, not me," the answer was: "Monsieur, to us you are worth more than ten thousand men."

On facing page and above: *Some technical plans of siege warfare according to the theories of Vauban as represented in old illustrations (Rome, Central Military Library). Sappers are preparing a single deep trench protected by gabbions and sandbags on one side. When protection is raised on both sides the trench becomes "double." Spinola invented the single "flying trench" at Ostend (1601-1604) with empty gabbions which were filled by the sappers as they advanced. Below: Another example of a relief map from the collection of Louis XIV (Paris, Museum of Relief Maps). It is a model of large dimensions which shows a reconstruction of Namur in the time of the Sun King.*

TURIN (1706)

Nine miles underground in search of the Throne of Spain

In 1700, a short time before he died, the last Spanish Hapsburg, Carlos II, not having an heir, designated as his own successor a nephew of Louis XIV, Philippe of Anjou. At the time, Europe approached a crisis which shortly developed into the first world conflict of the modern age. The most important pretenders to the Spanish throne, that is, those who could boast legitimate family ties with the Iberian Hapsburgs, included the Emperor Leopold I, Louis XIV, King of France, and Vittorio Amedeo, Duke of Savoy. But when Leopold decided to interfere with the execution of the will and to impose his own rights by force, division developed so that on one side there stood Austria, the Holy Roman Empire, Great Britain, Holland, Prussia, Hanover, Portugal, and the Duchy of Savoy; and, on the other side, France and Bavaria. This was the origin of the so-called War of the Spanish Succession, which would be fought not only on the battlefields of Spain, Italy, Germany, and the Netherlands, but also on the oceans and the North Sea.

Vittorio Amedeo, in effect, waited until 1703 before aligning himself with the league against the French. He did this when he saw the soldiers of Louis XIV arrive in Carpi on the Adige (near Verona), in Chiari (near Brescia), and in Cremona, between 1701 and 1702, at the scene of operations of the Imperial armies of Leopold I, under the command of his cousin Eugene of Savoy, who had become one of the greatest military captains of his time. Vittorio Amedeo thought that he could control the Milanese, whose dream for some time had been to annex the Piedmont and had entered into secret negotiations with the Imperial forces. Later, when, on September 29th, 1703, at San Benedetto Po, the French disarmed the Savoyard forces which had been fighting at their flank, and made them prisoner, the Duke became offended and, leaving the French camp, passed over to the league. But the moment was not a propitious one. Eugene had to return to Vienna and Vittorio Amedeo found that he had to face the French by himself.

In the period between 1704-1705, the fortress of Verrua, in whose defense Vittorio Amedeo II had taken part, held the French tied down for six months. By the day that the surrender was finally forced, April 8, 1705, they had lost, during the long siege, six generals, five hundred and forty-seven officers, thirty military engineers, and twelve thousand soldiers.

Meanwhile, Louis XIV presented to Vauban a proposed plan for the siege of Turin. The famous engineer answered the King in these terms: "The siege of Turin will doubtlessly be the most important undertaking of the Italian campaign. The city is about the same size as

Lille, well populated and equipped with a defense system including seventeen or eighteen bastions. The fortifications are exceedingly strong. The citadel is mined within and without and is protected by deep moats and covered trenches in excellent repair."

Actually the bastions numbered sixteen, baptized with names of saints and disposed according to the Italian fortification system, although in many respects a precursor of the most modern trench fields. The citadel, built under the aegis of Emanuele Filiberto in 1564 and

Above: *Prince Leopold of Anhalt-Dessau charging at the head of the Prussians, an episode during the battle by which Eugene of Savoy and Vittorio Amedeo II succeeded in liberating Turin from the rigorous siege of Louis XIV. The painting, a copy of a fresco in the Hall of the Captains in the Berlin Armory, was given by Germany to the city of Turin in 1906 on the occasion of the second centenary of the siege of Turin (Turin, Pietro Micca Museum).*
Facing page: *Giuseppe Maria Solara della Margherita, a portrait by F. Marabotti (Turin, National Historical Artillery Museum). It is to General della Margherita, who was in command of the artillery in the citadel before and during the siege, that we owe the first account of the story of Pietro Micca. His account was based on the story told to him by a surviving soldier, the last one who saw the heroic miner alive.*

erected facing toward France as if in mistrust of that country, was constructed in the form of a pentagon with a bastion at each angle and long rectilinear walls on each side. Two gates connected the fortress with the outside. The gate facing the countryside was called "the Gate of Help" – "Porta del Soccorso" – and it came out on a bridge which united the fortress with the crescent fortification in front and for this reason was called the "Mezzaluna del Soccorso" (Crescent of Help).

As far as the counter mining so highly esteemed by Vauban was concerned, we may say that it involved a labyrinth of subterranean galleries with a comprehensive length of about nine miles, opening into "mine chambers," special locations for storing explosives to blow up or interrupt the enemy mining operations, or to destroy enemy batteries, or to impede the enemy advance in a possible invasion through the galleries themselves.

In August 1705 the thirty-year-old General Louis François Aubusson, Duke de la Feuillade, began siege operations, only to destroy these complexes on October 13th by order of Louis XIV. Within the city there were only four thousand Piedmontese soldiers. La Feuillade had twenty-one thousand, but the city was so strongly fortified that it could not be besieged in the normal way.

The real siege of Turin began on May 14, 1706, when the city was faced by an array of French-Spanish forces of forty-four thousand men.

Vittorio Amedeo II was able to leave the city with a small body of cavalry ready to scour the countryside, while waiting for Eugene to return with a relief army. Ten thousand two hundred and seventy men, for the most part Piedmontese, remained within the city. The command of the stronghold was given to the Austrian Weirich Philip Lorenz, Count of Daun, then thirty-eight years of age: an energetic and decisive man destined for a brilliant career.

La Feuillade, who was dedicated to having his own way, chose not to accept the advice of Vauban who suggested that he capture the nearby Mount of the Capuchins, from which it would be possible to dominate the city. Instead, sure of obtaining a quick success, he decided on a direct attack.

It began by a storm of cannon fire over the city: more than eight thousand projectiles a day. The inhabitants of Turin – after a first moment of panic when Vittorio Amedeo, in the full light of day and before their eyes, had left the capital to take to the country-side – regained their courage and decided to support the garrison.

The lack of powder was very serious. The Duke had been aware of this and had left orders to use it as sparingly as possible. Daun therefore decided to intensify mine warfare, more effective than cannon fire and, at the same time, less wasteful in the use of powder. The intricate establishment and organization of the galleries and passageways, which we have already discussed, extended from the main galleries which extended from each principal bastion of the citadel and, after the crescent, ran deep and in a straight line with a slight downward incline toward the countryside down to a depth of forty-five feet and beyond the last bastion. Here they ended in a cluster of mines. Parallel to these main galleries, referred to as "low" passages, there ran about twenty to twenty-four feet higher, starting from the moat, the "high" main galleries. These too were equipped with mine chambers and also were used for listening to enemy movements.

On July 8th the Piedmontese "heard" the French searching for the low main gallery under the bastion of Soccorso. Their location was plotted and they were allowed to proceed for another six days until, when it was calculated that they were about to penetrate into the gallery, Count Daun ordered the most advanced mine cluster to be exploded. With the explosion, an abyss opened under the French operating on the surface. Forty men were buried in less than a second.

On August 7th the French succeeded in penetrating two main galleries but the danger was soon removed by other mines. Underground battles began, which were among the most tragic recorded in history. In the blackness of the galleries men groped for each other, found each other, and killed each other, with a rage increased by fear. The ones first to light the fuse saw the enemy die like moles, and then had to flee wildly toward the exit so as not to die in turn themselves from the gases released by the explosion. Carbon monoxide gas

Facing page: *A wall gun, a typical siege weapon of the XVIII century (Turin, Pietro Micca Museum).* Below: *Detail of a large painting preserved at Turin at the Risorgimento Museum, illustrating one of the decisive moments of the battle for the liberation of Turin. In the rear can be seen the city washed by the Po (above and to the left) and by the Dora Riparia in its winding course. The routed French are fleeing towards its bridges and its banks in search of safety.*

The finding of the body of Pietro Micca, *an oil painting by Luigi Di Giovanni, in 1884, preserved in the Pietro Micca Museum of Turin, where is also preserved the miner's lantern from the XVIII century, reproduced* below *beside the saber donated by the Piedmontese Royal Artillery Corps in May 1849 to Pietro Micca, last descendent of the hero and honorary sergeant of artillery (Turin, National Museum of Artillery).*

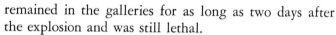

remained in the galleries for as long as two days after the explosion and was still lethal.

The galleries were filled with corpses. Convicts offered to go in and take them out in return for their liberty.

After the middle of August the French succeeded in establishing a battery of fourteen guns on the counter-escarpment of the moat, in front of the crescent of the Soccorso bastion, and began to bombard the walls of the escarpment in order to open breaches for the assault. On August 24th twelve of these guns sank into the ground as a result of four mine clusters which were exploded in perfect synchronization.

On August 27th a cluster of French counter mines exploded under the wall of the counterscarp of the Soccorso crescent. A short time after midnight the French appeared on the parapet in waves and were able to advance. At dawn they were thrown back into the moat by a counterattacck of a regiment of the Grenadier Guards, and there slaughtered by infiltrating artillery fire from the bastions. It was a scene of terrible carnage. Towards evening the French asked for a truce and permission to go down into the moat and gather their wounded who were crying for help. But Count Daun would not agree. The walls were breached and a surprise was still possible. He did not wish to take the risk. He ordered firewood to be thrown down into the moat. One thousand six hundred carts of brush and other inflammable material were dumped down over the dead and wounded, without pity. Then it was set on fire.

Towards midnight of August 29th, a French detachment of twenty men crossed the Soccorso moat and entered into the gallery which had its exit there and, overcoming the Piedmontese guard, proceeded to the ladder which brought them to the gallery referred to as the "low" main gallery. This gallery after only two hundred and twenty yards led to the citadel.

The ascent was guarded by some Grenadiers and, in addition, was mined. Two men were conducted into the gallery. One was called Pietro Micca, nicknamed "Passe-partout" (Slips-in-anywhere). When it was seen that the French were breaking into the high main gallery, the Piedmontese barred the gate to the passageway. While the French worked to open it, the Grenadiers fell back.

Micca ordered his companion to follow the Grenadiers and save himself. When his comrade seemed to hesitate, Micca shouted at him: "You are longer than a day without bread," and sped him on his way. He then regulated the length of the fuse so that the mine would explode at the very moment that the French were passing through the entrance. He lit the fuse and rushed toward the ladder. The blast hit him while he was turning into the low gallery and hurled him into the passage forty paces toward Turin. There he died from internal wounds and from the gas of the explosion. The comrade whom he had sent to safety was able to hear his last cries.

The following day, at dusk, while the battle was

going on, the Duke sent rocket signals from the Superga hill that Eugene had arrived and that together they were about to relieve the city from the terrible pressure of the enemy.

The French commanders once again found themselves with conflicting opinions. Duke Philippe II of Orléans, cousin of the king, having on that day arrived from Paris with fresh forces and now in command of operations, wished to raise the siege and to deploy the army for battle. His generals thought it would be better to stay where they were and to wait for the attack behind the fortified works. Louis XIV supported the generals.

Therefore, on September 7th, at the moment of the Austrian-Piedmontese attack, the French were dispersed along an extensive front. The right wing, under Orléans, broke under a charge of Piedmontese hussars and was forced to retreat. The left wing, anchored on the castle of Lucento, held out as long as possible and then fell back after destroying powder magazines and bridges. At that point twelve battalions issued from the city and attacked the French on their flanks and rear. For a while the struggle seemed favorable to the French but then Vittorio Amedeo launched his cavalry to the attack and the situation was definitely reversed.

The Battle of Turin *in a sketch for a painting of the same title, the work of Massimo d'Azeglio (Turin, Gallery of Modern Art). The battle would perhaps have had a different ending if the French generals had been in accord with the opinion of their chief, Philippe d'Orléans. When the Austrian-Piedmontese relief army approached he wished to raise the siege and to deploy his army for battle. But Louis XIV himself shared the opinion of his generals and for that reason the French awaited the attack behind their counterembankments. This dispersion of forces on an extremely long front had fatal results for the French.*

LILLE
(1708)

*Prince Eugene and
Marshal Bouflers
share a horsemeat steak*

The siege of Lille was the culminating point of the career of Marshal Louis François de Bouflers, portrayed here in a print from the Bertarelli Collection of Milan. Right: *The dress sword of Louis XIV (Paris, Museum of the Army) and, above, Eugene of Savoy, the great and knightly rival of Bouflers.*

On July 17, 1708, during the war of the Spanish Succession, the famous battle of Oudenarde was fought in the course of the campaign of Flanders. The forces opposed were the Austrian-Anglo-Dutch troops under the command of John Churchill, Duke of Marlborough, and Prince Eugene of Savoy, and the French of Louis XIV, led by Louis Joseph, Duke of Vendôme, and the Duke of Burgundy, heir to the throne of France. After winning a brilliant victory, the Allies considered bringing the war to French territory and aiming at Paris. Prince Eugene suggested that they should first obtain control of a stronghold which could serve as a base for future operations. The choice fell upon Lille, and the Prince himself was given charge of the undertaking.

The operations were not on a small scale: Lille had been formidably fortified by Vauban and was defended by the Marshal de Bouflers, the hero of Namur. He was now over eighty years old but extremely active, and he stood at the head of fifteen or sixteen thousand men. Prince Eugene perceived the need for haste, since the army of the Duke of Burgundy was on the move in the surrounding country. The Duke with his hundred thousand men could seriously endanger the siege operations.

On August 18th he began the investment of the city with fifty thousand Austrian and Imperial troops, one hundred and twenty cannon, forty-eight mortars, and a train of about three thousand wagons of munitions. The Duke of Marlborough entered the campaign with seventy thousand men to follow the movements of the French forces concentrated at Mons. In effect, the Duke of Burgundy established himself at Lille in order to attempt its liberation but was unwilling to confront the

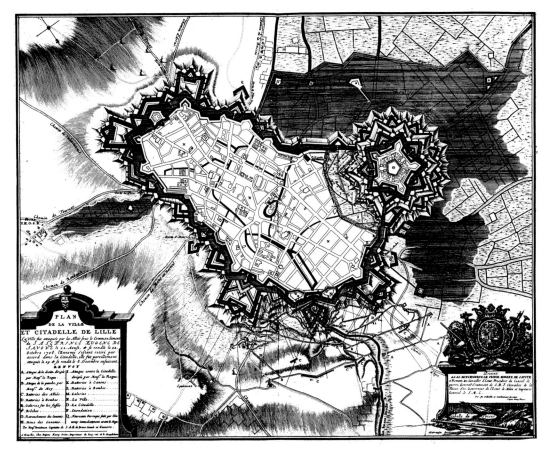

same troops which had defeated him at Oudenarde.

One of the problems facing Bouflers was the scarcity of powder for the cannon. A French officer, the Chevalier de Luxemburg, decided to replenish the supply by means of a daring plan. Choosing two thousand five hundred men from the cavalry, he had them put on Dutch insignia and carry on each horse two powder bags, and on a dark night brought the detachment through the Imperial lines. He had with him an officer who, when challenged by a Dutch sentry, was able to reply in perfect Flemish that the detachment came from the army of Marlborough. Even the officers in charge of the pickets were deceived by this Flemish speaking officer, and the convoy was able to pass. But one of its members in the rear of the column was heard to gave the command to close up in clear and recognizable French so that it was no longer possible to continue the deception. The Imperial troops opened fire in time to scatter the convoy, but they were unable to keep the first part of the column from entering the stronghold.

On September 20th, one month after the digging of the trenches, after a long artillery preparation, Prince Eugene ordered the attack. The attack column rushed through the breach but was driven back, and though twice renewed it achieved no result other than the loss of a great number of soldiers.

Placing himself now personally at the head of the assault column, the prince, sword in hand, led it once more to the attack. Hit by a musket ball in the head he collapsed, but suddenly he was once more on his feet, urging on his soldiers and leading them on to a fourth assault. At the end of the day the dead were so many that he made the request to Bouflers for a truce of two days to bury the dead. Bouflers refused; he feared that the operation would allow Austrian engineers to reconnoiter his positions, and he sent word to Eugene that he planned to bury them himself. On the following night he scattered the enemy from some trenches which he later filled in with some five thousand bodies.

Bouflers resisted the prince for still another month of combat characterized by chivalrous overtones. When he learned that a marksman of Lille had picked out Eugene and was preparing to kill him with a shot Bouflers threatened to imprison the man if he did so. But on October 24th the commander of the stronghold, worn out by the continual cannon bombardment, and by the tenacious and continuous attacks of the prince, gave up the city and continued resistance with the few troops remaining to him, about five thousand men. Eugene wrote to him in admiration: "Spare yourself and your brave garrison. I so esteem you that I promise in advance to accept all the conditions you may set."

But the old marshal, who wished to die rather than surrender, replied that there was no hurry. When he finally capitulated he did so at the express orders of Louis XIV. Prince Eugene received him with great cordiality. He then accepted an invitation from Bouflers to dine, on condition that he be served the same food that the citadel was able to offer its defenders. This is how it happened that Eugene of Savoy-Soussons, Lieutenant General of the Holy Roman Empire, and Louis François de Bouflers, Marshal of France, two of the greatest military captains of all time, came to share, like good comrades, a thin horsemeat steak.

PRAGUE (1757)

The grenadiers refuse extraordinary service

The Seven Years War developed in many successive campaigns between 1756 and 1763. The first campaign began on August 29, 1756, and witnessed the occupation of Saxony by Prussia under Frederick II, the Great.

While diplomacy hurled at Prussia the thunderbolts of Austria, Russia, France, Sweden, and Poland, leaving England as Prussia's only ally, Frederick began a second campaign in the spring of 1757. He employed his usual strategy: that of attacking the strongest enemy, beating him, and then turning back to the others. At the end of April the Prussian army began its march in four columns. These penetrated Bohemia in depth, defeated the Austrian garrisons, captured their plentiful supplies, and

Frederick Wilhelm von Seydlitz, founder of the Prussian heavy cavalry under Frederick the Great. He was, together with his cuirassiers, among the principal contestants in the battle of Kolin, which ended the siege of Prague (Cornwall-on-Hudson, New York, Todd Collection).

turned toward Prague, around which had gathered the first army to be beaten, that of Austria. This army was sixty-six thousand men strong and was under the command of Charles Alexander of Lorraine, brother-in-law of Maria Teresa of Austria.

On May 5th the Prussians probed the defenses of Prague and, finding them too strong, gave up the assault. During the night they crossed the Moldava River and on the following day they attacked the Austrians in the open field. This was one of the most bloody battles of the century. The Prussians lost fourteen thousand dead and wounded as well as four thousand prisoners.

On May 7th Frederick demanded the surrender of the Austrian forces who had sought refuge within the stronghold of Prague. The answer was an unequivocal refusal. Thereupon he completely surrounded the great city with his troops and placed his siege batteries certain to be able to capture it through artillery fire and by starvation.

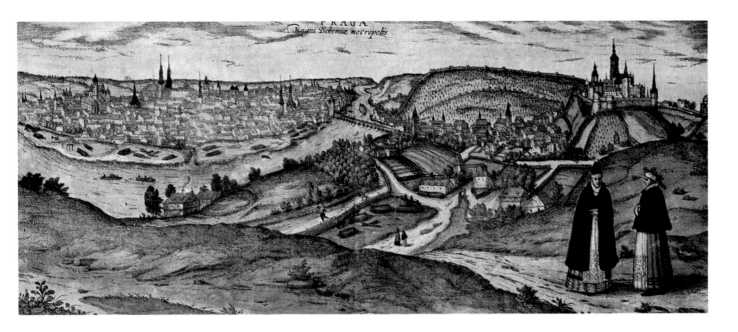

Any hesitant sortie on the part of the garrison was quickly frustrated. The Prussian incendiary bombs set vast fires within the different sections of Prague, while insufficient food supplies and increasing sickness began to be felt. The surrender seemed inevitable.

Meanwhile a strong Austrian force under the command of Marshal Leopold Joseph Maria, Count von Daun (son of the defender of Turin in 1706), was concentrated near Kolin and was joined by about sixteen thousand men who had not been able to find refuge in Prague. Thinking he could overcome these troops, King Frederick ordered General von Zieten to attack them with his hussars. When the desired result was not obtained, he was forced to send also the Duke von Beveren with a special corps. But von Daun, instead of accepting the challenge, retired slowly toward the Austrian frontier, continually picking up reinforcements along the way.

On June 13th, since he had not yet been able to resolve the situation, and since Duke von Beveren continued to vacillate, King Frederick, taking along many units from the forces which were then besieging Prague, marched on von Daun who, in the meantime, had collected enough forces to form a relief army and who had changed the direction of his march toward the besieged city with the intention of liberating it.

On June 17th the Prussians made contact with the enemy but on the following morning it was evident that the Austrians had once more disengaged. Frederick then marched on Kolin and from the inn called The Golden Sun was able to observe the Austrian deployment. He noted that the weak point in the battle order was on the right wing. Therefore, after having rested his soldiers, he set off to the attack at noon.

After five hours of massacre, with a third of his sixty thousand men lying on the battlefield, he retreated to Prague, lifted the siege, and retired to Bohemia.
During the battle when Frederick had attempted to inspire the grenadiers with his famous phrase: "Rogues, do you wish to live forever?" one of them was heard to reply: "For today's pay we have done enough."

A view of Prague shortly before the time of the siege described here. The city had previously had to endure another very severe one in 1741. Below: The famous mitered helmet of the Prussian grenadiers. This headpiece had no visor in order not to interfere with the typical action for which the soldier who wore it was trained, the hurling of hand grenades.

QUEBEC (1759)

"Do not weep, my dear. In a few moments I shall be happy."

During the Seven Years War the dramatic events taking place in Europe became involved with the colonial conflict going on between France and England, beginning with the great French victory in Minorca (April, 1756) and then turning favorable to the English in India and in North America.

On this latter front, England, then under the government of William Pitt, concentrated all its forces in the region of the St. Lawrence, with a view to the conquest of the immense territory of Canada.

At the end of July, 1758, the fortress of Louisbourgh, equipped with four hundred cannon, fell after a long siege. This fort guarded the entrance of the St. Lawrence from the Gulf of St. Lawrence. The next year a fleet of twenty ships, under the command of Admiral Charles Sanders, went up the river carrying as far as Quebec the nine thousand men who were to take it. They were led by one of the most unpleasant officers of the entire British army. He was thirty-two years old, tall and thin, pale, taciturn, and humorless. This was General James Wolfe, who concealed under a disagreeable exterior exceptional qualities of bravery and heroism.

On June 27th, 1759, English troops landed on the Ile d'Orléans, and still others on Pointe Levi, two positions on the St. Lawrence on the opposite side from the location of the city to be conquered, which was located in a strong natural position.

An attempted attack from the east, on the left bank, was carried out by a detachment under the command of General Townshend, which landed of July 31st. But the French, under the command of Marquis Louis de Montcalm, repulsed them, inflicting a loss on the English of five hundred men. On September 3rd Townshend abandoned the left bank and moved to the Ile d'Orléans. The Governor General of Canada, the Marquis de Vaudreuil-Cavagnal, sent word to Versailles not to worry, since Quebec was impregnable. Montcalm was less optimistic.

He avoided a pitched battle and forced the English into an inactivity which, accompanied by the torments of dysentery and mosquitoes, as well as ambushes by Indians in search of scalps, and the noisy quarrels of the prostitutes who followed the army, brought the nervous system of Wolfe and others of his command to the breaking point.

He decided to take the initiative and, on August 29th, called his staff together and proposed to try another attack from the east. His officers proposed, on the other hand, to go up the river and attack from the west. In any case it was necessary to hurry, before the autumn changed the river into a lake of ice. Wolfe accepted the second plan.

On the morning of September 7th, having left one thousand two hundred men at Pointe Levi as a reserve, he went up the St. Lawrence, against the current, with another three thousand six hundred. Towards evening he found a favorable place to disembark, many miles to the west of Quebec, and ordered a reconnaissance. When this was completed (it took several days) Wolfe ordered a landing at a location much closer to the city.

When this was going on, it was already past midnight on the night of September 12th. The river current was strong and the soldiers landed at a place more to the east than had been planned. An advance guard of volunteers found themselves confronted by a steep cliff which was nevertheless scaled without hindrance, under a driving rain. The first volleys were exchanged only when the English had reached the top. The few French members of the garrison who were

Above: *The death of General Wolfe in an old print (Milan, Bertarelli Collection). The thirty-two year old conqueror of Quebec had already been wounded twice during the decisive battle. The third wound, in the chest, was fatal. His adversary, the Marquis de Montcalm, commander of the French garrison, died on the same day of a single wound. The Governor General of Canada, the Marquis de Vaudreuil-Cavagnal, tried in vain to retake Quebec in the spring of 1760. But the French were abandoned by the local militia as well as by their Indian allies and the immense territory of Canada passed under English control.* On facing page: *A French sapper (Paris, Library of the Museum of the Army).*

stationed at that point retreated and, when dawn came, four thousand four hundred redcoats were to be seen deployed on the plain west of Quebec, called the Plains of Abraham, while the English cannon opened an inferno of fire over the city. Montcalm observed: "C'est sérieux" (This is serious) and essayed to repair the damage. But before his troops were deployed in line of battle it was nine o'clock. The rain had stopped and the sun was shining. The French fixed their bayonets and advanced, on a front more than half a mile long, deployed in a formation six ranks deep on the weakest points as well as some other sections of the long line. Five hundred and fifty yards away the English awaited them, drawn up in the same order. When the lines were about one hundred and seventy yards away from each other, the French opened fire. Many of the English fell. The rest remained immobile in their positions, without returning the fire. Nor did they fire when a second French volley opened

new holes in their ranks and when the enemy had reached a point about one hundred yards away. But when at a distance of fifty yards the French had broken ranks and were charging, the voice of Wolfe, who had already been wounded twice, was heard giving the order to fire, and then the voice of each regimental commander, one after the other, was heard repeating the order. The English were so well trained in collective fire that the six volleys seemed to be six cannonades. A moment later the fire was repeated, aiming into the smoke. When this cleared, Wolfe ordered the charge. But the battle, one of the shortest in history, was already decided. The French continued to resist in isolated groups, on a field covered with a thousand six hundred dead and wounded. Among the latter was Montcalm himself, his chest torn by an explosive bullet. The loss along the red lines was counted as six hundred and sixty dead and wounded. Wolfe, wounded for the third time, had barely time to order his men not to allow the French to retreat to the north. When a soldier begged him not to die he said: "Do not weep, my dear. In a few minutes I shall be happy." Then he died, closing his eyes on a spectacle of a victory that would be decisive to the destiny of the new continent.

The surviving French retreated to Quebec where, because of the number and strength of the fortifications, they would have been able to hold out forever. But the Marquis Vaudreuil-Cavagnal preferred to retire to Montreal and, on September 18th, the English were masters of the city.

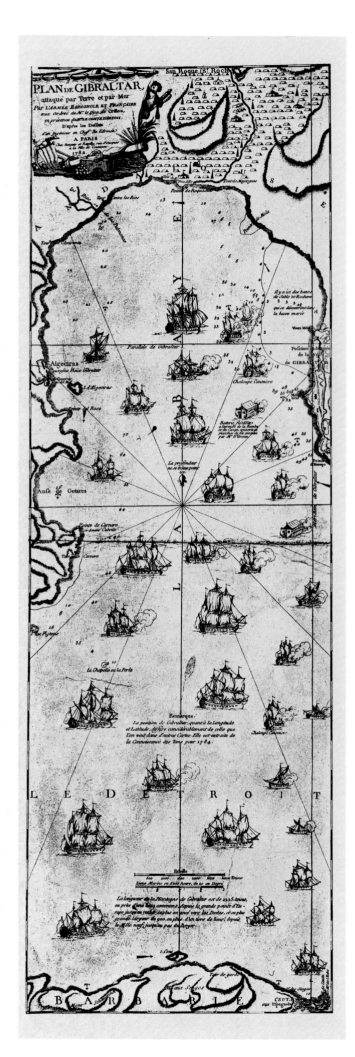

GIBRALTAR
(1779-1783)

*Two and a half million
sandbags do not get to the Rock*

In 1704, during the War of the Spanish Succession, the English seized control of Gibraltar, occupying the Rock (the Peñón, as the Spanish called it) which they have held ever since.

Spain never ceased considering the possibility of getting back the stronghold, and seized every occasion to make things difficult for the English garrison.

The most propitious of these occasions arose in 1779 during the revolt of the British colonies, supported and aided by France. In the early months of this same year, Spain offered her services as mediator and did what she could to settle the differences separating the belligerents. But, when the good offices of Spain were refused, King Carlos III allied himself with France, principally with a view of using her aid to regain possession of Gibraltar.

The blockade by sea and the siege of the English base from the land side were begun at the end of July 1779 and were still continuing on January 16, 1780, when a strong British naval squadron under the command of Baron George Brydges Rodney met a rather small Spanish fleet under the command of Don Juan de Langara near Cape Saint Vincent. The Spanish fleet, forced into combat, was completely defeated. Don Juan de Langara lost the greater part of his ships, and he himself fell prisoner to Rodney. This naval encounter destroyed the effect of the long siege which had been laid against Gibraltar since the stronghold was now abundantly furnished with food and ammunition by sea, despite the still very efficient blockade by land.

Carlos III established diplomatic negotiations with the British government and, with a view to making them more feasible, lifted the blockade of Gibraltar. But, during the delays in the course of negotiations, the situation again changed: some successful Spanish naval operations and the improvement of relations with France gave a new prestige to the Spanish monarchy. And France, fearing a move for a separate peace on the part of their ally, was ready to give all military aid possible for the reconquest of Gibraltar. Therefore, in August

Left and on facing page: *Two scenes of the siege of Gibraltar — part of a single drawing made in 1782 by an "ingénieur en chef" (chief engineer) of the French army. The action of the floating batteries deployed along the east coast of the peninsula is particularly impressive. In reality, however, the English batteries rapidly silenced them with their counterfire.*

of 1781, Spain again demanded restitution of the fortress. Following new and unsuccessful diplomatic moves, siege was again laid to Gilbratar in 1782.

The French Duke de Mahon, Louis Crillon, who, on February 15th of that year had brilliantly taken Minorca from the English while in the service of Spain, accepted the command of the undertaking from Carlos III. He gathered together at the site of the projected siege an army of about forty thousand men and directed various approach works, the most famous of which was accomplished during a single night, that of August 14th, 1782. It concerned the employment of about two and a half million sandbags and the labor of ten thousand men for the erection of an immense bastion, behind which the besiegers took up their positions.

Meanwhile, on the sea, the so-called "floating batteries" were being prepared. These were the idea of the French engineer D'Arzon: they were, in effect, pontoons protected by a covering of wood and wet sand on their sides and covered by a thick slab of lead, especially angled so as to diminish the effect of enemy fire. They were armed, altogether, by two hundred and twenty cannon and were considered practically invulnerable. Their success appeared so certain that many senior officers from the French and Spanish forces gathered near the field of operations to witness the general attack and the capture of the Peñón.

On September 9th the bombardment and land attack began. On the 13th came the attack from the sea. Four hundred cannon stormed the Rock; five thousand men attacked the town. But the defenders were able to return blow for blow and the troops of the garrison held on firmly to their positions. On the same night of September 13th many of the "floating batteries," hit by precise enemy fire, caught fire and were destroyed. Others were blown up by the Spaniards, to prevent them from falling into enemy hands. In winning their victory, the English were greatly helped by their sudden artillery attack and the use of *boulets rouges* ("red cannon balls"), the precursors of modern incendiary projectiles. It was, however, only a partial victory. Gibraltar remained cut off from supplies and ammunition and, if it were not possible to supply it within the shortest possible time, surrender would be inevitable.

The surrender, however, never took place. On October 10th, 1782, Admiral Richard Howe arrived from England with a squadron of thirty-three ships of the line and a convoy of reinforcements and munitions. He found himself faced by a French-Spanish squadron under the command of Admiral Córdoba, superior in equipment and in the number of ships. However, by expert seamanship, Admiral Howe was able to seize a favorable moment, during which the opposing fleet had been carried some distance off by the wind, to bring the convoy within the port of Gibraltar as if by magic. The siege continued, since the two contestants each wished to have something to say at the peace conference. This came one year later, on September 3rd, 1783, and, in effect, it left things just as they were. El Peñón remained the Rock.

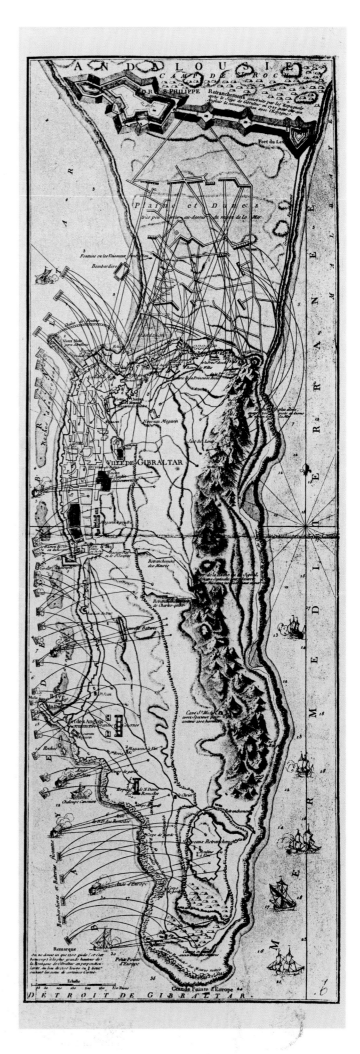

YORKTOWN (1781)

The great eve of American independence

The War of American Independence, which lasted from 1775 to 1783, witnessed its last great encounter at the siege of Yorktown.

Sir Henry Clinton, the successor of William Howe since 1778 as commander in chief of the British forces, sent orders from his general headquarters at New York to Lord Charles Cornwallis, the British leader at the dubious victory of Guilford Courthouse (March 15th,

George Washington and Lafayette at the siege of Yorktown, in a painting by Van Blarenberghe (Versailles Museum). The conquest of the town by the "rebels" against the British crown marked the beginning of the decline of British supremacy in North America. Among the prisoners who fell into the hands of the Franco-American forces was Count August Neithardt von Gneisenau, future chief of staff of the Prussian army, then twenty-one years old.

1781), for him to occupy a strong and easily defended position on the coast, to which the British fleet could have access. Lord Cornwallis, who had been in command of the forces in South Carolina since 1780, marched along the York peninsula and occupied Yorktown in August, 1781. Yorktown was suitable for the fleet to land safely.

The French general, Marie Joseph Paul Yves Roch du Motier, Marquis de Lafayette, who, with his army, had followed the movements of the English, indicated to General George Washington that Cornwallis could be trapped in Yorktown. Washington, with a force of more than six thousand men (two thirds of which were French) set his troops in motion on August 19th, 1781, from his general headquarters on the Hudson and, by forced marches, reached Chesapeake Bay on September 14th.

Meanwhile, on August 31st, Count Françoise de Grasse, in command of a French fleet of twenty-four ships

of the line, had dropped anchor in the waters of the York River. He debarked four thousand infantry, who completed the encirclement of Cornwallis' forces. On September 5th, the British naval squadron, under the command of Rear Admiral Thomas Graves, who had received faulty intelligence reports concerning the French fleet, appeared in Chesapeake Bay. He suffered a severe defeat and was forced to sail north toward New York. This was a harsh blow for Cornwallis, who now found that he was obliged to give up the prospect, on which he had so much relied, of being supplied by sea. And worse was to come. Another French flotilla appeared, under the command of Count De Barras consisting of ten ships loaded with matériel and siege cannon escorted by eight ships of the line.

The meeting of Washington with Lafayette brought the number of men available to besiege Yorktown to about sixteen thousand. This was at the end of September 1781. These troops were assigned to three divisions, under the respective commands of Thomas Nelson, Lafayette, and Baron von Steuben. The artillery of ninety-two cannon was assigned to General Henry Knox.

The besieged forces numbered more than seven thousand five hundred and had sixty-five cannon, mostly light-caliber guns, the famous eighteen-pound cochorns. Small detached units garrisoned the Gloucester advance post on the other bank of the river. On September 28th the Allies began their advance toward the town. The swampy ground, traversed by many streams, made artillery transport particularly difficult. On October 1st it was observed that the British had abandoned their first outer defense line and were drawing back, shortening their front. On October 6th, the Franco-American forces opened their first parallel and on the 9th they began bombarding. It is reported that Washington in person prepared the fuse for the first shot.

On October 13th the Americans, striking from a second parallel, took the outer British defense works by assault. Cornwallis held out in hope of help or of finding means of evacuating his position. But the only escape was by sea and this was blocked by French warships.

On the night of October 14th one French and one American assault unit, under the command of Alexander Hamilton, captured two redoubts at bayonet point. At dawn on October 15th the English made a sortie with three hundred and fifty men. The results were meager; several cannon were silenced, but were soon put back into action by the Americans. Cornwallis then played his last card. On the night of October 16th, abandoning the sick and the wounded, and leaving war materials and all supplies, he attempted to flee across the river by boat. A violent storm, however, ruined his plan, wrecking the boats and claiming many victims among the crews.

On October 17th Cornwallis offered to surrender. Washington wished to repay an insult to an American garrison which, captured in Charleston, was not given the honors of war. He required that the English leave Yorktown with folded banners to the sound of an English march called "The World Turned Upside Down."

An officer of the Corps des Ingénieurs Géographes Militaires *(Corps of Geographic Military Engineers) of the French Army, often employed in overseas operations (Paris, Library of the Museum of the Army). Below: A French battery in front of Yorktown (Rome, Central Military Library). The French contribution to the American struggle for independence was considerable, either because of the hostility of France against England, her great rival in colonial expansion, or because the insurgents were fighting for the principles advanced by French philosophers, such as Montesquieu and Rousseau. French intervention, first left to volunteers like Lafayette, became official after Saratoga (December 1777).*

TOULON (1793)

Captain Bonaparte wins his general's epaulets

Victorious military events celebrated the birth of the Republic in France in 1792. When the monarchy fell on August 10th with the assault on the Tuileries led by Danton, the Assembly followed the wishes of the people, suspending the king from his functions and establishing elections by the Convention. From that moment the events of the revolution were entwined with the events of war against foreign powers, which Austria and Prussia waged against France until April 20. The French were beaten at Longwy (August 27th) and at Verdun (September 2nd), and the Austro-Prussian forces, under the command of Karl Wilhelm Ferdinand, Duke of Brunswick, marched on Paris. But on September 20th, at Valmy, the famous "miracle" took place under Generals Charles Dumouriez and François Kellerman. This was what gave to revolutionary France a realization of her own military possibilities. France took the offensive, won a victory over the Austrians at Jemappes on November 6th and invaded the Netherlands. This was an attempt to carry out the revolutionary program: "Wage war on the kings to liberate the people." The kings, however, accepted the challenge and, while the Con-

vention, on September 21, 1792, was officially proclaiming the Republic, England, Holland, Spain, Sardinia, Naples, the Papal States, and Russia took the field at the side of Austria and Prussia. This was the so-called First Coalition. Angered by the execution of Louis XVI (January 21, 1793) and by the excesses of revolutionary extremism, at this time approaching the unbridled violence of "la terreur" (the terror), the kings attacked France again, reconquering the Netherlands with the battle of Neerwinden (March 18, 1793), and prepared to invade the national territory of France. The foreign enemies of the revolution were aided by attacks from internal enemies. Entire provinces such as Vendée, Brittany, Anjou, and Lower Normandy rebelled against the government of Paris. In the south, Provence, which had supported with enthusiasm the project of a constitutional reform, joined the anti-Jacobin movement against the execution of the king. Two counterrevolutionary centers arose in Marseille and Toulon, where the Jacobins were arrested or summarily condemned and where the counterrevolution had won the support of part of the armed forces.

When Paris mobilized two expeditionary corps to reestablish republican rule in the south, Marseille sent a request for aid to Viscount Samuel Hood, Commanding Admiral of the British fleet in the Mediterranean. He replied that he would intervene under three conditions: that his aid would be temporary; that a naval squadron composed of French émigrés would accompany the English, and that the purpose of the expedition would be the reestablishment of constitutional monarchy in France. However, he would land at Toulon, which he considered more adaptable as a base of operations.

The city of Toulon was located on an inlet called the Petite Baie (Small Bay), which was across a strait more than half a mile wide and about seventy-five feet deep. This communicated with the roadstead called the Grande Baie (Great Bay), which opened into the Mediterranean. Two promontories marked the limits of the smaller bay. The western limit, called the Aiguillette, with its attendant fortifications, dominated, for all practical purposes, the port of Toulon. In fact, the distance from its batteries to the deepest seaway of the straits, through which the larger vessels had to pass, was about three hundred yards. For this reason the main Republican efforts were aimed at the Aiguillette.

Meanwhile, on August 28th, 1793, the British and Royal French fleets dropped anchor at the Toulon roadstead and landed twenty thousand soldiers. Samuel Hood assumed supreme command of the sector whose outer defense line extended from the Ollioules straits to the island of Hyères.

In preparation for the attack, which would put in the hands of the Coalition an excellent base from which to invade southern France, Paris ordered General Carteaux (sometimes written Cartaux), commander in chief of the Republican garrison forces of Nice and Marseille, to expel the English from Toulon. Carteaux, who had twelve thousand men in his command, left four thousand in Marseille and with the rest, on September 8th, attacked Ollioules and captured it.

Meanwhile, General Brunet, who was then at Nice in command of the Army of Italy, had sent another army corps of about six thousand men to retake the Hyères batteries, to the east of Toulon. In this way the city would be attacked from two directions.

On September 1st, Dammartin, a commander of artillery in Carteaux's army, was put out of action, having been wounded in the Ollioules straits. It was suggested by Cristoforo Saliceti, Corsican deputy to the Convention, that his place be filled by Napoleon Bonaparte, then twenty-four years old, an artillery captain in the army of Italy. The latter, returning to Nice from a trip to Marseille, where he had visited his family, joined Carteaux's general headquarters on September 12th and immediately went to work, characterized by an intense activity markedly in contrast with Carteaux's own ineptitude. Fortunately the army artillery was commanded by Brigadier General Teil who, recognizing Napoleon's genius, entrusted to him the artillery command of one of the army's three divisions.

Carteaux's cannon were positioned near Montauban Castle in a position from which it was impossible to reach the British vessels anchored in the bay. For this reason Bonaparte, on the night of September 17th, advanced a battery of five pieces, named "la Montagne" (the Mountain), one thousand seven hundred yards to the heights of St. Laurent (today Piédardan), placing under his own fire some of the ships which were in the roadstead. However, this battery was constantly bombarded by the fire of the English cannon from the fort of Malbosquet.

On the night of September 19th, from the heights of Brégaillon, Bonaparte positioned a new battery of guns, eight in number, called the Sans Culottes. The fire of this battery obliged Admiral Samuel Hood to retire his own ships from the small bay, some days later, and to have them seek shelter in front of the promontory Aiguillette. On October 14th the English tried to capture

On December 18th, 1793, Napoleon, already a colonel (he will be a general within four days) observes the English rout as they endeavor to reach the ships which will take them back to England. The hundred and ten days of siege are over.

the two batteries but were repulsed and counterattacked by Bonaparte and his men.

On October 21st Bonaparte positioned a third battery of nine pieces, this one called the "Convention," on the Arene hill in order to bombard Fort Malbosquet, which was causing considerable trouble to the besiegers.

Meanwhile, the British were constructing strong fortifications at Fort Mulgrave, which barred access by land to the Aiguillette, strengthening it with forty-four heavy caliber pieces and garrisoning it with their best troops. They referred to it as "Little Gibraltar" and a British officer, by way of emphasizing its invulnerability, declared that if it were ever occupied by the French he himself would become a Jacobin. This was the position that Bonaparte, holding it to be the key to the entire system of fortifications, considered indispensable to take in order to capture Toulon.

On October 23rd, a former Savoyard doctor, Doppet, replaced Carteaux, but the situation did not improve. On November 15th he ordered an assault on Fort Mulgrave, although Bonaparte had warned against it, considering the operation to be premature. The great Corsican nevertheless took part in the action and received his first

wound, in the head. While he and his troops were about to penetrate the fort, Doppet sounded retreat, after seeing one of his adjutants fall by his side. It was reported that Napoleon exclaimed: "The fool that ordered this retreat has lost us Toulon!" The soldiers, for their part, demanded "degradation" of the "damned doctor." On November 20th Doppet was replaced by Jean-François Coquille du Gommier, better known as Dugommier, and from that moment on the real siege operations got under way.

The English, considering the battery positioned by Bonaparte on the heights of Arene to be very dangerous for the Malbosquet fort, decided to surprise and capture it. At dawn of the 30th, a column of about seven thousand British troops, under the command of General O'Hara, the British governor of Toulon, left the city and marched on the battery. An early success favored the attackers but a series of counterattacks, led by Bonaparte and Dugommier in person, prevented the recapture of the lost position and resulted in the wounding and capture of General O'Hara.

A short time after the arrival of Dugommier a parallel was opened to Fort Mulgrave, concealed by an olive grove, and three batteries were installed. But as soon as the position was discovered, the enemy commenced a furious and continuous bombardment of the position with terrifying effects on the French. Bonaparte then ordered Sergeant Junot, an excellent calligrapher, to write in big letters, on a placard: "Battery of the Men without Fear" and to put it well in view facing the gabions that protected the guns. From that moment on the artillerists competed with each other to show who was the more courageous and, following the lead of their commander, who, standing on the parapets, directed the fire, opened a bombardment on the 14th and did not interrupt it until an hour after midnight on the 16th, when the infantry moved to the attack. At three in the morning of December 17th, Fort Mulgrave fell into French hands. The loss of this "Little Gibraltar" imperiled the entire outer defense system of Toulon. This forced the British to abandon the Aiguillette and Bonaparte promised his "Fearless Ones": "Tomorrow or the day after we shall eat our rations in Toulon."

On the day of the 18th, French grenadiers occupied the outer forts of Saint-Antoine, Artigues, Faron, and Malbosquet. The English held the fort of La Malgue to the end, as it was necessary to protect their retreat, now inevitable. But before abandoning the stronghold, Admiral Sydney Smith caused the general storehouses to be set on fire, as well as the arsenal and the shipyards, in which there were nine high-seas vessels and four frigates.

On the same day, December 18th, the Coalition and the French Royalist Troops of Toulon evacuated the city and on the 19th Colonel Cervoni, with a small advance guard, entered Toulon. The siege was over.

It has long been considered that the solution to the problem of the Aiguillette and, therefore, Toulon, was exclusively the work of Napoleon. But Dugommier was an intelligent man and certainly guessed that the key to the siege was the point west of the Small Bay. If it is true that Bonaparte, pointing it out to his artillerists, used to say: "Toulon is there" it is also true that Dugommier wrote in his report: "Whoever was familiar with Toulon knew that its weak point was the Aiguillette promontory. At the council of war held at Ollioules its capture was decided upon."

Many years later, at St. Helena, Napoleon would say to Bertrand: "The conquest of Toulon was owed to Dugommier." For Napoleon it was the beginning of his ascent. When he appeared at Ollioules, on September 12th, 1793, he was, as we have noted, but a captain. On the 29th he became an acting major (chef de bataillon) and was confirmed as such on October 19th. On the 27th of the same month he became a brevet colonel (adjutant-général chef de brigade) and this was confirmed on December 1st. On December 22nd, also on a provisionary basis, he was promoted to brigadier general and on January 7th, 1794, this rank too became definite. On that day he was given command of the artillery of the Army of the Var, already called the Army of Italy. The eagle had begun his flight.

The British and the Toulon Royalists leave the city after the capture of the Aiguillette by the Republicans had forced the city to surrender. Flames are rising from the arsenal and from the French ships, which Admiral Sydney Smith had set on fire. A glorious relic is also burning, the seventy-four gun vessel Le Heros, *flagship of Pierre-André de Suffren de Saint-Tropez, who, ten years previously, had beaten the British in five consecutive battles in Indian waters (1782-1783).*

GENOA (1800)

André Masséna refuses to capitulate but surrenders by "agreement"

Right: *A view of Genoa under siege with British warships blockading the port. From the land, the batteries at the foot of the Lighthouse can be seen in action and, at the extreme right, those of the "Quarry" and the "Witch" (Genoa-Pegli, Civic Naval Museum).* Below: *André Masséna directing the defense of the Palazzo Doria, present headquarters of the Bank of Rome, on the Piazza De Ferrari. This is an illustration from the already mentioned* History of Napoleon *by de Norvins, who dedicates a great deal of space to the siege of Genoa. After having labelled it "one of the greatest deeds of arms in history," he continues: "Masséna... will eternally live in the memory of posterity."*

On October 9th, 1799, Napoleon, who had left the Army of Egypt to Kléber, landed at Fréjus. A month later he carried out the *coup d'état* of the 18th of Brumaire which gave him control of France. The four year period of the Consulate was beginning, the brightest years in the whole era of Napoleon. Meanwhile, however, dark clouds were descending over France.

At the end of 1798, England had organized the formation of a Second Coalition against France, and it had been joined by Austria, Naples, Russia, and Turkey (which had already entered the field in Egypt and Syria). In September 1799, General André Masséna, victor in the Battle of Zurich, referred to as the "new Valmy," revived the fortunes of France, which had then reached a low point, and was able to rush to the defense of Genoa, the last foothold in Italy remaining to France after a series of defeats suffered at the hands of the Russians of Field Marshal Alexander Suvorov and the Austrians under General Baron Michael von Melas.

Savoy too was included in the area to be defended so as to maintain open lines of communication along the shore line to France.

The city of Genoa possessed a double line of walls: an inner wall which enclosed almost the whole city and an outer wall which ran along the hills which crowned it to the north. The latter wall was equipped with various forts and batteries.

The defenses against attack from the sea were no less effective, with batteries at the Lighthouse, the Old Jetty and the New Jetty, besides those called "the

Quarry" and "the Witch." In order to prevent surprises and attacks against the port, light and heavy gunboats were arrayed outside the port.

Toward the end of '99, perhaps in the belief that the city would not have to suffer a siege, no food supplies against such an eventuality, especially grain and flour, were stored within the city. These, in effect, were prepared in the ports of Toulon and Marseille and there would be no way of getting them to Genoa. In the days before the end of the year, in fact, the populace was more concerned with amusements and, in particular, country festivals. One of these took place in October at Campi, within the villa of the imperial "citizen," the ex-prince of Sant'Angelo de Lombardy, Ugo Foscolo, now Lieutenant of the Cisalpine Hussars, who had come to Genoa at the end of July with the rear guard of General Macdonald.

The governor of Liguria cherished the illusion of increasing his territory at the expense of Piedmont, once the storm was over, and the French consul Belleville maneuvered him with fine diplomatic art. A conspiracy of Pasquale Adorno, involving noble émigrés and inhabitants of the city, further complicated the issues. Adorno, who usually met with the leaders of the conspiracy at the Osteria of Marc'Antonio Solari, outside of the gate of San Tomaso, proposed to occupy the Ducal Palace, eliminate the leaders of the police, get rid of a certain number of already designated persons, and open the gates to the Austrians. Discovery of the plot necessitated repressive measures against the conspirators and strict police decrees. On December 7th, following a proposal by Emanuele Montebruno (perhaps under advice of Miollis, the French commander, and of the already mentioned Belleville) the legislators abolished the Directory, suspended the counsellors, and nominated a Commission of Government with legislative and administrative powers. This is how the body of the "Men of November" was formed. They then proceeded to name General Marbot commander of the forces of Liguria. Meanwhile the food situation was getting worse: it was down to two ounces of bread daily per person.

This was how affairs stood when Napoleon appointed André Masséna commander in chief of the Army of Italy. Masséna arrived at Genoa on February 9th, 1800, several days after the arrival of General De Giovanni, his adjutant. Masséna assumed command on the 10th and established his general headquarters in the piazza San Domenico (now called De Ferrari) at the Palazzo Doria. On the day of the 12th he visited the Ducal Palace on a visit to the Commission of Government where he cut short all speeches of welcome with a few short and brusque words. He then visited the fortifications and advanced forts and divided his forces (about fifteen thousand men) into garrisons covering the valleys which led to Tuscany, Emilia, Lombardy, and the Piedmont. He strengthened all these positions and particularly the stronghold of Gavi, the impregnable bastion close at hand. Finally, since the scarcity of grain was beginning to cause some agitation, and since it was impossible always to distribute to the citizens the "two ounces for each one," Masséna, in agreement with the Commission of Government, established at various points of the city centers for the preparation and distribution of "good and nutritious soup" at a low price.

Meanwhile the Austrians were on the move and were able to get help from the citizens of Fontanabuona who caused so much trouble to the forces of Masséna that they became known as "the new Vendéens."

After some unimportant skirmishes, the enemy attacked in three columns, and despite a determined resistance, was able to reach Prato di Bisagno. To the west, General Melas, with twenty-five thousand men, attacked the defenses toward Savona, besieged the city, vanquished Sassello and drove the French to Varazze.

Masséna counterattacked with an action that gave him two thousand five hundred prisoners, among whom was the Baron d'Aspre and his general staff. Continuing their advance the French reconquered Borgo Fornari, Casella and Savignone.

Meanwhile, at Voltri, a corps of five thousand French established themselves later to march on Sassello, while the Austrians arrived at Acqua Santa, having vanquished Capanne di Murcarolo.

On April 9th Masséna, after having left the city in the care of the National Guard, who established guard patrols on its walls, left for the east to make contact with the forces that were besieged in Savona. After prodigies of bravery, the French reached Albissola but, being outnumbered by the enemy and lacking reinforcements, they were forced to retire. On the 17th, while Masséna was returning to Genoa, they established their lines at Voltri.

From this moment the daily bread ration was reduced to only one ounce per person. And even to obtain this, it was necessary to spend hours in line at the food shops designated for this distribution of bread.

The French, under the pressure of the Austro-Russians, retired to a point in front of the Sturla to the east and to Palmetta in the Polcevera valley in the west.

Toward the end of April, General Marbot died from an infectious disease. The Commission of Health, in an effort to face the possibility of an epidemic, which was already giving signs of breaking out, evacuated the hospitals and proposed to prohibit the burying of the dead in churches (the first beginning of the building of cemetaries outside the cities).

The lack of all kinds of foodstuffs continued to be felt, notwithstanding the skill and bravery of the corsairs who were engaged in food running and who, flaunting the British blockade, were able to bring in some supplies of grain. The most famous among these sea dogs was Captain Giuseppe Bavastro, a native of Sampierdarena and a former playmate of Masséna in Nice, where he had moved as a boy. They met in Genoa during the siege and Bavastro performed prodigies of bravery. One night he was taking General Oudinot through the blockade, bearing a message from Masséna to Soult, who was cut off at Finale Ligure. On his way back, still during the night, the boat was seen by the enemy and forced to proceed against the wind, on a stormy sea, in utter darkness. Rather than fall prisoner, Bavastro turned toward Cornigliano and sailed the craft to the reef where it broke up and sank. Then, with Oudinot and the crew, he escaped by swimming.

He performed another act of daring on board an old galley, called the *Prima* and equipped by him with a hundred prisoners at the oars and fifty fusiliers. With this force he dared to attack the British corvettes which were bombarding Genoa. This time too he had to escape by swimming.

At the end of April the enemy launched a general assault and succeeded in carrying different important positions to the east and also endangering Fort Diamante, a pillar of the defense positions. Masséna organized a counterattack to the west then, at night, transferred his forces to the east and recaptured the lost positions by bayonet charges.

On May 2nd Ugo Foscolo was wounded at Due Fratelli as well as Ceroni and Gasparinetti, both officers of the Cisalpine regiment. General Giuseppe Fantuzzi met his death at the same time.

On March 8th the English gunboats bombarded at night the town of Sampierdarena, then a summer resort, and on the 9th, again at night, they carried on the same action against Albara.

A general of a division of the French army and his aide-de-camp in uniforms reconstructed by Philippoteaux (Paris, Museum of the Army).

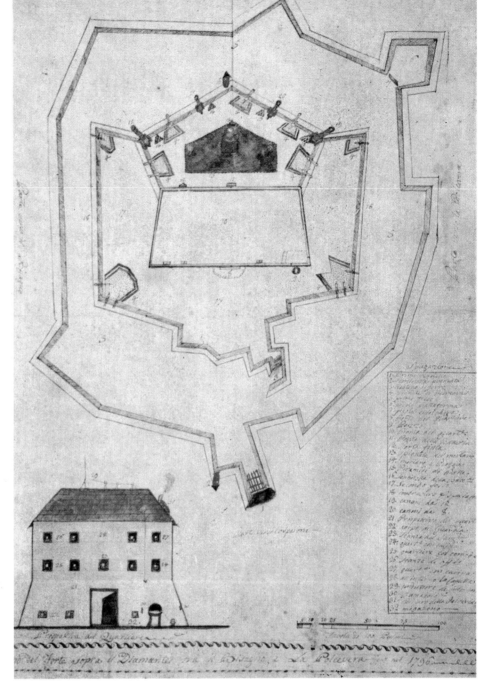

The day of the 10th saw Masséna lead the last action worthy of note. He made a frontal attack on Mount Fasce, in order to give time for a column to go up the valley of the Bisagno and to take the besiegers from the rear. With this action the defenders were able to penetrate as far as Nervi, permitting the besieged to renew in some measure their food supply.

On May 14th, with the courage of desperation, the military deputation declared to Masséna that they could no longer answer for popular support nor for public tranquility and requested the beginning of negotiations for a capitulation. When he was about to begin negotiations, however, a message from the first consul, Napoleon Bonaparte, arrived which required that resistance be prolonged to the last days of the month, since he, Bonaparte, planned to come to the relief of the city.

The Genoese were reduced to eating cats, dogs, rats, and even spiders. The blood of the animals was carefully collected, according to the historian Carlo Varese, "to be mixed with honey forming various little cakes considered excellent."

The Austrian prisoners, kept in the Customs building on the docks, first ate their shoes, and then tried to eat each other. Only the intervention of the sentries kept cases of cannibalism from appearing.

On June 2nd Masséna, beseeched on all sides for an end to suffering, finally proceeded with surrender negotiations. The Austrians, who feared the eventual arrival of Napoleon, granted conditions that were not too severe. They even gave up their demand for the arrest of Masséna himself.

On June 4th, at nine o'clock, the "agreement" of surrender was signed at Cornigliano. Masséna did not wish that the document be called a "capitulation" because, he said: "I never surrender." The Austrians accepted even this. "Your defense," they declared, "has been too heroic for us to deny you anything."

SARAGOSSA (1808-1809)

The Virgin of the Fount does not want to be French

After the treaty of Tilsit (July 1807) which put France and Russia together in an equivocal and uneasy joint control over Europe, Napoleon activated his gigantic plan concerning the so-called "continental blockade." This plan was to have the effect of vanquishing England economically, preventing her from acquiring grain in Europe and from exporting to the continent the products of her own industry and of her colonies.

An essential condition for such a blockade was the

Augustina Zaragoza, called Augustina de Aragón, according to a painting preserved at the Lazaro Galdiano Museum, in Madrid. This heroine of the first siege of Saragossa was seen, wearing her decorations, by Lord Byron on a visit to the Prado of Seville when the war was over. The poet mentions her enthusiastically in Childe Harold's Pilgrimage, *where he called her "The Maid of Saragoza."*

creation of an uninterrupted coastal blockade. To this end, Napoleon took steps to involve in this blockade, whether or not they wanted to be involved, all the nations of Europe. Whenever it was necessary to obtain their cooperation, he used force. This was the case with Portugal, invaded by the French in 1807; with Pius VII, dethroned and imprisoned in 1808 and 1809; with Spain, where King Ferdinand VII was replaced by Joseph Bonaparte, already King of Naples, on whose throne he then put Joachim Murat (1808).

The first violent reaction against the continental blockade came from Spain. It was a national reaction, and the French found it necessary not only to fight against an army, but against an entire people. The true sieges suffered by Saragossa in 1808 and 1809 furnish a striking demonstration of this phenomenon.

Saragossa, chief city of Aragon, lies on the Ebro, about two hundred miles northeast of Madrid. At that time it contained about sixty thousand inhabitants and it lacked defense works up to the standards of the era. The garrison was under the command of don José Rebolledo Palafox y Melzi, then twenty-eight years old and an officer of the Spanish army.

The insurrection of Madrid on May 2nd had created a state of ferment throughout Aragon which was ready to explode in open rebellion against the French, Thereupon the two divisions charged with the maintenance of order within the territories found themselves faced with a rebellious nation, swarming with insurgent bands and resolved to fight to the very end.

One of the divisions was under the command of General François Joseph Lefèbvre-Desnouettes, Duke of Danzig. He arrived in Saragossa on June 25, 1808, and, on the 28th, he captured Mount Torrero, one of the key positions of the city's outer defense. On June 29th General Verdier arrived with the other division. He was assigned the overall command of operations.

On June 30th the city was shaken by a tremendous explosion. A powder warehouse had exploded, destroying an entire street. While the inhabitants were attempting to rescue the victims of the disaster, the French subjected the city to a violent artillery bombardment and, at the same time, launched an infantry attack against the Portillo battery which, however, was repulsed with much bloodshed. In these circumstances Augustina Zaragoza made her appearance on the scene. She was popularly known as Augustina de Aragón, a young woman of the district which Byron would immortalize in *Childe Harold* (I, 54-56). She was ordered to carry food to a gun crew (one of whom, according to Byron, was her lover).

This XIX century Spanish print, by the Barcelona lithographer Hijo de Paluzie, numbered 367 of a series of pictures like the Epinal prints, represents the French assault of the Portillo battery (June 30th, 1808), and the intervention of the heroic Augustina de Aragón taking the place of the wounded member of the gun crew and firing on the French. On the wall, can be read: "The Virgen del Pilar says that she does not wish to be French and that she wants to be the Captain of the troops of Aragón."

Augustina arrived at a crucial moment of the struggle and she is reported to have taken the place of a fallen artillerist and to have fired a cannon herself, jumping up by the cannon and saying that she would not leave it while she was still alive. At another gate, an eleven-year-old boy, having received a banner from the hands of a wounded standard bearer, took it and waved it while invoking the help of the Virgin of the Fount, rousing the troops and citizens to new heights of valor. On all sides the resistance of the citizens was strong enough to repel the French, who had succeeded in penetrating within the city. On that day the French appeared to have lost two thousand men, six standards and six cannon.

On receiving reinforcements, Verdier emplaced new batteries and, on August 1st, resumed bombardment. The bombardment attained a terrible intensity on the 3rd, striking, among other points, a hospital. Since there were no victims in the latter instance, although the building itself was ruined, the news was spread that this was another miracle of the Virgin of the Fount, a proof of her protection which increased the patriotic and religious fanaticism of the Saragossans.

On August 4th, in the vicinity of the Carmen and Santa-Engracia gates, the French batteries began to fire in order to make a breach. They succeeded in making one in front of their line of fire and in killing all the artillerists of the Spanish batteries who were in position at these points. At ten o'clock in the morning three thousand French left their trenches for a general attack through the breaches and one hour later, they began to advance within the city from three different points in spite of desperate resistance. When they arrived at the plaza de la Misericordia they found themselves faced by a small group of Spaniards intent on forming a battery with some cannons taken from the lost positions. They were invited to surrender. Instead they raised a banner saying: "Conquer or die for Ferdinand VII" and opened fire. Other French soldiers, who had entered houses for the purpose of pillage, were seen to fly out the windows. Nevertheless, by seven o'clock in the evening, half the city was in French hands. This was when Verdier sent the following laconic message to Palafox: "Capitulation." Palafox, no less laconically, responded: "Guerra á cuchillo" – that is, "War to the knife" – and hoisted two red flags at the highest point so that eventual relief forces might know that the city was still resisting.

And, in effect, the struggle continued into the following days with increasing bitterness. Priests and monks, armed to the teeth, fought along with the people. One of them, Don Santiago Sas, who had been appointed captain by Palafox, in one engagement killed seventeen Frenchmen with his own hands. Nor were women far behind in their efforts. They organized the company of health and subsistence under the command of the beautiful, young, and delicate Countess Zurita.

On the night of August 13th and the morning of the 14th the French artillery opened fire with terrible intensity. But when the Spaniards began to fear the worst Verdier ordered retreat and the French voluntarily relinquished the part of Saragossa which they had conquered at so great a price. Verdier's decision was caused by news of the defeat of other French troops, under Pierre Dupont de l'Etang, on July 19th at Bailén, in Andalusia, by Francisco de Castaños. The French governor had been forced to evacuate Madrid with King Joseph Bonaparte at the head of his troops and Marshal Junot remained cut off in Portugal. (One week after Verdier had left Saragossa on August 21st, 1808, Junot, the former "fearless one" of Toulon, would be beaten at Vimeiro, losing Napoleon's favor and plunging into a state of despair which would lead him to commit sucide in 1813.)

Four months after Verdier's retreat, Napoleon, taking over personally the command of the army, took the offensive again and sent the army corps of Marshal Bon Adrien de Moncey against Saragossa, reinforced by that of Marshal Edouard Mortier. On December 19th the French forces, about thirty-two thousand men strong, assembled at Xiloca and began intense preparatory work. The artillery train, under the command of General Dedon, was increased by sixty siege cannon. The engineer corps, under the command of General Lacoste, prepared a hundred thousand sandbags, twenty thousand entrenching tools, and four thousand gabions. Once again the operations began with the French conquest of Mount Torrero, which was accomplished on the night of December 21st. An action which was supposed to be carried out at the same time on the left bank of the Ebro was not successful, thereby leaving the road open for a Spanish sortie that might prove decisive. But Palafox preferred to not take a chance and to wait for events. On the 22nd he received a message from Moncey, urging surrender. Palafox refused to capitulate and replied: "Spanish blood covers us with honor and you with shame."

Moncey now developed a planned attack in three phases. On December 29th he had the first parallel dug. On the 31st, when the last ones were about to be finished, the Spanish made an unsuccessful sortie. The following day, the end of the year of 1809, they made a second attempt, and on January 2nd, a third, just when Junot

A series of Spanish infantry uniforms at the time of the Peninsular or Spanish War against the French, grouped in an allegorical manner. The last one to the right is one of the irregulars forming a relief army which attempted to liberate Saragossa from the second siege conducted by Marshals Moncey, Mortier, Junot and Lannes in January and February of 1809.

was arriving at camp Andoche to replace Moncey in command of the 3rd corps and to convey to Mortier the order to move to Catalayud with one division, in order to keep communications open with Madrid which, in the meantime, had been reconquered. Thus the besiegers suffered an unexpected reduction of nine thousand men. Nevertheless, they were able to take Fort San José on January 11th. On the 21st a hundred Spaniards made a sortie from Saragossa in the vicinity of the fort and, with incredible audacity, were able to pass the second parallel, reach the first, and try to spike the battery of mortars positioned there. Only thirty remained alive as prisoners.

Meanwhile twenty thousand Aragonese insurgents had been organized into a relief army and, under the command of the Marquis of Lazán, the brother of Palafox, threatened to close a fatal pocket around the besiegers of Saragossa. Napoleon guessed the danger and sent Mortier to the side of Junot and entrusted the supreme command of the siege to Marshal Jean Lannes. The latter quickly sent Mortier against the Aragonese who were surprised at Nuestra Señora de Magallón, beaten and scattered. On January 26th fifty French cannon began again to effect a breach in the walls and, on the 27th, at noon, a column was sent to the attack. The French were successful in establishing a strong point within the breach itself in spite of the explosion of a Spanish mine.

Other points of the circle of walls were overcome and the battles in the streets started again. General Lacoste was killed, among many others.

Finally, on February 19th, Palafox hinted that he

The surrender of Bailen, as it appears in a painting by Casado del Alisal, preserved in the Museum of Modern Art of Madrid. Francisco de Castaños, commander of the three thousand Spaniards who defeated the twenty thousand French of Pierre Dupont, Count de l'Etang, is rendering homage to the defeated. The disaster of Bailén would force the French General Verdier, who was besieging the city of Saragossa and succeeded in penetrating within the city, to retreat and to raise the siege. Below: A typical firearm of the period.

was ready to negotiate and on the 20th Lannes received secretly a deputation of the citizens council. He indicated to its members the existence of an enormous mine which would be able to destroy the entire city in a second and asked for a discretionary surrender. A pact was made to avoid the reactions of the extremists, who favored last-ditch resistance. The latter, however, when they learned of the surrender, threatened to take control of the artillery and to continue the fight. Good sense finally triumphed however and, on February 21st, 1809, the siege of Saragossa, the second in nine months, was over. It had cost the lives of fifty thousand persons.

SVEABORG (1809)

Psychological warfare causes the fall of "the Gibraltar of Finland"

Sveaborg is the Swedish name for the present Suomenlinna, a fortified complex in front of Helsinki.

After the disaster of Poltava (1709), following which Sweden lost its place among the great powers, consideration was given to the construction of a fortress which could represent a strong base for what remained of the territories held by the Swedish crown which at this period also included Finland, united with Sweden within a single nation. Helsinki was chosen as a convenient site facing on the open sea where Sweden still held considerable power and could assure the fortress support from its high seas fleet.

The engineer entrusted with the construction of this stronghold, Augustine Eherensvärd, was an artillery officer when he began this project in 1748. He chose as a base six islands in front of Helsinki with a total area of about one hundred and fifty acres, and on these he established an immense fortified area with six defensive lines, with a citadel on the largest island, called Vargön. While he was proceeding with the building of the fortress, Eherensvärd organized a military unit unique in history, the "fleet of the archipelago," that is, a flotilla of ships adapted to operations within the labyrinth of islands which characterizes the southern coast of Finland, a series of waterways inaccessible to warships of the high seas. This organization was not under the navy but—and this was the unusual element in its organization—it was under the command of army officers. It was based in Sveaborg which had a drydock capable of servicing fifteen frigates and this construction was also a work of amazing ingenuity. Eherensvärd basically followed the principles of Vauban when he designed the base of Sveaborg. But he modified them with extremely interesting variations, suggested by the topography of the area, such as, for example, not using slopes on the land but substituting for them the use of steep reefs in the sea, and the changing color of the walls, owing to the characteristic colors of the stone, quarried in the area. The founder of the island fleet worked on the fortress for twenty-two years, with occasional interruptions due to the political situation of overriding interest to the country. The work force was furnished by the army which provided him with a regiment at a time. The money was supplied by gold sent by France. In the Autumn of 1771 he asked to be relieved. His health did not permit him to continue. In September of 1772 he was named Field Marshal. Two weeks later, on October 4th, 1772, he died and King Gustav II provided that he be buried within the fortress, in "Vargöns Borggard."

Others continued to work on Sveaborg after him for another eighteen years with the result that it became not only a fortress and a naval base but also a city of about four thousand inhabitants, without counting the ten thousand soldiers who were to make up the garrison. The different styles of architecture as well as those of the fortifications formed a complex that was unique in the world, fully worthy to be called, as it was, the "Gibraltar of the North."

But so much effort was rewarded by history with an ephemeral glory and with an incredible, unjust humiliation. That which we are about to narrate was the most bitter.

In 1807, at Tilsit, according to the famous treaty which established an artificial agreement between the Napoleonic Empire and that of the Czar, Alexander I of Russia pledged himself to convince Sweden to cease her hostility toward France. As compensation she would receive Finland, which, as has already been mentioned, formed a single nation together with Sweden.

Faithful to his agreements, the Czar sent his army to invade Swedish territory at the end of February 1808. The Swedes worked out a defense plan, providing for their forces to retire to the north while Sveaborg, in the south, would resist until the return of good weather. Then, with the spring thaw, all waters would become navigable once more and the country could be reconquered using "The Gibraltar of the North" as a base. The Russians were well aware that their success in the war would depend on the speed with which they could capture the fortress and they therefore directed all their forces to its early conquest.

When the hostilities broke out, Sveaborg had a garrison of six thousand men, equipped with seven hundred and thirty-four cannon (Eherensvärd had projected one thousand three hundred cannon), great reserves of food and ammunition and, in addition, the support of the island fleet. The command of Sveaborg was held by Rear Admiral Carl Olof Cronstedt, who had at his disposition a full month's time to put the fortress on a war footing before the arrival of the Russians.

The Russians entered Helsinki on March 2nd but the siege of Sveaborg did not begin until twenty days later. After a brief artillery duel, negotiations began on the 21st of March. Apparently the parlays were not successful and on March 28th the Russians resumed the bombardment. Five days later when shots fired on the forces had reached a figure of one thousand five hundred and sixty-five, without, however, having caused any important damage and resulting in a total loss of six dead and thirty-two wounded, negotiations started once more. On April 6th the cease fire was sounded. Sveaborg had missed its rendezvous with destiny: in effect the stronghold had capitulated although the Russians had occupied only three islands and they themselves had not expected to occupy the stronghold until the beginning of May.

This has given rise to one of the most mysterious chapters in the history of warfare. Cronstedt declared several times that he had powder enough for only two weeks. This was true; but only if he fired consecutively all the seven hundred and thirty-four cannon at the stronghold for two weeks. It therefore appears that he had other motives for surrender. What could they have been? Since Cronstedt carried his secret with him to the grave, historians have only been able to guess.

The most fascinating solution is certainly the one advanced by Cronstedt's biographer, Wilhelm Odelberg, who suggests that the Rear Admiral was a victim of psychological warfare employed by the Russians. The commander of the Russian army, General Peter van Suchtelen, must have known, as was later made evident, that around Cronstedt there was wound a web of treason and betrayal on the part of his closest staff members and that his senior officers were of so little worth that the junior officers were about to instigate a mutiny. This was confirmed by the fact that the soldiers of the garrison, once surrender was made, preferred to go north to join the nothern army and to rescue their own honor and the honor of the army instead of going to their own homes. With such information at hand van Suchtelen could not fail to obtain the result he achieved from a Cronstedt clearly overcome by events too big for him.

According to agreement, however, the Imperial Russian flag was not hoisted over Sveaborg until half past eleven on May 8th, 1809. It would fly there for one hundred and ten years, until May 12, 1918, at which point the young Republic of Finland would start on its own way, under the guidance of Carl Gustav Emil Mannerheim (1867-1951).

Rear Admiral Carl Olof Cronstedt, as portrayed in a miniature kindly lent by the Cronstedt family for purposes of reproduction. On facing page, above title: A watercolor by an unknown artist portraying the surrender of the island of Susisaari (Vargön in Swedish), on May 6th., 1809. The original is preserved in the Museum of Suomenlinna, the present name of Sveaborg. Susisaari is the largest of the islands on which the enormous fortress of Sveaborg was emplaced.

CADIZ (1823)

The surrender of the Trocadero rehabilitates the "Italian Hamlet"

In January of 1820, a strong contingent of Spanish troops were about to embark at Cadiz for South America, where revolutionary movements had broken out against Spanish dominion. Part of these troops rebelled when the order was given to embark and demanded that the constitution of 1812 be reestablished and that amnesty be accorded to political prisoners. This was the signal for a revolt on the "carbonare" pattern which soon extended as far as Madrid, forcing King Ferdinand VII to reestablish the constitution but, as a result, angering the conservatives and, above all, giving the Holy Alliance a chance to intervene. This was decided at the congress of Verona in 1822, which assigned the French monarchy the task of reestablishing order in Spain.

In January of 1823, a hundred thousand men, under the command of Generalissimo Louis Antoine d'Artois, Duke of Angoulême, gathered in the Pyrenees which they crossed on April 7th. The French advance did not stop until the 24th of June in front of Cadiz, where the Spanish constitutional forces ended their long retreat, taking with them King Ferdinand VII as prisoner. While Rear Admiral Hamelin blockaded the city from the sea, General Bodesoulle, charged with coordinating land and sea operations, set siege to the city.

At five o'clock in the morning on July 16th the besieged made a spirited sortie. But they were repulsed with serious losses. Desertions began the next day and increased on successive days, with news of other reverses for the constitutional forces especially that of General Ballesteros, reportedly stopped while on the way with a relief army.

The Duke of Angoulême, who had entered Madrid on May 24th, left on July 28th, having established a regency there in the name of Ferdinand VII. He entered Cadiz on August 16th. On the 18th he held a war

The attack on the Trocadero, according to an old print (Paris, Carnavalet Museum). The French troops, in water up to their belts, are crossing the canal and are about to assault the fortress. The canal was really crossed at night at a quarter past two on August 31st, 1823. Among these men was Major General Carlo Alberto de Savoia-Carignano, future King of Sardinia.

council and decided to attack as soon as possible the most important port of the city, the Trocadero. This was located in an extremely strong position around an open area called San José and protected a deep channel. It was garrisoned by seventeen hundred men with forty-five cannon. The assault, prepared with absolute secrecy, was carried out on the night between the 30th and 31st of August. Three columns, under the command of Generals Gougeon, d'Escars, and Obert, led by officers who on the night before had accurately explored the fords of the channel, moved forward at ten o'clock on the evening of the 30th. Half an hour after midnight they entered into the trenches excavated by the engineers, reached the second parallel in complete silence, made a single column, waded across the channel at half past two without waiting for low tide, therefore making their surprise to the enemy more complete, since they did not usually maintain a careful guard at high tide. The first column took a quarter of an hour to reach the enemy and to kill all the artillerists by bayonet action. The second column reached a redoubt called Molino de la Guerra and took the garrison prisoner. The third soon arrived inside the Trocadero, now the prey of terrible confusion. In order not to run risks and to give the cartridges time to dry, the French stopped and waited for the day. Thereupon the 34th and 36th line regiments entered the fort with a rush.

With the forces employed against the Trocadero, and precisely within the column commanded by General Gougeon, was Carlo Alberto de Savoia-Carignano. This was the "Italian Hamlet" who, guilty of having promulgated a constitution on the same model as the Spanish one, during his brief period of regency in Piedmont in 1821, had come to rehabilitate himself in the eyes of the Holy Alliance, fighting personally against the constitutionalists of Spain.

The fall of the Trocadero decided, for all purposes, the fate of Cadiz. But the city continued to resist. On September 2nd another strongpoint fell, the fort of Santi-Petri. The constitutionalists forced Ferdinand VII, who was still their prisoner, to sign several letters to the Duke of Angoulême, to the end of setting in motion negotiations for surrender. But "the Prince" replied that he would deal only with the King "alone and free." On the 23rd the fleet began a bombardment of the city of which the effects were, to tell the truth, more moral than material. Revolts occured among even the most trustworthy troops, and the citizenry arose and demanded capitulation. On the 28th the *Cortes* decided to let the king go free in order to entere into negotiations with the Duke of Angoulême, but Ferdinand, blocked by the extremists, was unable to reach the French camp before the 1st of October, after having promised that, as soon as he was on the throne again as absolute sovereign, he would grant a general amnesty. But those who were most compromised did not trust this promise and, boarding neutral vessels, which the French fleet let go by, they fled to Gibraltar and from there to England or America. In Spain, for them and for the constitution, everything had been lost.

Uniforms of the Spanish army at the time of the war of 1823. In February of that year the army numbered eighty thousand men in the regular army which was soon joined by another thirty thousand recruits by levy proclaimed for the special circumstances. The irregular troops, or militia, numbered about sixty thousand. Not all of these, however, took the field to contest the French advance, either since many components of the regular army were against the constitutionalist's ideas, or because of the difficulties connected with the assembling of such disparate forces. Nevertheless, at the beginning of the campaign, four army corps were ready to take the field: that of Catalonia, twenty-five thousand men under the command of General Mina; that of Navarre and Biscay, under General Ballesteros, thirty-six thousand; that of Galicia, with fifteen thousand under Morillo, and, finally, that of Madrid, with a reserve under the orders of Abisbal.

ANTWERP (1832)

*Sixty-three thousand French
cannon rounds for an
independent Belgium*

On August 25th, 1830, in Brussels, the presentation
of the opera *The Guard of the Porticos* by Auber,
through its revolutionary content, lit the fuse of Belgian
separatism in regard to Holland, of which Belgium then
formed the southern part. The economic advantages
intrinsic in the union of the two countries were not
sufficient to interfere with the proclamation on October
5, 1830, by a provisionary government, announcing the
independence of Belgium, confirmed on November 18th
by the National Congress. A conference called at London
by the great powers succeeded in establishing a truce
between Belgium and Holland, but in 1832 the situation
suddenly became worse, following the Dutch refusal to
give up the citadel of Antwerp. France, who sympathized

*Left: French mining engineers installing a mine cluster in
the escarpment of a fortress. Above: The final scene of
the siege of the citadel of Antwerp from a contemporary
print. Overpowered by about seventy-three thousand
cannon rounds, the four thousand men and a hundred and
thirty-five officers of the Dutch garrison under the command of
General Chassé capitulated and surrendered the fortress
to the French of the Armée du Nord, commanded by
Marshal Gérard and seventy thousand men strong.*

with the new state, set in motion the seventy thousand
men of the *Armée du Nord* (Army of the North) under
Marshal Etienne Maurice Gérard on November 15th.
On the 22nd he laid siege to the disputed citadel. Having
cut communications by land to Breda and Berg-op-Zoom
as well as those along the Schelde, and having concluded
preliminary works, Gérard sent an ultimatum to General
Chassé and his garrison of four thousand men on November 30th. Chassé was summoned to surrender and
was told that, in order to spare the city, the French
would attack from the side on which the citadel faced
the country. Chassé declared that he would resist and
also that he could not consider Antwerp an open city if
a single cannon shot was fired from outside fortifications
against the citadel. This declaration alarmed the population and they began to evacuate most of the city.

The trench was opened in the night between the 29th and 30th of November and, in spite of the cold and the rain which forced the sappers to work in the freezing mud up to their knees, on December 3rd the first and second parallels were ready and on the 4th the artillery opened fire with a hundred and four cannon. Aided by bright moonlight, the besieged replied, also at night, with very effective fire. On the nights between December 10th and 14th the mining engineers, led by their captain Jallot, crossed the moat with the aid of pontoons under the Saint-Laurent lunette to mine the escarpment. Thereupon the sappers threw into the moat itself three great pontoons, and succeeded in preparing a bridge for the three companies of the 65th line regiment chosen for the assault to be made through the breach after it had been opened by the mines. The mines exploded at five on the morning of the 14th but the explosion ruined part of the bridge and more time had to be lost in repairing it. Finally the three companies got into action and, by means of an irresistible bayonet attack, dislodged the Dutch from the lunette.

Encouraged by this first success, the French multiplied their efforts, opening over the citadel an infernal barrage of artillery fire which Chassé himself declared to be without equal in the history of sieges: "No fewer than fourteen projectiles were constantly striking at the same moment." In spite of this, the besieged held on and replied with all the fire they could muster.

On December 21st the breach batteries commenced action with such disastrous effects for the citadel that on the morning of the 23rd Chassé declared himself ready to surrender provided that he be permitted to retire to Holland with the garrison. Gérard replied that he also wanted the nearby forts of Lillo and Liefkenshoek. Since these were under another command, it was necessary to call on the King of Holland, William I, for a decision. While awaiting reply, the French entered the citadel and the Dutch marched out, putting down their weapons. "This is the saddest day of my life," Chassé wrote in his report to the Minister of War, "since I have tried to die without succeeding."

The king praised Chassé but refused to accept the cession of Lillo and Liefkenshoek. Marshal Gérard, who had detained Chassé and the survivors of the garrison, treating them with the regard due to brave soldiers, told the heroic defender of the citadel that he would honor the condition of their free return to Holland if he would promise not to fight again against France and her allies, particularly Belgium. Chassé refused this proposition and chose to go, along with his men, to prison in France.

MONTEVIDEO
(1843-1851)
The Red Shirts of Garibaldi at the baptism of fire

After having won her own independence, with the aid of Great Britain, from Brazil in the battle of Ituzaingó (1827), Uruguay plunged into civil war. Manuel Oribe, leader of the party of the Blancos, and José Rivera, leader of the Colorados, won out over the other factions and engaged in an open and violent struggle. Supported by the Argentine dictator, Juan de Rosas, Oribe marched on Montevideo, then held by the forces of Rivera, in 1843. Since he was unable to capture the city by assault, he laid siege to it in February.

The city then contained thirty thousand inhabitants, many of whom were European liberals who had fled from the political persecutions of their countries. The Italians numbered about four thousand. Among them was Giuseppe Garibaldi, condemned to death for rebellious activities in 1834 by the Piedmont of Carlo Alberto and who had found refuge in South America. In 1840, after having participated in the operations which the state of Rio Grande was carrying out against the Brazilian Empire, Garibaldi put himself at the disposition of Uruguay. Rivera entrusted him with the command of the fleet, which then had only three ships but which soon would become stronger.

Then, under the threat of the siege and above all following a defeat suffered by Rivera in Arroyo Grande in November, 1842, Garibaldi organized the Italian Legion, endowing it almost by chance with the red shirt that was to become legendary. The first Red Shirts were actually a shipment of scarlet tunics destined for the butchers of Buenos Aires persuasively obtained from a merchant of Montevideo.

With the uniform completed by the addition of a plumed hat, the legionaries, although Garibaldi was absent, entered into action. Their first action was not a very brilliant one, but very soon they redeemed themselves, attacking again, with Garibaldi at their head, the Argentine forces at the Cerro, a hill to the west of Montevideo, which was a key point of the siege plan. Garibaldi and his men took forty-two prisoners. This episode took place in June, 1843. A short time later the main force of the fourteen thousand Argentines that Oribe had deployed around the city again attacked the Cerro, under the command of General Núñez. When affairs seemed at their worst Garibaldi launched his legion and reversed the situation. Núñez was killed along with many of his soldiers. Others were taken prisoner.

Instead of taking advantage of this success, the Uruguayan general staff allowed Oribe time to reorganize and to attack once more. The Uruguayans were forced to retreat under the protection of the Red Shirts.

The siege, meantime, proceeded in a desultory fashion. The commander in chief of the Uruguay army, José María Paz, who succeeded Rivera after the defeat of Arroyo Grande, attempted a field operation to the rear of the enemy in the hope of freeing the situation and dividing the forces of Oribe from those of Rosas. But Rivera, who still had command over some regiments, and who was supposed to await orders from Paz before entering into action, became seized with impatience and perhaps also with the desire to acquire for himself merit from the victory. He attacked Rosas at Indias Mortas and suffered a disastrous defeat. The Argentine dictator

Giuseppe Garibaldi (in the center, marked with the number 4) with his two hundred Red Shirts of the Italian Legion, sustained a charge of a thousand two hundred Argentine cavalrymen under Servando Gómez at San Antonio del Salto.

subjected the two thousand Uruguayans who had fallen into his hands to terrible tortures which horrified the entire world. France and England ordered Rosas to cease hostilities and, when he refused, they blockaded Buenos Aires in 1845. At this point an expedition of fifty armed vessels was organized and was entrusted to Garibaldi who, with two hundred Red Shirts of the Italian Legion and three hundred Uruguayan cavalrymen of the regular army, sailed up the Uruguay River and reached the cataract called El Salto. Here Garibaldi debarked and fortified his camp, making it into a base for successive operations. On February 8th, 1846, at a place called San Antonio, he sustained a charge of one thousand two hundred cavalrymen under Servando Gómez. Garibaldi won a defensive victory with only two hundred men.

The Red Shirts remained at El Salto until August 20th, 1846, and then returned to Montevideo and then once more to El Salto. The siege of Montevideo in the meantime continued in its usual listless fashion and would still continue when Garibaldi had left Uruguay to rush with his sixty-eight most faithful followers to the irresistible summons of the Italian events of 1848. Finally on October 8th, 1851, the Argentine General Justo de Urquiza, chief of a rebel party against the dictatorship of Rosas, led Colorados, Brazilians, and Paraguayans against Montevideo, where he defeated Oribe and ended one of the longest sieges of history.

VENICE (1848-1849)

"Sickness rages, bread is lacking: the white banner is waving over the bridge."

The year of Forty-eight was a year of political uprisings so deep and so convulsive for Europe that it became, at least in Italy, practically proverbial. The spark of revolution broke out in Paris on February 24th when Louis Philippe was forced to grant power to the Republicans. On March 3rd Kossuth roused Budapest in the name of Hungarian liberty and, on the 13th, Metternich was forced to flee from Vienna. On March 18th, while King Friedrich Wilhelm IV in Berlin was granting the constitution, in Italy there began the Five Days of Milan and the revolt of Venice against Austrian dominion. On the same day Count Palffy, the governor of Venice, had to agree to the liberation of the patriots Daniele Manin and Niccolò Tommaseo as well as the formation of a Civic Guard. By evening two thousand joined its ranks, under the command of an ex-officer of Napoleon, Angelo Mengaldo.

On the 22nd the Venetian insurrectionists obtained control of the arsenal and Daniele Manin, addressing the people, proclaimed the Republic of San Marco.

The other cities of the Veneto followed the example of the capital and, after expelling the Austrian garrison, sent declarations of their allegiance to the republic. Marshal Radetzky, who commanded all the imperial forces in the Lombardy-Veneto region, took refuge within the famous Quadrilateral, bounded by the forts of Mantua, Legnago, Verona, and Peschiera, and awaited events. Carlo Alberto, with Piedmontese troops, entered Lombardy to conduct the first war for Italian independence.

Pope Pius IX sent troops from Rome, and Ferdinand II sent other troops from Naples, but these did not arrive quickly enough and when they did reach Lombardy they received orders to return. Both General Guglielmo Pepe, in command of the Neapolitan troops, and General Giovanni Durando, in command of the papal army, refused to obey the orders. Pepe rushed to put himself at the disposition of Venice and Durando went to defend Vicenza. In June the operations slackened and while the Piedmontese wore themselves out besieging Mantua, Radetzky reoccupied all the rebel cities of the Veneto. Only Osoppo and Venice remained free.

Despite the unhappy turn which events had taken, the Republic of the Veneto decided on its own annexation to the Sardinian kingdom on July 4th and on August 7th three Piedmontese commissioners assumed the power of government in the name of Carlo Alberto. Daniele Manin ("I was, am, and remain republican") abandoned his post as president of the republic and entered into the Civic Guard with the rank of captain, although with duties of a much more modest nature such as, for example, that of sentry. Meanwhile, at Custoza on July 26th and under the walls of Milan on August 6th, Radetzky won two decisive victories and forced Piedmont to the armistice of Salasco (August 9th, 1848). On August 11th the Venetian populace tumul-

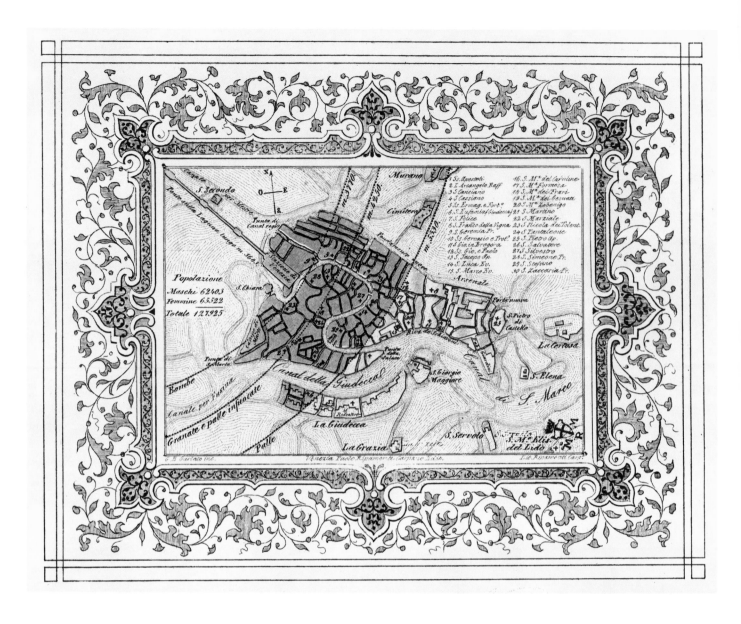

Map of the siege of Venice, indicating the zones subjected to Austrian artillery fire, according to their range and type of projectile (Milan, Bertarelli Collection). The bombardment started on July 28th, 1849, and continued for twenty-four consecutive days, forcing the population to take refuge in the sections of the city beyond the range of fire. Overcrowding favored the spread of cholera which finally claimed two hundred dead each day. The lack of supplies and muntions, and the epidemic, caused the Venetian surrender.

tuously proclaimed once more the establishment of the Republic and on the 13th gave full powers to the "dictator" Manin. The Austrians were now at Mestre and were about to prepare to carry out their siege.

The second half of 1848 went by in comparative calm. Osoppo, after six months of heroic resistance, surrendered to Marshal Laval Nugent, Count of Westmeath, and Venice was left alone to defend the revolution. Its hopes were placed, in part, in the success of the mission which Tommaseo had led to Paris to obtain French support (not forthcoming) and, in part, in the great patriots and military men who had come to Venice. These included the already mentioned Guglielmo Pepe, a Calabrian from Squillace, an ex-officer of Napoleon and

conspirator during the period of 1820-1821, who was entrusted with the supreme command for the defense of Venice; Giuseppe Sirtori, from Milan, Garibaldi's future chief of staff, the Cadornan agitator Pier Fortunato Calvi, Alessandro Poerio, Gerolamo Ulloa, Enrico Cosenz, and others.

The Venetian land forces, on October 22nd, 1848, carried out an audacious sortie against the fort of Tre Porti al Cavallino which captured two cannon from the enemy, two ships with arms, food supplies, and munitions. Another sortie was carried out on October 27th at Mestre and cost the Austrians two hundred dead and wounded, fifty prisoners, twelve cannon, and more booty. The Venetians lost Alessandro Poerio, who was gravely wounded (he would die on November 3rd). On the sea, Giovanni Battista Cavedalis, ex-director of works of the Liviana-Vienna railroad, contributed in no small degree to maintaining the spirits of the people of the city by his harassment of the enemy with sudden and daring attacks. But on March 12th, 1849, Carlo Alberto denounced the Salasco armistice and, on the 20th, he resumed the war against Austria. He lost it within three days, during the tragic day of Novara (March 23rd, 1849). Radetzky could now concentrate all his forces against Venice and conduct the siege with the utmost vigor.

The fortress of Marghera, put under siege in April and submitted to an intense bombardment, resisted for more than a month and surrendered only after a peremptory order from Manin. On June 27th an Austrian bomb hit the powder reserve of the Sant'Antonio battery on the bridge connecting Venice to the mainland, causing great damage. Cesare Rossarol, from Naples, a veteran of Greece in '33 and former defender of Marghera, was in command of the battery. He died while attempting to restore the damage, struck by a cannon ball. Against the battery, the Austrians tried a surprise attack on the night of July 6th but were repulsed.

On July 28th the Austrian artillery, arriving within range with its guns, began the bombardment of twenty-four days, which was the most splendid (and for the Venetians the most unfortunate) action of the entire siege. The Austrian grenades fell in an uninterrupted rain on two-thirds of the city, forcing the inhabitants to seek refuge in parts of the city that were still out of range and thereby causing these quarters to be overcrowded. This was one of the reasons for the spread of the enemy most to be feared: cholera. To their already severe sufferings, arising from the scarcity of food, the Venetians now had to add an epidemic, which daily cost them two hundred dead. But they showed steadfastness and did not surrender until August 24th, when, as specified in the act of capitulation, the city had to surrender, "through lack of munitions and bread, to famine and contagion, not to peril or to the force of the enemy."

The Lion of Saint Mark surmounted by the Hapsburg eagle, an ironically symbolic union of the Austrian rule in Venice in an old woodcut preserved in the Bertarelli Collection in Milan. Below: An impressive night view of the Austrian bombardment of Venice with the "flaming cannon balls throwing off fire" (the expression of the poet Arnaldo Fusinato), which, coming from batteries located at a distance of less than three miles from the city, rained on the western quarters of Venice (Rome, Museum of Engineering).

SEVASTOPOL (1854-1855)

Vauban's parallels conquer again

The war in Crimea which, in the period of 1853 to 1856, pitted Russia on one side against the other, consisting of Turkey, England, France, the Kingdom of Piedmont and Sardinia, was only one of many episodes of Russian expansionism in the Balkan Peninsula. It was caused by the negative reply on the part of Turkey to the demand of Czar Nicholas I to place under Russian protection the twelve million orthodox Christians subject to the Ottoman Empire. The Czar tried without success to involve Austria and England in his plan for breaking the Turkish power and then he ordered his troops to invade Moldavia and Walachia as well as that part of Armenia subject to the sultan. On October 4th, 1853, the Sublime Porte declared war on Russia and obtained some success in the first land encounters. But on the naval front, on November 30th, the Russians obtained a victory known as the "massacre of Sinope," on the Black Sea. This caused the great powers, alarmed by this disturbing of European equilibrium, to decide to intervene in favor of Turkey. Only France and England did so with armed forces, in March 1854. They were followed, a short while later, by Piedmont, wishing to have the right to sit at the peace table in order to bring up the question of Italian unity. Actually France and England had requested the help of Piedmont, but they desired to have the Sardinian troops in their service as mercenaries. Cavour, Piedmont's prime minister, refused this plan, although he continued to negotiate.

On March 31st, 1854, the first French contingents landed at Gallipoli, on the Dardanelles, under the command of General François Certain Canrobert. Another fifty thousand French, under the command of Marshal

A contemporary print brings together in an allegorical exultation the "occidental" victors of Sevastopol; Italians, French, and English. The Turks are not depicted although it was to aid them that the three countries intervened against Russia. Below: Cossack horse drawn artillery. Facing page: A general view of Sevastopol during the concluding moments of the siege.

Kosaken Artillerie.

Piedmontese cavalry in Crimea. The Italians distinguished themselves at Chernaya, on August 6th, 1855. On seeing them in review General Adolphe Niel, who had commanded the French engineers in the siege of Rome, exclaimed, "What good looking soldiers!" Alfonso Lamarmora, with the next battle imminent, added: "I am convincend that tomorrow he will say 'What good soldiers!'" Below: *The Russian strongpoint of the Grand Redan after the siege.*

Armand de Saint-Arnand, and twenty-five thousand English, under the orders of seventy-year-old Lord Fitzroy James Henry Somerset Raglan, a veteran of Waterloo, set foot on Turkish territory in May.

From Varna, today in Bulgaria, troops were sent to landing points established about thirty miles north of Sevastopol, aboard ships of insufficient capacity. Never had so many armed men been transported by sea for a single military action. Organization broke down and serious deficiencies arose in provisioning, in the equipment, and in the sanitation. Cholera commenced to rage among the soldiers and could not be stopped.

On September 16th, 1854, the Franco-English army landed in the Crimea and, on the 19th, began their march to Sevastopol. On the 20th they won the battle of the Alma, a river noted for its banks. Thirty thousand Russians under the command of Prince Alexander Menshikov were routed in five hours of bitter fighting.

Sufficient advantage was not taken of this success and the war, which could have ended the same day, continued. While the French commander, ill with cholera, embarked to return to France (he would die on September 29th), Canrobert, who replaced him, and Raglan, who did not get along at all well with Canro-

bert, decided they would lay siege to Sevastopol.

On November 5th there was a battle at Inkerman, a village at the mouth of the Chernaya River (in Russian, Chernaya means "black") and the Russians left twenty thousand dead on the field. Other actions developed around the city, but the communications between Sevastopol and the hinterland were never completely cut by the Allies, thus permitting the continual arrival of supplies and reinforcements. The siege became, to a certain point, an artillery duel. On both sides the contending forces had emplaced on land heavy cannon from their ships, which were served by the ships' sailors.

Winter came and despite the relative mildness of the Crimean climate, operations languished. The two armies, practically stationary on the two banks of the Chernaya, limited their encounters to artillery duels.

Meantime, Cavour had finished his diplomatic labors and fifteen thousand Piedmontese were able to leave Genoa, under the command of General Alfonso Lamarmora, the brother of Alessandro, creator of the bersaglieri corps. He too accompanied the expedition in command of the second of the two divisions (with a brigade in reserve) into which the expeditionary corps was divided. The Sardinian army arrived on May 8th, 1855. On the 19th Canrobert quarreled with Lord Raglan and he left. The command of the French expeditionary corps passed to Amable Pélissier. On June 18th a first assault was decided upon against Sevastopol, was carried out and repulsed. Ten days later Lord Raglan was carried off by cholera. The English command passed to General James Simpson. On August 16th, at the Chernaya, Italian

An encounter between Russian cavalry and Allied infantry in the Crimea. The war which witnessed important and bloody battles like those of the Alma and Inkerman and the very famous Balaclava, has passed into history as one of the more luckless campaigns from the point of view of organization and strategy, arising from the poor attitudes of the commanders and their rivalry.

infantry and bersaglieri troops would prove their worth.

Finally, at exactly twelve o'clock on September 8th the general assault was sounded. The Zouaves of Patrice MacMahon, with an epic rush, appeared over the parapet of Fort Malakov, the key to the defense. The English attacked another strongpoint, called the Grand Redan. On the left wing, with the others, a Sardinian brigade made its advance. From the bay the English fleet, in spite of there being a rough sea, carried out a diversionary action, bombarding in turn another point of the fortification. Here and there the Russians counterattacked, forced the allies to fall back on the parallels, which had been established according to the still valid principles of Vauban, but the entire defensive art was now engaged and Pélissier was able to concentrate his forces on Malakov, where MacMahon pronounced his famous phrase: "J'y suis, j'y reste!" (I am here, I stay here!) "Night hardly descended," Pélissier wrote in his final report, "fires arose on all sides. Mines exploded, powder reserves went up, and the spectacle of Sevastopol in flames, lit by the Russians themselves, appeared to the eyes of all the army as one of the most imposing and saddest spectacles in the history of all wars."

GAETA (1860-1861) *The cannon has a new bore*

On the same day that Garibaldi entered Naples in triumph, September 7th, 1860, Cavour, wishing the Savoyard monarchy to assume an active rôle in such a decisive moment of national unity, sent an ultimatum to the Pope. On the 11th he gave the army orders to move. Two army corps under Generals Enrico Cialdini and Enrico Morozzo della Rocca, under the supreme command of General Manfredo Fanti, invaded the Marche and Umbria, won a victory over the papal troops at Perugia (September 14th) and Castelfidardo (September 18th) and entered the Kingdom of Naples. On September 23rd Stefan Türr's division of Garibaldian troops suffered at Caiazzo the only defeat of the Red Shirts in the entire campaign. But on October 1st and 2nd, Garibaldi destroyed, with some difficulty in the open field, the last Bourbon hopes of return. Nothing remained to Francesco II except the fortress of Gaeta. He enclosed himself within with his beautiful young wife Maria Sofia of Wittelsbach, and a garrison of twenty thousand. Cialdini, who was given command of the siege, at first had only eighteen thousand men, but he had at his disposition one hundred and eighty artillery pieces, a third of which were equipped with rifled barrels, accord-

Above and on facing page: *Two tempera paintings by C. Bossoli preserved at the Museum of National Revival at Turin, respectively depicting the Castle of Gaeta (of Swabian origin) and the march past of the Bourbon troops who are leaving the stronghold after the surrender.* Above: *A portrait of Francesco II, King of Naples, who had placed his last hope of saving the throne on the resistance of Gaeta. He was incapable of properly utilizing his army, which wished to fight in the name of military honor and fidelity to the dynasty.*

ing to the system introduced by Giovanni Cavalli, one of the most famous artillerists of all time, who, at Gaeta, also began the use of his first rear charging cannon. Because of the rifling of his cannon, the Piedmontese artillery could bombard Gaeta while remaining outside the range of the Neapolitan cannons. Actually, five of the latter were also rifled but the remainder of the Bourbon artillery, composed of five hundred and thirty-nine cannon and another hundred and thirty smooth bore howitzers and mortars, was revealed to be inadequate to the needs of the siege. In the ninety-four days of the blockade, from September 6th, 1860, to February 12th, 1861, the defenders of Gaeta fired thirty-five thousand rounds, causing a loss to the enemy of forty-six dead and three hundred and twenty-one wounded. The Piedmontese fired fifty-six thousand rounds, killing eight hundred and twenty of the Bourbon forces and wounding five hundred and seventy. The rifling of the barrel gave the projectile a rotary movement which increased its penetration and the stability of its trajectory and gave it the possibility of changing from the form of a sphere to that of a cylinder. In sending the projectile to the target loaded with a great quantity of explosives, it was no longer necessary to depend on heavy caliber guns. The weight of the projectile was now independent of its diameter and the cannon, of smaller caliber, was more manageable with greater range. It was a true revolution. The range of artillery suddenly increased from two thousand to six thousand meters and the enclosing walls lost their historic importance.

Francesco II and Maria Sofia, besieged in Gaeta by the pursuing advance of the Piedmontese, did not despair of recovering the throne through a change in the international situation. England, in effect, favored the unity of Italy but the France of Napoleon III seemed still ready for any eventuality. Meanwhile the French fleet prevented the Piedmontese fleet from blocking Gaeta by sea. However, when the Bourbon General Ruggiero tried to enter Rome with certain Neapolitan forces destined for a future recovery of power, France denied him entrance to the Papal State so as not to give to Victor Emmanuel II a pretext to resolve the "Roman question" by arms. Later the French permitted the Piedmontese fleet to undertake the blockade of Gaeta.

Convinced then that there was a need for haste, the Piedmontese attempted to shorten the resistance of the stronghold by employing two fireships loaded with five hundred barrels of powder, to be launched against the defenses facing the sea. General Francesco Menabrea, in command of the Piedmontese engineer corps, made ready two small boats for the task. But when everything was ready Cialdini revoked the order, declaring that so much deception was no longer necessary. Gaeta, shaken by continuous artillery fire and weakened by the epidemics that had broken out among its defenders, would not have been able to hold out much longer. Capitulation, in fact, took place on February 13th, under honorable conditions. While Francesco II took refuge in Rome with his family, Cialdini directed an order of the day to his men in which he stated, among other things: "We fought against Italians and this was a necessary though sad task. Let us pray for the peace of the heroes who have died during this memorable siege while fighting in our ranks as well as on the enemy bastions."

PUEBLA (1863)

The frock coat of Juárez fails to stop destiny

A moment during the fierce struggle of Puebla according to an Epinal print (Rome, Gasparinetti Collection). The Mexican enterprise was desired by Napoleon III as a prelude to placing Maximilian von Hapsburg on the throne that used to belong to Montezuma. This would create a Latin-American empire to serve as a counterweight to the increasing power of the United States. It would also serve to compensate Hapsburg Austria soon to lose her possessions in the Veneto.

Benito Juárez, the Indian of bourgeois aspirations, who would make his frock coat a symbol, an institution, and almost a banner against the robes of the clergy and the uniforms of the military caste who dominated Mexico in the first half of the 1800's, was still the "young man dressed in black" when, in 1859, the Mexican government presided over by General Miramón became fearfully indebted to various European powers. When Miramón was overthrown and forced to flee, Juárez succeeded him and fell heir to the crushing debt. In December of 1861, while the United States was paralyzed by the Civil War, Juárez suspended payment of the debts, bringing on thereby a demonstration of force — the blockade of Vera Cruz — on the part of England, Spain, and France. Although the first two countries retired from the scene the following spring, Napoleon III's France, desirous to counterpose a Latin-American empire to the growing power of the United States, designated Maximilian as ruler of Mexico and sent French armies to help him on his way to the throne. This was the first act of the

tragedy that would end on June 19th, 1867, at Querétaro, whe na platoon of the regiment of Nuevo León would execute, by shooting, the "reborn flower of Hapsburg."

Meanwhile, on May 5th, 1862, five thousand French of the expeditionary corps of General Count de Lorencez arrived in view of Puebla, then guarded by twelve thousand Mexicans. The city was dominated by several forts. Three columns supported by artillery and protected, on the flanks, by cavalry wings, made a vigorous assault and reached the walls, but were repulsed. The French, tired by a four-hour march and subjected to another four hours of combat, were unable to accomplish anything more and retired, after having lost two hundred and fifteen men dead and wounded. In the following months, expecting a new assault, the city multiplied its defenses, adding to forts Guadalupe and San Lorenzo, already in action at the time of the French attack of May 5th, Santa Anita to the north, San Javier to the west, Carmen and Totimehuacuan to the south, and Zaragoza and Misericordia to the east.

The new French attempt was carried out on March 16th, 1863, by the brigade of General Elie Forey, who had replaced Lorencez. The two divisions under his command were led by Generals Douay and François-Achille Bazaine, joined by Mexican conservative forces and foreign contingents: in all, thirty thousand men and fifty cannon took part in the new assault. Puebla had a force of twenty-two thousand and was defended by General Jesús Ortega.

Forey chose as a point of attack San Javier and in that sector he executed approach works which took until March 23rd. Meanwhile, the French forces occupied Cholula, east of Puebla, to impede the relief army under Ignacio Comonfort. The latter was engaged in making a sweep of the countryside in order to destroy all possible supplies that might be available to the French. On March 26th, after intense artillery preparation, San Javier fell into French hands. The Mexicans removed their guns and fell back on the city in order to organize a new line of resistance. Along this line which, joining the Carmen and Santa Anita forts, cut the city in half, the French made repeated unsuccessful attacks. Forey thereupon indicated new objectives to his men: the Carmen and Totimehuacuan forts. General Bazaine was charged with making the attack, while the line running across Puebla was again attacked on April 25th. Both attacks were again repulsed.

Since the food situation and the lack of munitions had become critical, Comonfort on May 4th and 8th attempted to bring reinforcements within the city. Bazaine, however, frustrated this operation and inflicted on the Mexican column, which was six thousand men strong, a severe blow at San Lorenzo. Comonfort fell on the field. The convoy of reinforcements and eight cannon ended up in the hands of the French.

Ortega then tried to initiate surrender negotiations but Forey preferred to take forts Carmen and Totimehuacuan by assault. This took place on the 16th and 17th of May. On the 17th itself, Ortega surrendered the city to Forey's soldiers.

Above: *Surgeon-Major of the Medical Service of the French army treats wounded on the field.* Below: *A beautiful steel model of a nineteeth century Mexican cannon (Turin, National Artillery Museum).*

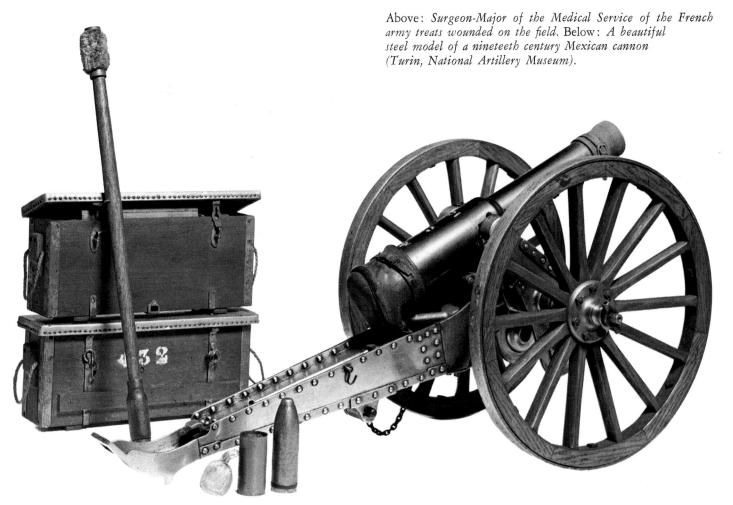

VICKSBURG (1863)

*"Oh, Susanna,
don't you cry for me."*

During the American Civil War the fortifications of Vicksburg were the key point of the defenses prepared by the southerners along the Mississippi. If they could be conquered the Union would have control of the whole course of the river and would be able to sever communications between the two blocs of Confederate States, that is, those to the west and the east of its banks.

Decisive operations against Vicksburg began in the winter of 1863, when Major General Ulysses S. Grant assumed command of a regroupment of forces which included the 13th army corps of General John A. McClernand, the 15th under General William T. Sherman and the 17th under General James B. McPherson. After attempts to surprise the city from the north had failed because of the swampy terrain and the resistance of Confederate sharpshooters hidden along many of the minor streams of the river, Grant worked out a plan of attack on the city from the south, and provided for, by the end of April 1863, a concentration of forces at a place called Hard Times, about 25 miles south of Vicksburg.

The chief of the Confederate forces of the Mississippi, General John C. Pemberton, became informed of this maneuver and hastened to reply to it by furnishing men to the garrison of Grand Gulf, a position of the Confederates facing Hard Times. He should have concentrated all his forces there but he was distracted by a diversionary northern action, destined to become famous

Right: *An episode during the siege of Vicksburg in a lithograph taken from an oil painting by Thulstrup, one of the noted painters of the Civil War. The painting is preserved in New York City, while the lithograph, part of the collection of Anne S.K. Brown, comes from the Brown University Library of Providence, Rhode Island. It shows the Union infantry attacking Confederate fortifications, forcing a barrier of sharpened stakes similar to those used by Caesar at Alesia.*
Left: *The Great Seal of the Southern Confederation, made in England and preserved in the Richmond Museum.*

because of its spectacular aspect. Under the command of Colonel Benjamin Henry Grierson, a hundred thousand Union cavalrymen made a raid seven hundred and fifty miles long from La Grange in Tennessee to Baton Rouge in Louisiana between April 17th and May 2nd. The reports that Pemberton received about the effects of this raid led him to send against Grierson all his cavalry and part of his infantry.

Taking advantage of this indirect success Grant inflicted on the Confederates, commanded by General John Bowen, a severe defeat at Port Gibson on May 1st. The following day the Confederates abandoned Grand Gulf. At the same time Grant learned that there was assembling at Jackson, capital of Mississippi, about fifty miles east of Vicksburg, an enemy army under the command of General Joseph E. Johnston, senior commander of all Confederate forces of the West (and therefore Pemberton's direct superior). On May 12th McPherson defeated a Confederate brigade at Raymond, about nineteen miles from Jackson. On May 14th, at four o'clock in the afternoon, Jackson was occupied by Union troops and Johnston was in precipitous retreat to the north. While Sherman stayed in Jackson, Grant moved west with two other army corps. On May 16th, Pemberton suddenly found himself facing the Federal army. The encounter took place at Champion Hill, about twenty-five miles to the east of Vicksburg. While McPherson energetically attacked on the right, McClernand found himself in difficulty on the left flank and was forced to slow down his march so much that the numerical superiority of the Union troops, who numbered twenty-nine thousand men against twenty-two thousand, was practically cancelled. Champion Hill was taken and lost several times during a day that can certainly be considered the most severe of all the campaign. It cost the Confederates four thousand men while Grant's losses were half of this. Finally Pemberton fell back on Vicksburg and fortified himself there, ignoring the order of Johnston, who wanted to make a general retreat. The last Southern bridgehead on the Big Black River was attacked on the 17th by Sherman (who had abandoned Jackson, immediately occupied by the Southerners), while McPherson and McClernand attacked a Confederate rearguard and, after an hour of struggle, captured eighteen cannon from the Confederates as well as a thousand seven hundred men. Aiming at Pemberton and his twenty thousand demoralized survivors, Grant arrived in front of Vicksburg on May 19th and, on the 22nd, tried to take it by assault. The Confederates resisted stubbornly, causing losses to the Northerners of more than three thousand men. Grant immediately understood that the city could be taken only by siege. Fearing that an operation of this kind would not only weaken his own forces but would also permit Johnston to reorganize the Southern troops and to attack him from the rear, Grant sought to make haste. He constructed trenches and ordered works of mining and countermining to be put into effect. Half of his seventy-one thousand men were deployed to the north and to the east in order to face an eventual return offensive by Johnston. Sherman's forces were deployed to the north of the city, those of McPherson to the east, and to the south of it those of McClernand (to be replaced by Edward Ord on June 18th).

Within Vicksburg, among increasing privations, thirty-one thousand men attempted through all means to make the city impregnable. The defensive works ordered by Pemberton ran for about eleven miles around the city and were garrisoned by the divisions of Martin Smith, John Forey, and Carter Stevenson, deployed respectively from north to south. General John Brown's division made up the reserve.

After the attack of May 22nd there were no more direct assaults on the city by the Union troops. From then on the siege, carried on along classic lines of artillery bombardments and blockade of reinforcements, found its principal expression in cannon, in snipers from the trenches, and in the increasing hunger of the besieged.

On May 24th the *Times* of Chicago wrote: "At Vicksburg Federal and Rebel forces are facing each other from trenches less than thirty-three feet away from each other." And the *Commercial* of Cincinnati reported: "The Federals can shoot the sparrows who alight on the Confederate positions." Actually the "Vauban" parallels of the Northern troops came to within seventy-five yards of the Southern fortifications. It is said that those of Sherman were so well protected against enemy fire that he could without danger send artillery and carts along its length. And hidden within their foxholes and shelters, sharpshooters of both armies carried on their work of marksmanship with terrifying diligence.

The other great protagonist of the siege was artillery. The Northerners rained down on the town projectiles of all kinds, from the normal explosive spherical charges weighing three hundred pounds to incendiary bombs loaded with inflammable materials, from cylindrical canisters loaded with grapeshot to massive iron balls attached two by two with heavy chains. Every twenty-four hours not less than seventy thousand projectiles of all calibers fell on the city. For their part, the Southerners were not far behind. One of their cannon, affectionately called "Whistling Dick" by the soldiers, has remained famous. Among the lesser known artillery pieces used at Vicksburg by the Yankee artillery was the eight-inch Dahlgren gun, so named by its inventor, Admiral John A. Dahlgren (1809-1870). It was constructed of fused iron and fired with an enormous noise, causing a notable psychological effect on the enemy. It was, however, of little practical effect and fell into disuse as more pratical weapons came into existence.

On June 25th the Confederates realized that the enemy was about to explode a mine under a fort held by the 3rd Louisiana regiment. The soldiers abandoned the position just in time to avoid being blown up by the explosion, which was an extremely violent one. Then they returned to the ruins to expel the Northerners who had entered with a rush. A second mine, which was exploded on the 29th, caused many victims among the infantry of the 3rd Lousiana.

The 4th Minnesota Regiment Entering Vicksburg. *Painted by F.D. Millet, it is preserved at the Minnesota State Capital in St. Paul. It is ten o'clock in the morning of July 4th, 1863, and forty-eight days have passed since the Union forces put a siege around the city so tight that, in the picturesque phrase of a Confederate officer: "Not even a cat would have been able to leave Vicksburg unnoticed." The fall of Vicksburg with the contemporaneous defeat at Gettysburg (July 1st to 3rd, 1863), cut the Confederacy in two and wiped out forever the possibility of a Rebel victory.*
Below: *One of the famous siege guns of the Civil War: the "Dictator," used by the Northern forces. It was so heavy that it had to be transported on a railway car.*

At three o'clock in the morning of July 3rd, Pemberton sent to Grant a message saying that he wished to negotiate a capitulation for the sole reason of avoiding more shedding of blood. Actually, the message concluded, he felt that he could hold his positions indefinitely. The dawn had not yet broken when Pemberton received a reply from the enemy. Ulysses Simpson Grant—faithful to the nickname which the soldiers had given him, from the initials of his first and middle names, "unconditional surrender"—sent word to Pemberton that there were no conditions to negotiate: Vicksburg must surrender and the garrison must surrender as prisoners of war. They would be treated as they deserved for the courage and firmness shown in the defense: "with all respect." But this was all that the government of the United States would concede to the "Rebels."

At eight o'clock in the morning Grant and Pemberton met near Fort Hill, accompanied by some of their officers. Bowen, who had been defeated at Fort Gibson, asked for the honors of war for the garrison as well as the possibility of leaving the city with the light artillery. He was brusquely silenced. This hasty conference was followed by a later exchange of messages between the two commanders, which took place on the following night. Toward midnight of July 3rd Grant's son, Fred, saw his father receive a note, open it, scan it, and break out with a sigh of relief, accompanied by the calm words: "Vicksburg has surrendered."

PARIS (1870-1871)

From the telegram of Ems to the Commune - the long Calvary of France.

L'année terrible *(The Terrible Year). This drawing from an English engraving of 1871 conveys a clear allegorical message. France, militarily humbled, is divided by factions (Paris, Hartmann Collection).*

In 1868 Queen Isabella of Spain lost the Spanish throne following a military coup. The Cortes of Madrid thereupon offered the crown of Spain to Prince Leopold von Hohenzollern Sigmaringen, a relative of the King of Prussia. He refused it. But France was so resentful of the offer that she demanded that Prussia pledge herelf not to accept similar offers in the future. Gramont, the French Minister of Foreign Affairs, wishing to achieve a diplomatic success, succeeded in angering the Prussian court to such a degree that as a result the famous telegram of Ems was sent, which Chancellor Bismarck had purposely composed so that it would read in a dry and impolite manner. The French felt humiliated and fell into a trap, declaring war on Prussia on June 19, 1870. This was the war that Bismarck had long dreamed of.

The Prussians seized the initiative of operations which, under the leadership of Marshal Helmut von Moltke, had the benefit of a detailed plan of attack and also, through the operations of a well-organized intelligence service, was able to prevent the enemy moves in advance by occupying Alsace and Lorraine. Marshal François-Achille Bazaine, put at the head of the most powerful French army, soon found himself blockaded in Metz, while MacMahon, who, with a second army, was getting ready to defend the capital, and who had received orders to relieve Bazaine, concentrated all his forces on the heights around the fortress of Sedan.

The attack of the Bavarians under General Von der Taun, and the wounding of MacMahon, resentful and careless because of his new orders, were the principal elements which contributed to the negative outcome (for the French) of the famous battle which takes its name from Sedan and which ended on September 1st in the greatest military disaster ever suffered by France: Napoleon III himself fell prisoner.

The Prussians now had the way open to Paris and it was clear that they would use it. Following a strategy which became a typical tactic of the German army, the advance guards would leave the elimination of pockets of resistance to the forces that followed them and would proceed directly to the attack on the capital.

In the metropolis, and of course in all of France, the press had convinced the people that the German army was at the point of collapse and was throwing its last reserves into the battle. The disenchantment of the people was all the more cruel when they saw the frantic haste employed in fortifying the capital.

General Trochu, in command of the city from August 17th, acted to reinforce it with new artillery and with a corps of volunteers. The outer forts already possessed a considerable force of artillery which was brought to its full complement. The entrance and exit of the Seine were fortified and a flotilla of gunboats was put in action on the river.

The 13th corps of General Vinoy was already in Paris and this was joined by other regiments of reservists and recruits. Thereafter twelve thousand sailors entered the city and were mustered into a division under the command of Rear Admiral La Roncière de Noury. Since they were expert in serving heavy caliber guns, they were assigned to the defense of the principal forts, each one of which had a marine battery under the command of a naval captain. In all about four hundred thousand men were mobilized for the defense of Paris. Their morale was sufficiently high, in spite of the presence of survivors from the battle of Sedan, who had fortunately escaped from prison camp.

On September 2nd the capitulation of Sedan was signed. On the 4th Paris proclaimed the Republic and formed an emergency government presided over by Léon Gambetta. Jules Favre and General Trochu also formed part of the new government. Around Paris work proceeded apace. To clear the field for cannon fire from the forts, trees and houses were removed.

On September 12th the Prussian advance guards reached Chateau-Thierry and on the following day they were at Crécy. The Prussian 3rd and 4th armies, crossing the Marne and the Aisne, proceeded with their plan of surrounding the city. On September 17th General Vogel von Falkenstein's army corps occupied the heights of Villeneuve. On the 19th the encirclement was complete. Emperor Wilhelm I established his general headquarters in the Royal Palace of Versailles.

General Ducrot failed, in a conflict at Châtillon, in

Franc-tireur column on the march and at rest in the environs of Paris, at the time of the siege (Paris, Library of the Museum of the Army). The franc-tireurs *were among the most typical combatants of the Franco-Prussian War. Divided in autonomous units of several dozen men each, attired in picturesque uniforms and bearing evocative names, they included men like Stefano Canzio and Frédéric-Auguste Bartholdi, future designer of the Statue of Liberty in New York. The sculptor was then the representative of Garibaldi with the government of national defense in Paris and customarily wore the red shirt of Garibaldi's legions.*

his plan to cut the advance column in two and with this the French right wing collapsed. This forced other units, which up to then had fought extremely well, to retreat, leaving free passage to the Prussian forces.

The news of a successful sortie raised the spirits of the besieged. It proved to be, however, only a lucky local engagement in which the Maud'huy division occupied and held the position at Villejuif.

The surrender of the fortresses of Toul, Strasbourg and Metz allowed the Prussians to make other forces available for a total and complete siege. At this moment the capital could count for its defense only on the forces who garrisoned it and on its forts, well manned by the sailors who were considered the best disciplined and bravest of the defense forces.

On October 7th, Léon Gambetta succeeded in leaving Paris by means of a balloon, in which, after an adventurous flight, he reached Tours, where a provisional capital had been established. He lifted up the spirit of

Two tragic moments of the Franco-Prussian war: the Germans in Paris, on the Place de l'Etoile and, right: an engraving taken from a painting by Giuseppe Ferrari of the burning of the French flags at Colombey, on October 27th, 1890 (Milan, collection fo the author).
Below:
Uniforms of the army of the Loire. The first soldier to the left is a Papal Zouave (by Le Passefoil, Paris, Library of the Museum of the Army). Many volunteers gathered in France from all parts of the world: among the most famous were Garibaldi and his son Ricciotti, who, in January, 1871, contributed, with the Army of the Vosges, the brilliant victory of Pouilly-les-Dijon.

the French through his energy and, forming three army corps, he prepared to rescue the city of Paris.

At Paris, meanwhile, the Prussians were entrenching themselves with formidable earthworks, perhaps in expectation of the siege artillery capable of battering down the forts previously considered unassailable. In effect, no direct assault was ever made on these forts. On October 28th, the encounter at Le Bourget took place, a village that the besieged forces captured by a sudden move and subsequently held in spite of an enemy attempt to regain it. It was actually a position of little strategic importance but the action served to raise the troops morale.

To lighten as far as possible the constant privations to which the population was subject, enormous and spacious common canteens were established where the people could obtain something to eat without suffering the exactions of the black market, which was rapidly prospering. After a time, only the privileged social classes were able to afford certain foods; prices had risen sky high and meat, in particular, was unobtainable. Animals of all kinds were eaten and finally the point was reached where dog, cat, and rat meat were paid for in gold.

On November 29th and 30th, the besieged forces carried out their strongest sortie: a hundred and forty thousand men with four hundred cannon moved against the enemy and occupied the plain of Avron while the sailors of Admiral Sasset set up sixty-eight heavy-caliber guns to protect passage across the Marne. In the very heavy fighting a Bavarian army corps was destroyed. A Prussian counterattack was unsuccessful in expelling the French from the territory they had won.

Within Paris hopes rose again. But on December 4th, General Ducrot's column was forced to return to its starting point. The Army of the Loire, which was attempting to relieve Paris, was also defeated. On December 28th the bombardment of the city began. The enemy put into action all the heavy caliber batteries that it had, in the meantime, installed and incessantly bombed the city and forts with grenades and shells. The effect of the bombardment, together with the cold, increasing

Prussian officers and soldiers on a reconnoitering action before Metz, according to a contemporary lithograph (Milan, author's collection). After the battle of Gravelotte (August 18th, 1870) Marshal François-Achille Bazaine shut himself within the stronghold of Metz, on the Moselle, with a hundred and sixty thousand men. The Prussians, under Prince Friedrich Karl, nephew of King Wilhelm, immediately set siege to the city. On August 31st Napoleon III attempted to break Bazaine's encirclement with an unsuccessful sortie that cost France more than thirty thousand men. The following day France suffered the famous defeat at Sedan, but Paris still remained unconquered and new armies were forming in the provinces. Everything, therefore, was not lost. Nevertheless, on October 27th, Bazaine with his troops surrendered to the enemy Metz, and a thousand five hundred cannon.

sickness, and the lack of food, forced the city to surrender, after one last sortie toward Mont Valérien. On January 26th, 1871, at 8:30 in the evening, the firing stopped and a capitulation was signed on the 28th. Ten days before this, in the Hall of Mirrors at Versailles, Wilhelm was proclaimed Emperor of Germany by the assembled German princes, the culmination of the movement for the national unity of Germany.

The armistice following the capitulation of Paris gave rise to the convocation of a National Assembly to discuss the peace conditions imposed by Germany. The assembly met at Bordeaux and proceeded to appoint Adolphe Thiers to the post of chief executive. Under his régime France acceded to the Treaty of Frankfurt on May 10th, 1871.

Meanwhile, however, the sufferings of France and of Paris were not yet over. In February the revolution of the Commune broke out. This was principally the result of a spirit of anger and protest against the social classes who had brought the German legions to Paris.

When the Germans left the city, popular fury broke out against Thiers. Anger reached its height when Thiers ordered the dissolution of the national guard.

The guard, about thirty thousand strong, occupied the Palais de Ville (City Hall) and forced Thiers to retreat to Versailles while the Commune organized itself into an autonomous workers government. This was on March 20th, 1871. Thiers, with the regular army – "the army of Versailles" – blockaded and then launched Mac-Mahon against the "Communards" for the reconquest of Paris. The Paris Commune fell on May 29th, after an extremely bloody repression of the rebellion.

On June 29th, at Longchamp, Thiers reviewed the army. At the end of the review he faced MacMahon and embraced him. Jules Cambon, who witnessed the episode, reported that the two men "approached each other, seized by an emotion also shared by the crowd. The soul of France was present, and one felt that the nation herself, wounded but not dead, was getting herself together again as a proof of her will to live."

Left: *An allegorical painting by Meissonnier dedicated to the siege of Paris (Museum of the Louvre). The cannon aimed at the enemy and attended by sailors celebrates the contribution made to the defense of the capital not only by the heavy artillery from within the fortifications, but also by the cannon of the flotilla of gunboats operating along the Seine. The severe sufferings of the civilian population during the siege is also noted.*

Above: *An affectionate caricature of Garibaldi, from a lithograph by Faustin, carrying an eloquent title indicating the general's popularity and the hopes placed in him by the French: "The Commander needed by the National Guards of Paris."*

The "Josephine" 190 mm. cannon (the maximum of the time) in Paris, 1870, from a painting by Guiaud and Decaeni (Paris, Museum of the Army).

The artillery depot at Montmartre, photographed March 18th, 1871, on the eve of the second siege of Paris by Thiers (Paris, Library of the Museum of the Army).

PLEVNA (1877)

The powder keg of Europe blows up and the Crescent dies amidst the wreckage

Officer of the Imperial Russian army of the 1st Guards brigade (Milan, Bertarelli Collection). Below: *Unusual hand weapon of the second half of the XIX century from the manual of Rudolf Schmidt,* Die Handfeuerwaffen, Basel, 1875 (Paris, Library of the Museum of the Army). Above right: *A picture from the* London Graphic *showing the Russian infantry on the march toward Plevna.*

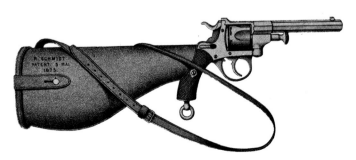

An unusual war was fought in the Balkans, the "powder keg of Europe," between Russia and Turkey from 1877 to 1878. After twenty years of peace following the Crimean war, Russia, rising as the paladin of the Slavic population subject to the Turks, intervened in support of Serbia, then engaged in a deathless struggle against the Sublime Porte. Czar Alexander II demanded that Constantinople disarm; Sultan Abdul Hamid II refused the Russian ultimatum and war resulted. Russia and Turkey did not have a common frontier in Europe. To make contact with each other the armies had to invade Rumania. Turkey abstained from doing so although Rumania was formally considered to be its "vassal," but Russia, on April 16th, 1877, made a pact with Rumania which permitted the passage of Czarist troops across Rumanian territory. Turkey, following the tactics of a defensive war, relied on the natural obstacles and on fortifications constructed here and there on the Balkan peninsula to stop the Russian advance. The first category included the Danube River. The Russians, however, under the command of Grand Duke Nicholas, younger brother of Czar Alexander II, crossed the Danube on the night of June 26th. The second category of obstacles to be overcome included Plevna (today Plevn, in Bulgaria), a fortified town which the Czarist army reached in the middle of July, after having taken Sistova (Svistov) and Nikopol.

Four Russian columns essayed an attack against the Ottoman defenses on July 19th, 1877, losing about three thousand men. Immediately afterwards there arrived in Plevna new Turkish forces under the command of Osman Pasha, one of the bravest generals of the time, who assumed command of the stronghold. The garrison, now increased by new arrivals to a strength of about

thirty thousand men, began to construct imposing defense works. Plevna became transformed into a true entrenched camp, with a perimeter of about 10 miles in length. Along this perimeter Osman deployed small garrisons while holding the greater part of his forces in Plevna, ready to rush to whatever positions were endangered. The extremely mobile Turkish artillery was also moved, according to need, from point to point.

The stronghold was again attacked by the Russians under General De Krüdener (thirty-six battalions, thirty squadrons, and twenty-three batteries) at seven o'oclock in the morning of July 30th, while the area was covered by a thick fog. Towards evening, when the entire Russian front was forced back, De Krüdener lay siege.

Plevna was not equipped with great reserves of food or ammunition and was thus dependent on reinforcements from the outside. Osman Pasha had organized so-called "operational lines" formed by access routes with stations garrisoned by three or four thousand men. Every two weeks great supply convoys were sent along these routes, which, in case of a Russian attack, could seek refuge within the closest station.

The new Russian attack against Plevna developed from the 6th to the 12th of September, against a garrison which had wall defenses manned by a powerful artillery corps. The Russians, now joined by Rumanian forces, had a hundred and ten thousand infantry, ten thousand cavalry, a hundred and fifty cannon of heavy and medium caliber, and others of light caliber.

On the morning of September 6th the Russian artillery opened fire to clear the way for the infantry. The Turkish earthworks, however, did not suffer much damage nor were there any serious losses within the Turkish camp, since Osman Pasha, as has been mentioned, kept the greater part of his forces in a sheltered spot, leaving a veil of troops in the outer works. In like manner, his artillery also avoided losses because of its great mobility. The weather also seemed to militate against the Russian attack, becoming suddenly wet and foggy. The attack, however, timed for September 11th took place punctually. The artillery became silent, and, under the eyes of the Czar, present on the battlefield, the infantry attacked at one o'clock in the afternoon, accompanied by fanfares of music and ruffles of drums. Some Turkish redoubts were overcome but finally the Russians had to return to their starting positions. Twenty-one thousand Russians had been put out of combat.

At this point the Czar called to Plevna General Frants Totleben, who, in 1854-1855, had directed the defense of Sevastopol. He advised blockading the stronghold, considering that Osman Pasha's reserves could not be very large, and that the town would soon fall from starvation. A hundred and twenty thousand men and five thousand cannon were placed around Plevna, completely surrounding it and subjecting it to an uninterrupted bombardment. Meanwhile, other Russian forces under the command of the young and brilliant General Osip Gurko scoured the countryside, attacked the supply stations between Plevna and Sofia and forced their garrisons to take refuge in Plevna or to flee to the mountains.

During early December Osman Pasha refused surrender after a demand by Grand Duke Nicholas, and on the night between the 9th and 10th of December, he tried to open a passage to Sofia for himself and twenty thousand men. But Totleben had forseen this and attacked at that moment. Osman Pasha, gravely wounded, fell prisoner. Gurko rendered homage to his valor, stating, with military simplicity: "I envy you."

KHARTOUM
(1884-1885)

The Dervishes dip their spears in Gordon's blood

In 1883, Egypt, which was nominally independent but which was in practice under the dominion of England, was faced by the famous Mahdist Revolt in the provinces of the Sudan. This revolt was a burst of Moslem fanaticism, a kind of holy war led by a certain Mohammed Ahmed, son of a Nubian carpenter. He had a passionate preoccupation with religion, and it is said that at the age of nine he had memorized the entire Koran. After having studied at Khartoum, the capital of the Sudan, Mohammed retired to the Isle of Abba, on the Nile, to meditate and fast in solitude. Convinced that he had been called by Allah to accomplish a great religious reform, he began to preach and to draw to him a constantly increasing band of faithful followers who saw in him the new Messiah, sent by Allah – the Mahdi. On May 11th, 1881, two hundred Egyptians landed on Abba where he was living in retirement, for the purpose of seizing him, dead or alive. They were cut to pieces. Thus began a series of very violent encounters, culminating in the massacre at Kashgal on November 3rd, 1883, when eleven thousand Anglo-Egyptians under the command of General William Hicks, called Hicks Pasha, were ambushed and massacred.

The British government then sent to Khartoum a soldier of great renown, General Charles George Gordon, called "Chinese" Gordon from his exploits in the Far East during the civil struggles China was suffering in the period 1860-1865. Gordon left Cairo on January 26th, 1884. When he arrived at Khartoum he realized that his forces were not sufficient for the task and requested reinforcements from London which were, however, refused. The reply to his call for help came to him when he was already cut off. In August the Mahdi personally moved on Khartoum at the head of two hundred thousand men to undertake its conquest. In response to the new and pressing demands of Gordon for reinforcements, the English prepared a column in Egypt and sent it on its way aboard eight hundred small boats by slow stages along the Nile. Sir Garnet Wolseley was in command. When the Mahdi was informed of the imminent arrival of the relief army, he hastened his plans and set siege to Khartoum. Early in November, while General Wolseley was still about a hundred and eighty-five miles from Khartoum, the situation within the city was already serious. Food and munitions were scarce and the native soldiers were continually deserting. The Mahdi kept sending his troops in a series of assaults on the city which the besieged were able to repulse with much bloodshed. By Christmas the situation was extremely critical.

The relief army was now south of Wadi Halfa, near Korti, and pleasantly celebrated the year end festivities by songs and distribution of small gifts. On December 30th, a courier from Gordon was able to reach Wolseley and inform him that Khartoum's resistance was approaching its end. Wolseley then detached one

On facing page, above title: *Egyptian soldiers of Hicks Pasha's expedition, massacred at Kashgal on November 3, 1883.* Above: *Arrival of the advance guard of Wolseley's relief army at Khartoum on four boats sent by Gordon to meet it. But it is already too late. The siege is over and Gordon has died horribly under the spears of the Dervishes. Both illustrations come from correspondents' reports to the* London Graphic *(Milan, author's collection).*
Below: *The last portrait of "Chinese" Gordon (Sandhurst, Army Museum). When he was in China, at the head of the "Ever Victorious Army," he used to lead the attack equipped with only a cane.*
The Chinese believed the cane had magic powers.

thousand six hundred men from a camel contingent and sent them as a rapid advance guard toward Khartoum. When the Mahdi learned of the advance of this detachment he sent ten thousand Dervishes to meet it. The encounter took place on January 17th, 1885, at a place called Abuklea, with favorable results to the British.

In spite of the severe losses they had suffered, they re-formed in time to face the attack of a second wave of Dervishes. Colonel Wilson, of the information services, especially distinguished himself at this time, although he had never been in command of combat troops. He was successful in repulsing the Mahdists and in reaching the river, where four boats sent by Gordon were awaiting him. Finally, on Febraury 28th, the reinforcements reached Khartoum. It was too late. The city had been in the hands of the bloody messiah since February 26th and Gordon had been killed on that same day. When the Moslems had swept over the city, killing without pity both civilians and soldiers, he had come out of the governor's palace, dressed in his white uniform and with a pistol in his hand. While he was demanding to be taken to the Mahdi, a spear struck him in the chest, killing him. The Dervishes fell upon his corpse, cut off its head, and sent it to their chief at Omdurman. The body of Gordon lay under the sun in the courtyard of the palace and, one after the other, the followers of the Mahdi approached to dip their spears in his blood. It was an atrocious end, which even the Mahdi condemned. The city was abandoned to the violence of the Dervishes. Four thousand people were killed by sword, the surviving men stripped naked, tied, and left to die under the sun. The women were distributed among the warriors.

PEKING (1900)

The "Harmonious Fists" defy Europe

The walls of Peking at the time of the siege of the Legations, an eloquent testimonial of the loyalty of the Clestial Empire to the outdated models of medieval-type fortifications (Milan, Bertarelli Collection).

The thousand-year-old Chinese isolation from the attention of Europe was broken in 1840-42 by England who, through the so-called "Opium War," forced China to accept the importation of the drug from India and to cede Hong Kong. Twenty years later, two Anglo-French expeditions (1858 and 1860) compelled the Celestial Empire to open another ten ports (including Tientsin) and to accept the establishment of Legations at Peking. Beaten in 1894 by land and sea by a modern and industrialized Japan, ancient China revealed all her weakness, arousing thereafter the cupidity of the great European powers. Between 1897-1899 a real race to dismember China brought the Russians to Port Arthur, the English to Wei-Hai-Wei, the Germans to Kiao-Chow, and the French to Kwang-Cho-Wan.

The Chinese Government reacted to such an invasion by fostering hatred of foreigners among its nationals and organzing secret societies, of which the most outstanding was the "Harmonious Fists," or Boxer. This movement, born in Peking, spread to the interior of the country and assumed an increasingly violent character. Acts of hostility against foreigners attributed to the Boxers became so frequent that on May 20th, 1900, the Diplomatic Corps sent an ultimatum to the Imperial Court demanding necessary guarantees.

The Empress Tzu-Hsi finally promised to meet the demands, but also permitted large groups of Boxers to carry out violent demonstrations in Peking, demanding the expulsion of the foreigners. The diplomats then asked their ships stationed at Taku to send, for the protection of their respective Legations in Peking, units from the different warships. Detachments came to the capital toward the end of May and the beginning of June of 1900. Almost at the same time the Imperial Chinese Army of General Tung-Fu-Siang arrived in the capital.

On the 19th of June the Legation received the ulti-to go to Tientsin by rail. The Diplomatic Corps answered through their dean, the Spanish de Calogan, asking for more time and an adequate escort. But the following day, when the German Minister, Baron von Kettler, was killed in the street by Boxers, the situation changed suddenly and it appeared clear that the diplomatic representatives were in a state of siege.

An entire quarter of Peking was occupied by the Legations. It was located within the so-called "Tartar City," next to the Great Wall, between the other two zones of the Chinese City and the Imperial City. The Legations were those of France, Italy, Japan, Russia, Austria, Holland, Germany, Spain, America, and Belgium. It was decided to shorten the line of all the Legations into a quadrilateral area more easily defended, to move women and children to the British Legation which was larger and less exposed, to abandon the Legations of Belgium and Holland, which were too decentralized, and to occupy several positions on the Wall to the south, for better observation of Chinese movements.

Pei-Tang, the residence of the Archbishop of Peking, was another isolated center of resistance and the site of the cathedral. The faithful were gathered there, Europeans and native, defended by a detachment of French sailors, later joined by some Italians. Some Europeans formed the nucleus of a group of volunteers aided by natives who took turns at guard duty and who often penetrated within the city to guide to safety groups that were still isolated. Each unit was assigned the defense of a sector while the sailors prepared the defense with the digging of trenches, the construction of barricades and sandbags. The combatant forces were composed of sixty-one English marines, fifty American sailors, twenty-four Japanese, thirty Austrians, forty-five French, fifty-one Germans, seevnty-two Russians, and thirty-one Italians.

The heaviest weapons were one American machine gun, one Austrian gun, one English gun, and a small caliber Italian cannon. Command was entrusted to Tho-

man, an Austrian, and then to an Englishman, Sir Claude McDonald.

At four o'clock in the afternoon of June 20th, the ultimatum having expired, the Regular Imperial Forces opened fire on the Legation defenses, arraying themselves in effect with the Boxers. Operations, marked by sorties and bayonet charges, ran down every so often as the combat changed to long silent pauses during which the Chinese, protected from the destruction, smoked and drank their tea. On the 9th of July some Chinese, having penetrated the French Legation, were captured, hung up by their pigtails to a tree, and interrogated. They admitted belonging to the army of Tung-Fu-Siang and declared that about eighteen thousand regular troops were surrounding the Legations. On July 13th two mines shook the French Legation without any result other than starting a fire. The Chinese soldiers appeared to fear making assaults by sword or bayonet and in general abstained, leaving such attacks to the Boxers. In the middle of July a truce was arrived at, and even an exchange of courtesies. The Empress sent two small wagons of fruit and vegetables to the besieged. Meanwhile the Declaration of War by China on the different Western Powers was announced, dated the 25th day of the 5th moon (the tragic 20th of June) and Europe mobilized. But the Legations could not expect reinforcements before too long a time and therefore available forces were concentrated in the immediate vicinity of Tientsin. During the middle of July, while the truce was in effect, the besieged received word that a relief column had left Tientsin around the 20th of July. On the 22nd of July the Russian, Italian, and English Ministers learned that

Picture No. 186 of the series Imagerie d'Epinal *of Pellerin (Rome, Gasparinetti Collection) shows a moment during the siege of the Legations in Peking. Unsuccessful in their efforts to penetrate the buildings held by the Europeans by assault, the Chinese are about to use their artillery which will cause considerable damage to the besieged. These were almost all sailors employed for the first time in battle, but they behaved like veterans.*

the column had not yet left and that moreover it would not move until the arrival of reinforcements. They kept this news secret so as not to increase the anxiety of the besieged, who were now menaced by hunger and the imminence of the rainy season which would hinder the progress of the forces coming to the relief of the besieged.

Finally, on August 9th, the Regular Chinese Forces left the siege positions to Manchu troops. This was a definite indication that the relief columns were approaching. Tung-Fu-Siang had in fact attempted to stop them. When, during the night between the 11th and 12th of August, the besieged heard at last the noise of cannon close at hand, they understood that the Chinese had not succeeded in their attempt and prepared to receive their liberators. These were seven thousand Japanese forming the first column and another ten thousand troops in a second column composed of English, Russian, American, French, German, and Italian elements. Russian cannon demolished the heavy gate of the "Chinese City" and entered it on the night of the 13th and the 14th. At half past three the English made the first contact with the Legations. The band of the "Harmonious Fists" was broken forever.

PORT ARTHUR (1904-1905)

A river of oriental blood sweeps away the myth of occidental invincibility

A salvo of twenty torpedoes from the torpedo boats of the Japanese Admiral Togo launched against the Russian ships at anchor in the bay of Port Arthur marked the beginning of operations against the famous Russian naval base in the Far East. The time was eight o'clock in the evening of February 9th, 1904. Thus, without the traditional declaration of war, began a conflict which would prove to be extremely bloody and would establish the technical and military progress made by modern Japan. This had been foreseen in 1894, during the Sino-Japanese War, sometimes called the war over Formosa.

Port Arthur had already been in the hands of the Japanese during the latter war, but they had been forced to evacuate in 1896 by the combined pressure of France, Russia, and Germany. Two years later, in 1898, China was forced by Russia to "rent" her Port Arthur. Czarist Russia immediately went to work to fortify the port and to equip it with all the services necessary to make it a great naval base. She then concentrated there the most important and most efficient units of her Pacific fleet. Vladivostok, which had formerly enjoyed this position, passed to a subordinate rôle. Obviously, the base was a menace directed against Japan, who after having tried to establish through diplomatic channels the spheres of influence of the two nations, was unable to obtain any other result than that of playing a secondary rôle to Russia. Japan therefore suddenly decided to leave the decision to the cannon and to the torpedo.

The city and port of Port Arthur situated at the end of Kwantung, a southern section of the Manchurian peninsula of Liaoutung, were circled by an amphitheater of steep hills, from about three hundred and twenty-five

to six hundred feet high and were connected to the open sea by a canal one thousand yards long and about four hundred and forty yards wide. The nature of the surrounding terrain had made it possible for first the Chinese and then the Russians to equip the stronghold with what seemed to be formidable fortifications. At the time that Togo's torpedoes exploded, the seafront of Port Arthur, five miles long, was fortified by twenty-two batteries, equipped with cannon of calibers varying from one hundred and fifty to two hundred and eighty millimeters. The greater part of these batteries were employed at points more than three hundred feet above sea level. Others placed at a lower elevation served to protect the defenses near the base. On a cliff called the "Electric Rock," which dominated the outer roadstead, there had been installed at a bomb-proof point an electric station which supplied four sub-stations of searchlights.

On the land front, the defense framework was composed of a fortified defense line fourteen miles long, enclosing the entire peninsula. It contained forts of permanent character, equipped with guns of medium caliber and capable of effective passive resistance; light defense works but with concrete casements which gave them a semi-permanent character; redoubts for field infantry, for field operations, and various batteries, giving a total of about six hundred medium- and small-caliber cannon.

The forts, to which access was gained over drawbridges, were capable of resisting rounds from cannon up to two hundred and eighty millimeters. The systems adopted by the garrison in order to increase the defensive capacity of the city which, in spite of everything, was still behind the times in necessary defenses against siege warfare, were nevertheless ingenious and anticipated some of those which would be used in World War I. Use was made of electrically charged barbed wire. In order to cut through this wire, the Japanese employed the first shears with handles covered with insulating material or long poles of bamboo full of black powder and gun cotton exploded by men protected by metal shields. In addition, in order to illuminate the battlefield, the Russians employed, besides searchlights, special rockets, called "starshells."

On their side, the Japanese constructed siege trenches which were completely buried. There were shelters designed to be resting places for the veterans of the assaults and there were also semi-buried trenches for winter quarters capable of housing fifty men. The besieged made frequent use of "wolf jaws," that is, man traps with steep sides, often equipped with sharpened stakes. Hand grenades were employed, constructed by using cartridge or shell casings with a wooden stopper traversed by a fuse. Torpedoes and land mines, set off electrically by conductors buried up to a depth of more than twelve feet, were used with telling effects. Finally the Japanese devised a system of launching bombs from very light wooden mortars, bound with bamboo.

The Russian garrison of Port Arthur, under the command of General Anatoli Stësel, commander of the 3rd Siberian army corps, included two divisions of Siberian light infantry, the 4th and the 7th, commanded in turn by General Kondratenko (who would later be one of the heroes of the siege), and another regiment, the 5th, also of light infantry. In all, the Russians had thirty-five thousand men, twenty-four thousand infantry and the crews of the ships anchored in the port.

The Japanese surrounding the stronghold were commanded by General Count Marosuke Nogi, and were divided into two divisions, composing the 3rd army, reinforced by a division of the 2nd army. A fourth division which arrived later brought the number of the besiegers to eighty thousand men. The artillery, made up of seventy medium-caliber pieces, was totally inadequate to the task. This would prove very costly to the infantry, who would be called upon to make unheard of sacrifices in the relatively absurd attempt to win the victory with bayonet charges.

Facing page, above title: *A symbolic drawing illustrating the Japanese victory of the war against Russia with a samurai and with the banner of the Rising Sun waving over the bay of Port Arthur. It is taken from the work* Japans Krieg und Sieg *(Berlin, Schall) as is the illustration reproduced above, describing, in all its cruelty, an episode of the siege. Japanese infantry are caught in ropes by the Russians during the siege and thrown back on those below. (Rome, Central Military Library).*
Below: *A detail from a page of the* Imagerie d'Epinal de Pellerin *shows a heavy caliber Russian naval cannon employed in the defense of the fortifications and served by sailors as it would be aboard the ship from which it came (Paris, Library of the Museum of the Army). The use of cannon of this kind during the siege is excellently described in the* Tales of Sevastopol *by Leo Tolstoy, who was an eyewitness of the siege of that city, described earlier.*

Before proceeding with the siege of the port, the Japanese had to interrupt railway communications between Manchuria and Port Arthur, and isolate the peninsula. Since the Russian engineers had destroyed or put in a safe place all the locomotives, the Japanese were forced to use the cars for short distances only, activating them by manpower. The stations, strongly garrisoned by special contingents of frontier guards, opposed unexpected resistance to the Japanese.

The city became cut off after the battle of Nanshan and was then besieged by the 3rd army, while the 2nd army turned to the north, aimed at Mukden, with orders to impede the advance of any Russian troops sent to the relief of the city.

Meanwhile, on April 13th the Russian fleet, commanded by Stefan Makarov, called the "Cossack Admiral," attempted a sortie with the aim of breaking the blockade of the Japanese ships of Admiral Heihachiro Togo. But Makarov's flagship, the battleship *Petropavlovsk*, hit by a mine, sank with the admiral and six hundred sailors. The rest of the fleet was forced to return to Port Arthur.

In June of 1904 the Japanese forces established themselves on a line distant six to fifteen miles from the city. Since the Japanese had already taken the city by storm during their war against China, they did not foresee a long siege. The Russian resistance therefore surprised them and even more of a surprise was the determined counteroffensive which the Russians launched against them in July. The Russians employed their naval artillery as well and were able to stop the enemy through the use of mobile troops operating outside of the fortified complex.

Meanwhile, the Russian command was making ready a defense line which would go across the entire Kwantung peninsula from Louise Bay to the Bay of Takei. Against the almost nine miles of line which protected the port and the center of the city from the fire of enemy artillery, the Japanese had to sacrifice four thousand men before they were able to overcome it, and then to reach, on June 30th, the outer fortifications.

On August 9th the Japanese were successful in occupying the heights of Takyshan and setting foot on the right bank of the Taho. They were then in a position to bombard, with indirect fire, the old city and the port. On August 17th Nogi offered Stësel the opportunity to surrender, sparing the garrison. But the offer was refused in spite of the fact that at that time the Russian naval squadron had disastrously failed in its efforts, following orders from the Czar, to leave the besieged stronghold and to join the Vladivostok squadron. As a result there was a direct encounter between Togo and Vitheft, commander of the Russian fleet, resulting in the decimation and dispersal of the latter.

The Russian admiral, hoisting his flag over the battleship *Czarevich*, left the bay on August 10th with three cruisers, five ships of the line, and various minesweepers and destroyers. At the head of the fleet sailed the cruiser *Novik*, the fastest in the Pacific. But this was the moment that Togo had been waiting for for some time. He attacked the Russians and in a series of combats destroyed the greater part of the fleet. Vitheft died on his flagship, and the *Novik*, which had first escaped from the enemy, was finished off by several cruisers. This proved to be a general rehearsal for Tsushima, the battle in which, on May 27th, 1905, Togo also destroyed the Russian Baltic fleet, which had arrived too late to save the Czar's naval forces in the Pacific.

All this had not succeeded in diminishing the combative spirit of the Russians, who inflicted on the Japanese losses of another fourteen thousand men, in encounters from the 19th to the 24th of August, forcing the enemy to suspend operations up to the 19th of September. After having made new approach works, the Japanese infantry returned to the attack, concentrating its efforts now on Fort Kuropatkin, on whose escarpments it left another ten thousand men to accrue to their losses. After overcoming the fort, the Japanese then prepared for a final assault.

The attack started on November 26th and continued for ten days, with enormous losses. It took the Japanese to the famous hills 203 and 210, which the Russians abandoned after savage hand-to-hand fighting only because they were so greatly outnumbered. On December 5th, under an inferno of fire, the Siberian light infantry left the summit, on which the Japanese could now posi-

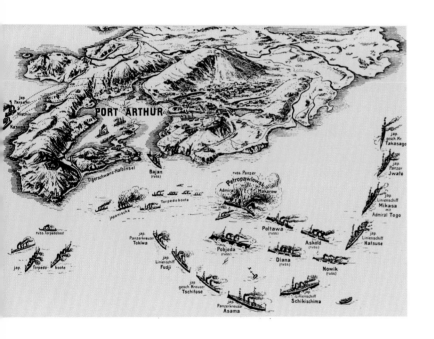

One of the most dramatic moments of the siege. The date is April 3rd, 1904. For two months the Russian fleet, under the command of Stefan Makarov, called the "Cossack Admiral," has been blockaded within the port by the squadron of Heihachiro Togo. On April 13th, Makarov attempted a sortie, but his flagship, the battleship Petropavlovsk, *hit a mine and sank, taking with it six hundred sailors. Makarov drowned with his men. The Russian fleet would not move again until the besieging Japanese would bring it under their artillery fire and bombard it from the hills. Then, under the command of Admiral Vitheft, it would again leave port and head toward Vladivostok. But Togo would be waiting and Vitheft too would not survive the battle.*

tion their 280 guns and open bombardment of the port and the Russian ships.

General Kondratenko lost his life on December 15th while he was engaged in countermining operations. On the 18th the Japanese succeeded in blowing up Fort Kikuan by means of a mine. This fort was located on the northeast front of the city and the Japanese, after repeated attacks, were able to occupy the ruins. Ten days later the same fate overtook Fort Ertung, which held out, however, for another four hours after the explosion of the mine. By the end of December the Japanese had been able to open a breach in the main defense front while they continued to bombard the city. On New Year's Day of 1905, a Russian emissary appeared at the Japanese advance posts to negotiate surrender. The document of surrender was signed January 2, 1905.

On the summit of Hill number 203 there was erected, in the following years, a singular monument, an enormous cartridge, pointed toward the sky, with the three numbers designating the tragic hill arranged vertically, as is customary, in Japanese characters. These characters also mean, in Japanese, "the hill of your spirit." Nogi, perhaps thinking of his younger son, who had fallen within sight of the hill (the other fell at Nanshan) composed a song which was popular in Japan for many years to come.

Some years later, the victor of Port Arthur committed harakiri in his silent house, while in the street outside the casket of the Emperor of Japan, of the family of the Sons of Heaven, was passing by.

Japanese infantry attacking a Russian position at Chan-bo-kan, the evening of August 30th, 1904. During the preceding ten days the Japanese lost fourteen thousand men. Some regiments were reduced to three hundred men with six or seven surviving officers. The heavy losses forced the Japanese to a halt in their offensive operations, which they undertook again on September 19th. The illustration is a part of the aforementioned work by Güdke, as is also the final reproduction, in which two wounded soldiers of the opposing armies, a Russian on the left and a Japanese on the right, rest under a palm tree symbolizing peace, in the light of the rising sun and fragile paper lanterns. It represents a pathetic attempt to tone down the horrors of a war which, in many respects, will remain one of history's most cruel. The sufferings of the Japanese infantry were particularly severe, as they were ordered by Nogi to make unheard-of sacrifices. Their losses were so great that they were scornfully criticized by the European nations.

LIÈGE (1914)

The "420" millimeter gun thunders for the first time by orders of Alfred von Schlieffen

When hostilities broke out between Germany and France on August 1st, 1914, introducing the First World War, the German General Staff was concerned before anything else with putting into action its attack plan, worked out in minute detail by Alfred von Schlieffen which postulated the invasion of France through the southern part of Belgium. According to the plan, a strong German right wing (formed by the 1st and 2nd armies), was to cross the Meuse between Huy and the Dutch border, turning the main French front, and then, taking advantage of surprise, turn toward the Channel coast. The same plan, more or less reexamined and corrected, was later applied by Adolf Hitler.

Above: A German seal-stamp dedicated to the artillery and to the siege of Antwerp which followed the siege of Liège (Milan, author's collection).
Below: Two pages of a curious satirical British brochure illustrating the "unexpected delay" experienced at Liège by the German invasion forces. Particular emphasis is given to the caliber of the German artillery which, at Liège, put in the field for the first time guns of 420 millimeters. Two lancers with spiked helmets symbolize the second corps thrown by the Germans into the operation.
Following page: A representation according to an Italian popular print of the encounter between the opposing cavalry forces at Liège.

According to exact timing, the two German armies were to carry out their preoffensive deployment in Belgian territory by August 16th and then wait for the order to proceed against France. The only real obstacle to the timetable exactness of the successful carrying out of the plan was the Belgian army and, in particular, the Belgian forces manning the forts. Specifically the fortress city of Liège was the great question mark from the point of view of the German General Staff. Liège was guarded by twelve forts, constructed with modern methods between 1880 and 1891, equipped with seventy-eight medium-caliber artillery pieces. Besides these, two old fortified works dominated the hill: the Carthusian fort and the Citadel.

On August 5th the garrison was increased to thirty thousand men while the Germans brought to bear six

brigades and the greater part of the 2nd cavalry corps of General Otto von Emmich, as well as the personal presence of General Erich Ludendorff, of the General Staff, who had a perfect knowledge of all details of the Schlieffen plan. Counting on surprise it was considered that it would be possible to occupy the city of Liège by infiltrating past the forts which would then be eliminated. The attack was begun on August 4th to the right and to the left of the city. The Germans encountered a vigorous Belgian resistance as well as the obstacle represented by the Meuse River because of the destruction of the Visi bridge. On the 5th, having established a temporary bridge, the German infantry was able to cross to the other bank and establish a bridgehead there despite serious losses. On the night of the 6th, the XXXIV brigade, passing between the forts of Liers and Pontisse, made a frustrated attempt at the city. A night attack by a Zeppelin dirigible was also unsuccessful.

Ludendorff, conquering all resistance, went through the line of forts and entered the city. At midday of the 6th his brigade arrived at the Carthusian, whose garrison was now reduced to fifteen hundred men.

On the night of the 7th other German forces entered the city while the garrison of the Citadel, now reduced to a thousand, surrendered. The Belgian command had retired the greater part of its mobile forces, leaving the duty of guarding the forts to the garrisons.

The governor of Liège, General Gérard Leman, took shelter in Fort Loncin to direct the last resistance. Meanwhile the Germans had taken control of the railroads and all bridges. On the 8th they took Fort Barchon while the supreme command, located at Aachen, ordered that the 7th corps, under the command of General Emmich, be assigned the task of capturing the forts. To this effect heavy artillery pieces were gathered and sent to Liège, including some heavier than ever used before. Mortars of such unusual caliber as 300 and 420 millimeters started the bombardment of the fortifications on the morning of August 15th. Fort Loncin fell under the shells and General Leman was made prisoner among the ruins. The forts of Hollogne and Flemalle finally raised the white flag on the 16th. Now the way was free for the Germans. While the Belgian and Allied forces retired toward Antwerp, the Germans reactivated the railways and, on the 17th, completed the deployment of the two armies. On the morning of the 18th they began their advance according to the instructions indicated on the maps of the late Alfred von Schlieffen.

TOLEDO (1936)

Around the Alcázar, the last romantic siege of history

This was how the siege of the Alcázar was interpreted by Vittorio Pisani for the Rome Tribuna Illustrata *in 1936, in showing an episode in which the besieged got control of a pump with which the besiegers were trying to spray the defense works with gasoline and then to set them on fire. The military cadets based at the Alcázar are generally mentioned as its defenders although, in reality, the cadet students were on summer leave at the moment of the siege. To defend the forthess, Colonel José Moscardó, who was in command, was able to count on only six hundred and fifty men of the Civil Guard and a few other soldiers.*

The word Alcázar was long used in Spain to designate royal palaces. The Alcázar of Toledo was noted more for its solid and unassailable walls than for its imposing architecture. These walls were ten feet thick. It was the seat of the Spanish Military Academy under the command of Colonel José Moscardó Ituarte, when, on July 17th, 1936, there broke out in Melilla, in Morocco, the revolt which would end in the installation of the régime of General Franco.

Two days later the government ordered Moscardó to send to the capital all arms and ammunition stored at the arms factory in Toledo. The Colonel replied that he refused to make shipment and that he was in support of the insurgents. His decision was considered treasonable and on the 21st government troops arrived in Toledo to arrest him and his rebellious supporters. Moscardó, realizing that he would not be able to hold the city, after some combat within the city ordered the local garrison of the Guardia Civil to enclose themselves within the Alcázar.

The occupants of the fortress rose to about fifteen hundred with this addition. There were 328 women and 210 children in the Alcázar, principally members of soldiers' families stationed in Toledo. The others, the fighting troops, were 650 members of the Guardia Civil and seven Academy cadets. Officers and noncommissioned officers numbered 147. Munitions were in abundance. The insurrectionists had at their disposal one thousand rifles, thirteen machine guns, and numerous hand grenades, all taken in time from the arms factory of Toledo.

On July 23rd the militia forces began a long telephone conversation with Colonel Moscardó, demanding immediate and unconditional surrender. When he refused, they put his son Luis, seventeen years old, on the telephone; he was being held prisoner at the palace of the provincial deputies. Luis informed his father that if the Alcázar was not surrendered within ten minutes he, Luis, would be shot. Moscardó replied: "Then commend your soul to God, shout 'Long live Spain' and die as a patriot." Several hours later, Luis Moscardó was shot, while his father proceeded with the final organization of the defense. The mules and horses (124 in all), destined to be the future food of the besieged (only six would be alive at the end of the siege), were lodged in the safest possible part of the stone fortress. The water was rationed: a liter a day per person. Through night sorties, Moscardó's men were able to transport within the Alcázar grain from a nearby storehouse. A rudimentary machine was improvised, run by a motorcycle motor, for the purpose of reducing the grain into flour.

Since the government forces had suddenly interrupted the water, telephone, and electric services, the besieged provided their own illumination through rudimentary lamps which burned animal grease. A small field receiving radio set permitted them to get news from the outside. The news was transcribed in a small bulletin distributed daily among the besieged.

In early August the fortress was surrounded by about eight thousand government soldiers. The Republican air force concentrated a good part of its planes in the skies of Toledo, carrying out 120 missions over the Alcázar. During this same period ten civil guards deserted the rock fortress. The total number of desertions was 35.

On the thirty-fourth day of the siege a plane flew over the Alcázar, dropping into the ruins of the fortress a message announcing the arrival of a Falangist relief column. Moroccan legionnaires were advancing on Madrid, and Andalusia was under the control of the nation-

"If in the struggle you see fall my horse and my banner — lift up my banner before you lift me." The inscription above is written on a monument to Carlos V which rises in the courtyard of the Alcázar and which was damaged during the siege.

alist General Varela: Colonel Moscardó was no longer alone. The besieged felt themselves renewed in spite of their sufferings and privations. On September 9th Moscardò was able to answer "No" to a government envoy, Major Vicente Rojo, who had come to offer conditions for surrender. A mission on the part of the canon superior of Madrid, Monsignor Vázquez Camarrasa, had no better success. The government ordered the Alcázar to be mined. The noise of the ensuing drills kept the besieged from sleeping.

On September 17th the Republican government caused the city to be evacuated in order to spare useless shedding of blood among civilians, and invited foreign journalists and war correspondents to witness what was to be the Alcázar's last resistance.

The mine exploded at six in the morning on September 18th, destroying the tower of the southeast corner of the Alcázar and opening a breach in the wall. Government and Falangist forces threw themselves at each other in a savage bayonet encounter which lasted three hours. A red flag appeared over the ruins only to be replaced a short while later by the red and gold flag of the Falangist nationalists.

On September 27th, while the troops of General Varela were deploying themselves around Toledo, another mine struck the northeast side of the building. At sunset the first members of the relief forces entered an Alcázar now in flames. The following morning Colonel Moscardó gave over the command of the half destroyed fortress of the Alcázar to General Varela, with the famous phrase: "Sin novedad" — (Nothing to report).

LENINGRAD (1941-1943)

"O city of Peter, uncontrollable Russia" (Pushkin)

Founded by Czar Peter the Great in 1703 at the mounth of the river Neva, on the Baltic Sea, Leningrad was capital of the Russian Empire from 1712 to 1917, under the names of St. Petersburg and Petrograd. On January 26th, 1924, when the Soviet government, after having overthrown the Czarist regime, had already established the capital in Moscow for five years, the city was given its present name, in honor of Nikoai Lenin, founder of the Communist International.

Hitler's Germany, together with Italy and Rumania, declared war on Russia on June 22nd, 1941. On the 25th Finland and Czechoslovakia also declared war against the USSR. Then the so-called Operation Barbarossa was put into effect, the plan for the rapid conquest of Russia by the German army, worked out by Hitler at the end of December 1940 and always rigorously kept secret.

The plan, whose name goes back to medieval Germany and to the Emperor Frederick Barbarossa, predicated a mass attack on all fronts by three groups: one to the north, one to the center, and one to the south.

The *Heeresgruppe Nord* (Northern Army Group) was commanded by General Ritter von Leeb and was formed by the 16th and 18th armies and by the Hoepner armored group, making a total of twenty-six divisions. It was this *Heeresgruppe* which, after having conquered Kovno, Dünaburg, and Pskov between June 23rd and July 8th, 1941, cut off the Soviet army of the Baltic and aimed at Leningrad. At about ninety-three miles from the city, von Leeb divided his army group into three columns and, advancing them in three different directions, attempted to encircle Leningrad.

An old Czarist fortress, Schlisselburg, transformed into a modern fort, resisted for five days, keeping open a narrow corridor toward the east. But the Germans conquered this obstacle as well and Leningrad was left cut off from the rest of Russia by land. Water routes remained open, the Gulf of Finland to the west and Lake Ladoga to the northeast, but German and Finnish aircraft and ships could interfere with reinforcements sent by this route.

Leningrad, crowded with refugees, had five million inhabitants during this period. They collaborated decisively in the construction of formidable defense works, transforming the houses in the most threatened districts into small fortresses with cement embankments and palisades of tree trunks. A stadium which was in construction was dismantled and artillery positions were constructed with the salvaged material.

The factories continued to function and to produce munitions, weapons, and even armored tanks. The Kirov factory, famous in Czarist times under the name of Pu-tilov, formed a special unit among its workers, called the Civic Guard of Leningrad. Deployed with other operational units, it functioned as an assault unit, engaging the Germans in the manner they most feared: hand-to-hand combat with the bayonet.

In the winter of 1942 the besieged were successful in establishing contact with outside supply centers by constructing a railway over the ice of frozen Lake Ladoga. To somewhat obviate the effects of the terrible cold and the lack of supplies for heating, the bottom of the port was dragged. It was considered that, since the port had been used for fifty years as a coal port, considerable amounts of coal must have sunk to the bottom. Indeed, it had. A quantity of no less than five thousand tons was retrieved.

In order to overcome starvation, which claimed victim after victim, every bit of cultivable land was put to use to grow food, preferably cabbage, which soon invaded plazas, gardens, courtyards, and terraces.

Meanwhile, the German artillery and bombing planes were engaged in demolishing the palaces and monuments which had made Petersburg so splendid and sumptuous a city. Against the bombers barrage balloons were raised, but nothing could be done against the artillery. Shells fell everywhere, killing people in the streets, unexpectedly. A Russian officer, interviewed by a reporter when the siege was over, reported that he had seen a man running during a bombardment who suddenly had his head cut off by a piece of shrapnel but who still kept on running, horribly, for several yards, without his head. (At Vicksburg something very similar happened to a cavalry officer, who remained sitting in his saddle for some seconds after his head was cut off.)

In December of 1942 the Russians recaptured the fortress of Schlisselburg and the situation improved. On January 18th, 1943, the same day in which the epic of Stalingrad began, the Germans raised the siege of Leningrad. During the last month of struggle, they lost seventy thousand men before Leningrad. They would lose others in their retreat, pursued by two Soviet armies charged with mopping-up operations around the city.

The siege of Leningrad would remain the most memorable of the Second World War. Its duration – sixteen months – and the unheard-of sufferings endured by its inhabitants and by the besieging forces themselves, have few equals, at least in recent history. And what is especially unique is the event which occurred in Leningrad – in which workers voluntarily formed themselves into a fighting unit – of a factory, the Kirov works, being awarded the two highest Soviet decorations: The Order of the Red Banner and the Order of Lenin.

Enormous siege cannon were put in action against Leningrad by the Germans, like this one depicted in an illustration of the Domenica del Corriere, May 3rd, 1942, one of the last by Achille Beltrame. Similar guns were used to bombard the stronghold of Sevastopol to which the Germans laid siege during the Crimean campaign of 1942.

STALINGRAD
(1942-1943)

*"The Sixth Army will hold out
to the last man:
I forbid surrender." (Hitler)*

The German 6th army under General Friedrich Paulus reached Stalingrad on September 13th, 1942. Conquest of this great industrial city signified, for Hitler, the availability of a navigable river such as the Volga, on whose bank was located the city which, since 1924, had born the name of the then Soviet chief of state, the Georgian, Joseph Vissarionovich Stalin. (Today it is called Volgograd.) Convinced of being able to take Stalingrad with a first easy assault, the Germans had sent against it only a single army, the 6th army of Paulus, supported by the 3rd Rumanian army, and the 8th air corps, under the command of von Richtofen. This great optimism came from the German conviction that the Russian army had ceased to exist. But fresh Russian troops were massing beyond the Volga, well trained, equipped with newly developed weapons, such as the T-34 tank, the terrible multiple rocket launchers Katiuscia BM-8 and BM-13, and the self-propelled CY-76 cannon. The Germans could not imagine this. Before them were only fugitives, remains of destroyed and disbanded armies. In their pursuit they had reached the Don and had crossed it at the nearest point to the Volga. And then they had come to Stalingrad.

The Soviet General Vassili Zhukov had organized the defense of Stalingrad as well as he could, collecting scattered units and opposing the 4th army of General Hoth, who was advancing from the south with three infantry divisions and a marine brigade.

On August 23rd Paulus reached the Volga to the north of the city, where forty thousand Russian civilians had died under the bombs dropped by six hundred planes. Three hundred thousand succeeded in fleeing across the river. The others huddled in the shelters and awaited events, together with the soldiers of the 52nd Soviet army. By September 3rd almost the entire city was in German hands. Two districts alone remained to the Soviets. But Paulus had already left unfulfilled part of Hitler's order, which was to take the city by August 25th. When Paulus succeeded in capturing the railroad station and cutting the city in two, after a series of deadly attacks and counterattacks, it was already October. On September 10th the Germans had reached the Volga to the south of the city as well, but now they had to fight house to house in a series of difficult struggles.

Meanwhile autumn was getting on, and the first blocks of ice appearing on the Volga served to announce the arrival of an even more formidable adversary, winter. The German deployment was now in the shape of a wedge with its vertex in Stalingrad, but with extremely weak flanks: the Rumanians to the left and Hoth to the right. The General Staff felt that it would be advisable to abandon Stalingrad and to rectify the front. But Hitler insisted: the city must be taken and held.

On November 11th Paulus undertook a last offensive but without success. On the 19th the Russian heavy artillery broke the Rumanian line, on which the tanks then fell like an avalanche. On the 22nd two Soviet armored corps, after having passed the Volga, made contact at Kalach on the Don to the rear of Paulus, one coming from the north, the other from the south. The 6th German army was encircled, and the besiegers had become the besieged. The house-to-house combat continued, especially in the center where the Russians were trying to join the two remnants of their 52nd army. The hunt began for enemy soldiers hiding in the ruins.

Hitler authorized Paulus to try for a breakthrough to the south, where Hoth was advancing to meet him; but Hitler reconfirmed his order not to leave Stalingrad ungarrisoned. Paulus could not divide his forces and thus did not move. On Christmas day the Russians recaptured the famous Red October factory. On January 8th and again on January 23rd, 1943, the Russians made proposals for an honorable surrender. But under Hitler's orders Paulus refused. Meanwhile, twenty-five thousand Germans died in one week. On January 26th the Russian relief forces, under the command of Rokossovsky and

Voronov, met with the forces of Zhukov, who had never abandoned the eastern strip of the city.

On January 30th Paulus informed Hitler that the 6th army could resist a day more, and that he would do it "for the Führer and for the Fatherland." Hitler replied by naming Paulus field marshal and then waited for news of his suicide. For no German field marshal had ever fallen alive into the hands of the enemy.

At 7:45 P.M. on January 31st, 1943, the radio telegraphs of the army command sent his last message: "The Russians are at the entry to the bunker. We are destroying the equipment." Finally came the signal CL-CL-CL, which means: "This station is ceasing transmission." Then, in silence, Paulus directed his steps to prison.

Facing page, above title: *The Soviets in action at Stalingrad, in a painting by a Russian artist (Milan, Rizzoli Archives).* Below: *Self-propelled flamethrower and German infantry in action among the ruins of the city in a illustration by Walter Molino in the* Domenica del Corriere *of December 6th, 1942.*

DIEN BIEN PHU (1954)

Giap's guerrillas open the history of Vietnam

The tragic story of Dien Bien Phu (which in the local language means "chief city of the province") about 78 miles from the Chinese border and 141 from Hanoi, started on November 30th, 1952. It was at this point, during the retreat of the French troops from Indochina, that the forces of Ho Chi Minh's communist liberation army installed themselves there. The move placed in great danger the only French base in the region, Lai Chau, which was threatened with encirclement.

The French General Staff thereupon prepared operation "Castor," with Dien Bien Phu as objective. This began at ten o'clock on November 21st, 1953, with a considerable parachute drop, followed by others on the succeeding days. The position was taken, and at the same time the French command ordered the evacuation of Lai Chau, which was then surrounded. The Dien Bien Phu basin (about two and a half miles wide and nine and a half miles long) was rapidly transformed into an entrenched field camp, equipped with its own airstrip (with a force of seventeen aircraft) and garrisoned by parachutists, French and native battalions, and some units from the Foreign Legion. The artillery arm was commendable: antiaircraft and heavy guns with heavy-caliber mortars. The garrison was under the command of the then Colonel Christian de Castries. Continuous work was performed in preparing hedgehog-type centers of resistance. They were given women's names, such as Huguette, Béatrice and Dominique, and were connected among themselves by communication trenches for the defense of the principal nucleus. All the services, the hospital and the command posts were installed within galleries to protect them from the incredibly strong enemy artillery fire. On December 8th the garrison of Lai Chau fell back on Dien Bien Phu, increasing the effective strength of the stronghold. Dien Bien Phu was frequently disturbed by guerrilla action but the first real contact came in February 1954, when General Vo Nguyen Giap besieged it with picked units. Repulsed, the Vietnamese commander decided to change tactics and began the long and continuous work of digging, attempting to reach the fort with tunnels while the French forces were kept busy on the surface through attacks.

On March 5th, 1954, after a bloody encounter during a sortie, a battalion of French parachutists, supported by armor, was forced to fall back on its own positions. From that moment the military situation became rapidly worse for the French, while the forces of General Giap increased in number and means, receiving also armor and a great deal of artillery of recent make. The bravery and sacrifice of the besieged was not successful in preventing the tightening of the circle and the successive capture of various strongpoints. Under the continual bombardment of shells from the Vietminh artillery (it was calculated that almost one hundred and fifty thousand were fired) the twelve thousand men at Dien Bien Phu, with few supplies and limited medical facilities (which arrived only by helicopter), nevertheless defended

themselves untiringly against continuous general attacks by the forces of Giap from March 13th, 1954, onward. The final assault took place on May 1st. Fierce fighting took place in the trenches with hand grenades, bayonets, and knives, the French getting the worst of the fight. On Wednesday, May 7th, the guerrilla forces captured the French general headquarters, and on May 10th, 1954, at dawn, silence reigned over Dien Bien Phu. Over the ten thousand fallen on both sides the jungle was beginning to extend its green mantle. By now it has become impenetrable.

A strongpoint of Dien Bien Phu during an attack by Giap's guerrillas in a diorama constructed by model maker Maurice Boverio, based on photographic material furnished by the Etablissement Cinématographique et Photographique des Armées de Fort d'Ivry (Milan, collection of the author). Trenches, weapons, mechanical implements, uniforms and equipment are faithful reproductions of those used in the siege. The soldiers are made of plastic, and arranged in action. In the foreground, on the left, can be noted the ladders used by the attackers to cross the barbed wire and later to mount the parapet according to the most ancient techniques of siege warfare.

INDEX

Cum Privilegio

LABORE E ... INDVSTRIA

A LEIDE,
Chez les ELZEVIERS. *1635.*

INDEX OF NAMES

SOURCES
OF ILLUSTRATIONS

CAPTIONS FOR THE ILLUSTRATIONS
ON THE FIRST PAGES

Siege to a hungarian fort by the Turks, in the XVI century. Oleograph by M. Ormai (1892), property of Aldo Martinetto, Milan: jacket.
Siege and bombardment of a castle. Engraving by Jost Amman, from the *Kriegsbuch*: pag. 3.
Medieval catapult. Courtyard of the Castel Sant'Angelo: page 4.
Atlas frieze of the XVII century (Milan, Bertarelli Collection): page 7.
Frontispiece of a XIX century work (Milan, Bertarelli Collection): page 9.
Frieze from the frontispiece of the *Theatri Praecipuarum Totius Mundi Urbium, Liber VI* of Braun, 1618 (Genoa-Pegli, Civic Naval Museum): pages 10-11.
Model of a Roman Ram (Rome, Engineering Museum): page 12.
Model of a catapult (Turin, National Artillery Historical Museum): page 13.
French field cannon of the XV century with gun carriage (imitation) of hammered iron with stave chamber, bands of iron, and operating device. The original belonged to Charles the Bold, and was captured by the Swiss at Nancy, where Charles was defeated and killed on January, 5, 1477. (Turin, National Artillery Historical Museum): page 14.
Above: Piedmontese siege mortar in cast iron, a 220-mm. caliber model of 1851. (Turin, Narional Artillery Historical Museum). Below: A Neapolitan stone mortar made of bronze, of the XVIII century with a caliber of 400 mm. (Turin, National Artillery Historical Museum): page 15.
Rear page: Ancient siege system referred to as "per coronam" (Library of the Musée de l'Armée, Paris).

Printed in Hong Kong
by South China Printing Co.